IMAGES of America

JOHN C. CAMPBELL FOLK SCHOOL

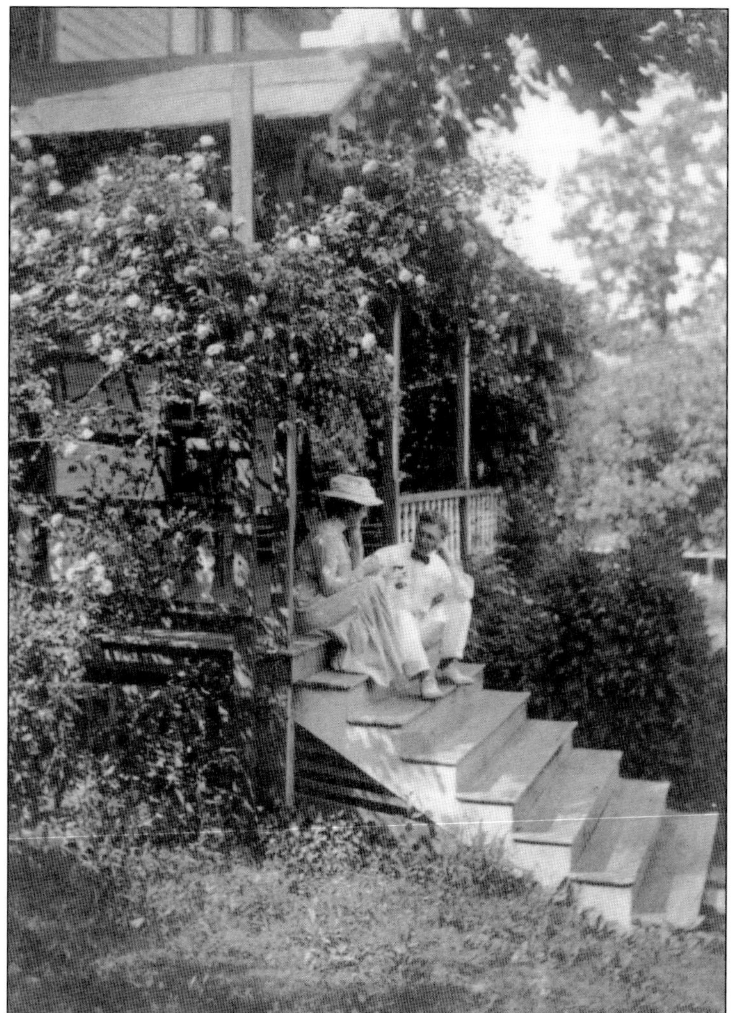

Olive Dame Campbell (left) and her husband, John C. Campbell (right), met in 1906 on a voyage to Scotland. By 1907, they were married. John briefly served as president of Piedmont College in Demorest, Georgia, and this 1908 image was captured on the front steps of their Demorest home. Between 1908 and 1912, the couple traveled on horseback and by covered wagon through eight states, discussing wants and needs with people in rural mountain communities that would provide social and economic development. Their travels inspired them to study the Danish folk school model and adapt it to Appalachia, enriching the lives of mountain people through farming, cooperatives, and the development of their art and craft skills. (Courtesy of John C. Campbell and Olive D. Campbell Papers No. 3800, Wilson Library, the University of North Carolina at Chapel Hill.)

On the Cover: Cathy Henson moved to Brasstown in 1975 and fell in love with John C. Campbell Folk School after attending her first Saturday night dance. She volunteered in many areas of the school in exchange for classes, joined the Rural Felicity Garland Dancers, and became a dance caller. She later started a garland team in Asheville, North Carolina. Henson credits her friendships with many people across and outside the country to the time she spent at the Folk School. This image was taken in 1978 by Johanna McConnell. (Courtesy of the John C. Campbell Folk School Collections and Fain Archives.)

IMAGES
of America

JOHN C. CAMPBELL FOLK SCHOOL

Kitty Taylor
Introduction by Bethany Chaney

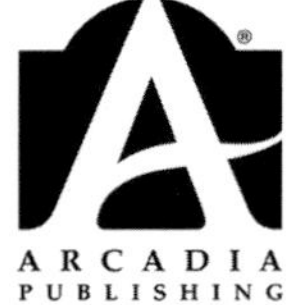

ISBN 9781-4671-6276-0

Published by Arcadia Publishing
Charleston, South Carolina

Printed in the United States of America

Library of Congress Control Number: 2025937194

For all general information, please contact Arcadia Publishing:
Telephone 843-853-2070
Fax 843-853-0044
E-mail sales@arcadiapublishing.com

Visit us on the Internet at www.arcadiapublishing.com

*Dedicated to the hearts and hands that have made
Folk School magic for 100 years. Thank you.*

Contents

Acknowledgments

Like the many folks who make weekly classes possible, the many folks who made the story of the John C. Campbell Folk School and this book possible number beyond what we can write. Robert Grand and Anthony Perrone turned a possibility into a proposal. E. Lane Gresham gifted her editing skills to the final content. Susanna Pyatt provided invaluable research guidance, and her current work on the story of the Brasstown Carvers can be found in chapter 10.

The John C. Campbell Folk School has been going for 100 years thanks to the dedication of countless people who provide clean rooms, nourishing meals, peaceful surroundings, joyful classes, meaningful programs, beautiful music, energetic dancing, and the thing we like to call Folk School magic. It is magic that can only be understood after being experienced, and it would not be possible without employees, volunteers, donors, and community members who still believe in Olive Dame Campbell and Marguerite Butler Bidstrup's dream. Every student, instructor, and staff member is a direct recipient of that belief, and they carry it forward in their work. From answering phones to turning a bowl, every act keeps the dream alive.

One more dream that lives on through this publication is the legacy of Olive Dame Campbell's work collecting songs. While traveling through Appalachia with her husband, John C. Campbell, she learned and recorded ballads she heard in churches, schools, and living rooms. Each chapter in this book has been given a title from her collection.

Unless otherwise noted, all photographs appear courtesy of the John C. Campbell Folk School Collections and Fain Archives.

Introduction

The John C. Campbell Folk School is a unique educational and cultural anchor in the far southwestern corner of North Carolina and the heart of Southern Appalachia. Founded in 1925 and celebrating its centennial year in 2025, it is the oldest surviving folk school in the nation, still delivering rich, enlivening educational and community-building opportunities in a manner faithful to the values and methods embodied by the Danish *folkehøjskole*—or "folk high school"—movement. Popularized in the late 1800s by followers of Danish theologian, philosopher, and politician N.F.S. Grundtvig, folk high schools were and still are "Schools for Life," with the aim of preparing students to be creative, active, free-thinking yet responsible participants in democratic society.

In 1922, founders Olive Dame Campbell and Marguerite Butler traveled abroad to learn about the folk school model and bring it back to Appalachia, adapting it to the conditions of the time and needs of the region. From the beginning, the school's fascinating history has not been without trial, error, or controversy, but its endurance across a century is testament to the clear vision and leadership of its founders, and to the contributions, creativity, and resolve of the community of Brasstown, which surrounds the serene, 274-acre campus. It is also important to acknowledge that the campus is situated on historic Cherokee land, in an area that was the focal point for Cherokee "removal" and the Trail of Tears just 90 years before the Folk School was founded.

The purpose of this book is to illustrate through archival photographs the story of the John C. Campbell Folk School, its founders and community supporters, and its evolution from its agricultural roots toward a hybrid school of the arts and humanities for primarily adult learners. Some of the photographs in this book are iconic to those familiar with the school. Others are being seen for the first time, the result of diligent archival collection, documentation, and digitization that will continue for years to come. The effort to organize and daylight the Folk School's archival collection demonstrates, in part, the organization's valuable role as a history-maker, history-keeper, and storyteller for the Brasstown community and Southern Appalachia.

Images of America: *John C. Campbell Folk School* is organized into 10 chapters, six that highlight people, events, and benchmarks over the decades and four that feature special aspects of the Folk School's legacy. In the first chapter, the reader will learn about the Folk School's founders, Olive Dame Campbell and Marguerite Butler, and community champions who supported their efforts. Some photographs and text offer a glimpse into the life of John C. Campbell, Olive's husband and the school's namesake, whose interests as a scholar, educator, humanitarian, and theologian are documented in *The Life and Work of John C. Campbell*, a book written and published by Olive after John's untimely death in 1919. While the school's curriculum through the 1930s focused primarily on agricultural practices, animal husbandry, and home handiwork, Olive's interest in the craft revival movement and traditional Appalachian music informed other aspects of the school's education and community engagement, including the formation of a craft cooperative and a credit union, convening regular community "singing games," and participation in the Southern Highland Craft Guild, which Olive Dame Campbell cofounded with other similarly minded peers in 1930.

The 1940s and 1950s saw growth and adaptation because of World War II, offering more opportunities for women to practice skills typically taken up by men and a program for veterans seeking a new sense of purpose upon returning from war. Director Georg Bidstrup, who married Marguerite Butler in 1936, also redoubled the Folk School's emphasis on Danish folk school elements, including music, dance, and gymnastics.

With a more fully developed and accessible public education system and affordable university education throughout Appalachia, in the 1960s and 1970s, the Folk School met with changing community demographics, needs, and interests. Its hands-on, less formal educational programs were attractive to "hippies" and conscientious objectors, causing some friction in the community. An established but costly dairy farm was eliminated, and leadership turned toward campus growth to support a robust arts and culture curriculum. Hallmark events like Fall Festival were founded during this period to attract regional visitors to the area. By the 1990s, the leadership and vision of Jan and Nanette Davidson resulted in the largest teaching blacksmith shop in the nation, the development of new programs such as cooking, and a recommitment to teaching and performing traditional music and dance. In the most recent decades, the Folk School has served an average of 5,500 adult learners annually with weeklong and weekend classes in craft, music, dance, nature studies, and foodways. Adult students come from all over the United States and internationally, sharing a desire for creative learning, respite from the digital world, and authentic community-building. Families benefit from the Little Middle summer program, intergenerational programming, dance and music classes, and more. Emerging craftspeople seeking to grow their practice and arts-based income also find a home here as students and instructors and as participants in intensive learning programs.

To offer a deeper, more nuanced examination of the contributions of the Folk School to the community, four special sections are included in this book. These highlight the lively and unusual music and dance programs of the Folk School, Doris Ullman's extraordinary portraiture of Brasstown residents, the long history and accomplishments of the Brasstown Carvers, and the evolution and importance of Fall Festival. For those interested in understanding folk school education in the United States more generally, the Folk Education Association of America is a very fine resource: www.folkeducation.org.

Ultimately, the story of the John C. Campbell Folk School and Brasstown is the story of so many Appalachian communities, one of economic and social interdependence between institutions and community members, of evolution and endurance, and of change and resistance to it. The leaders of the Folk School across the generations have faced different challenges, including changing needs, demographics, political and social morals, and macroeconomies. They faced competing visions between the institution and the community and between staff, students, and board members. Some even faced financial difficulties that put the school on the brink of closure.

This book, of course, highlights the contributions of many of these directors and champions, but there are too many over 100 years to mention, and so many stories that have yet to be fully explored. Apart from the founding women who conceived of and birthed the John C. Campbell Folk School, no person in particular can be credited with influencing the Folk School the most significantly or in the most positive ways. In fact, it is a fundamental tenet of folk schools that everyone is both a learner and a contributor—teachers, students, and administrators—not always equally in all ways but always meaningfully. The key individuals noted here may be the best known, but the enduring impact and importance of the John C. Campbell Folk School must be credited to the tens of thousands of students, instructors, staff, donors, board members, hosts, work studies, dancers, musicians, and community members who have both created and found joy, enlightenment, friendship, and purpose upon entering the famous red door of Keith House. It is to all of those who are not mentioned that this book is dedicated and to whom future leaders of the Folk School will always be indebted.

—Bethany Chaney
Executive Director

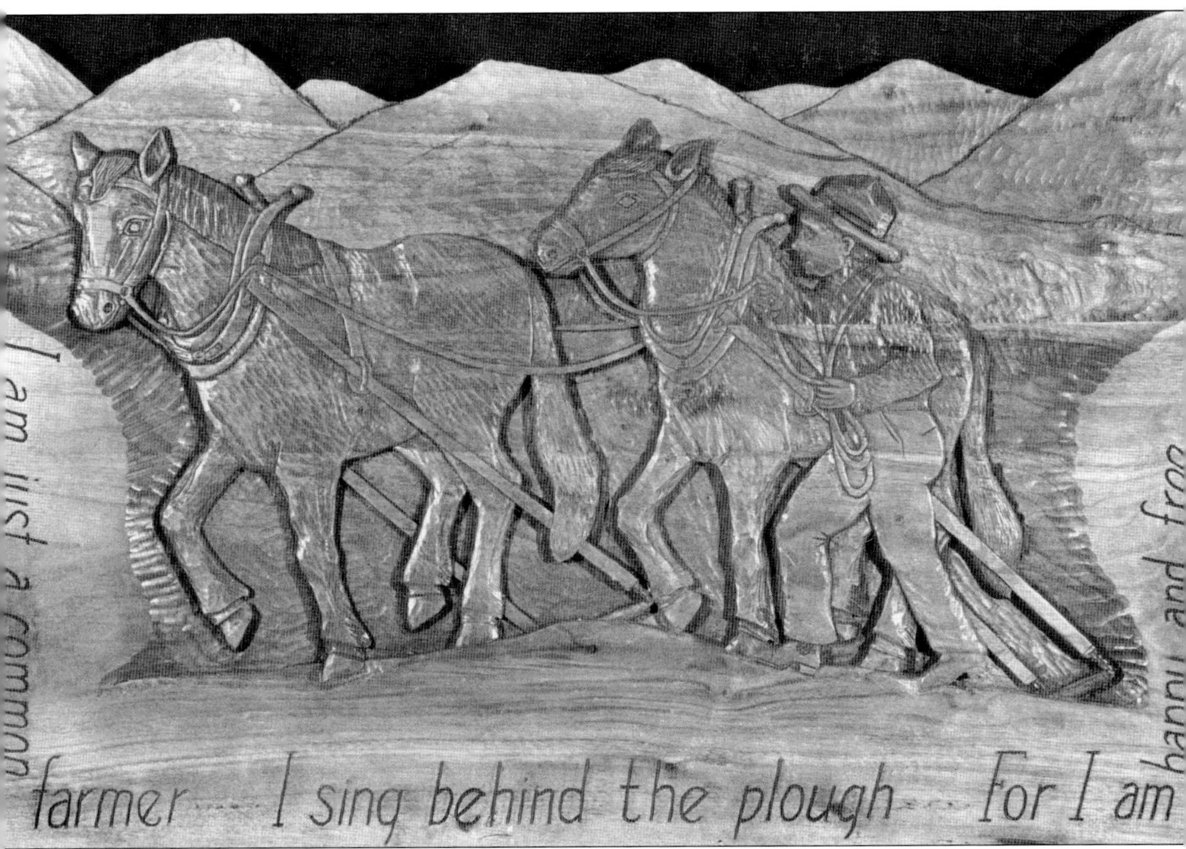

Olive Dame Campbell adapted the Folk School motto, "I Sing Behind the Plow," from a poem by Danish farmer and poet Mads Hansen. One translation of the poem reads, "I sing behind the plough and to the sound of the mowing. Hills and woods give back my song. And when I am weary with toil and day is done, my spirit is fresh, my mind at ease, I am happy and free." It is a reminder that people can find joy and creativity in everyday tasks. This rendering of the school's logo and motto was completed in 1981 by Elmer J. Tangerman, a well-respected carver who published a number of books on the craft. His work hangs in one of the common areas of Keith House, a building where those everyday tasks turn into conversation, connection, and community.

Set your feet fast in the common soil,
There are the roots of life.
There you must learn to stand.
Begin on the plane of every day
not in the blue of the heavens
and grow upward.
Must you not plough the field
before you gather in the harvest?
Love life.
Hate no one.
With joy and sorrow, hope and faith,
you shall build here on earth
a bridge up to the stars.

Olive Dame Campbell's translation of a favorite Danish folk-school song

The Olive Dame Campbell Dining Hall was dedicated in 1992. Included in the program was this section of a favorite Danish folk school song, translated by Campbell herself. The values in these words have been carried forward through 100 years of the John C. Campbell Folk School story. As the song says, it is a story filled with joy and sorrow, hope and faith, a story of how people still sing behind the plow.

One

1920s

Go Round around the Valley

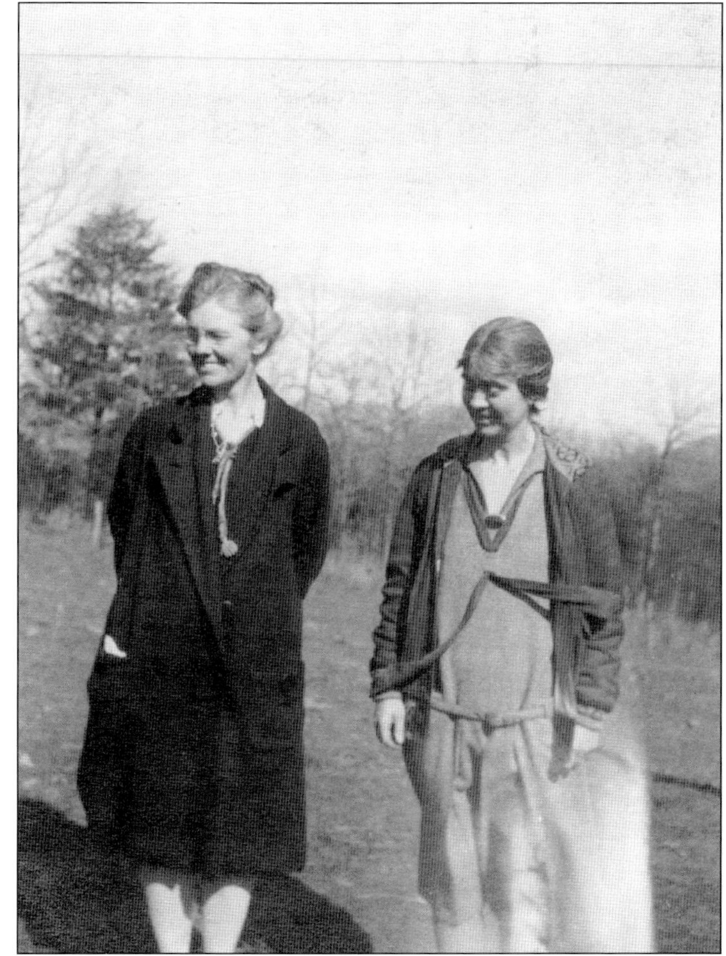

The official establishment of the John C. Campbell Folk School can be traced to the people and promise of Brasstown, North Carolina. The origin story of the John C. Campbell Folk School can be traced to two women, Olive Dame Campbell (left) and Marguerite Butler (later Bidstrup, right). In the 1920s, their ideas merged with the hopes of a small community and brought a new school to life.

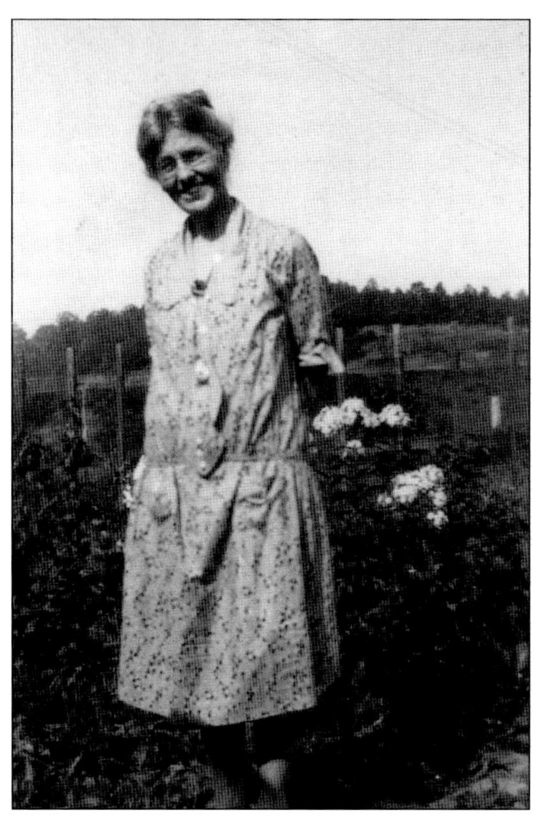

In the early 1900s, Olive Dame Campbell traveled with her husband, John C. Campbell, through eight states in Southern Appalachia. She kept records of their excursion, which found them in conversations with residents who could and did speak to the needs and wants of the region. She also collected ballads along the way and studied handicrafts. He researched social conditions in the mountains and interviewed farmers about their agricultural practices. After their travels, both were convinced that education could improve the quality of life and that traditional crafts of the region needed to be preserved. John died before their hopes were made manifest, but Olive Dame Campbell carried the vision forward.

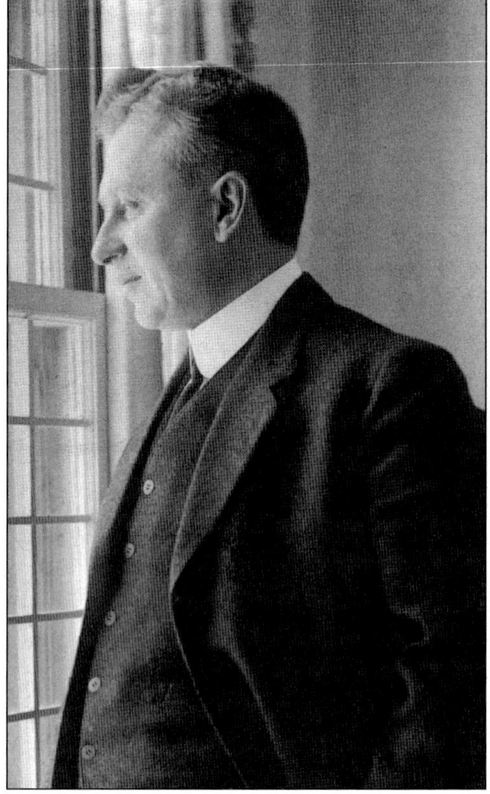

Marguerite Butler met Olive Dame Campbell at the 1919 Conference of Southern Mountain Workers. Their shared interest in service took their friendship to Denmark in 1922, where they studied the Danish *folkehøjskole*, meaning "folk high school." These "schools for life" focused on process, community, and transformation. Three years after these travels, Butler and Campbell opened the John C. Campbell Folk School.

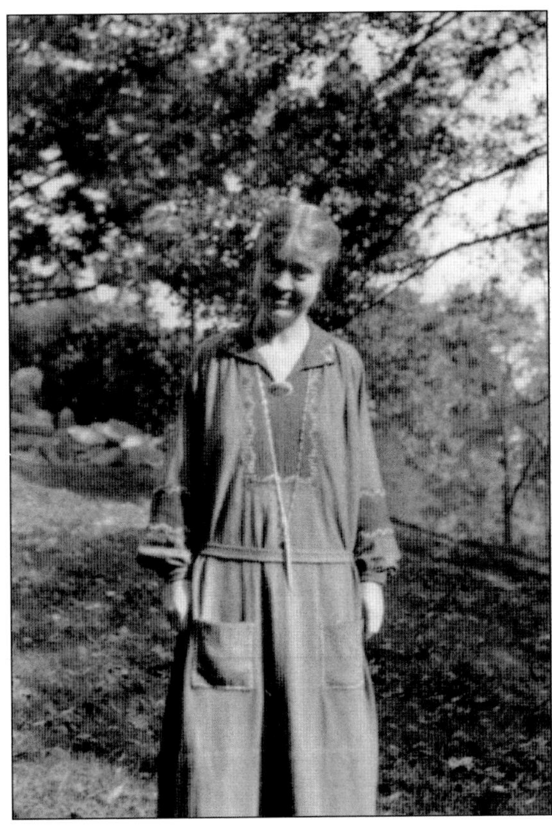

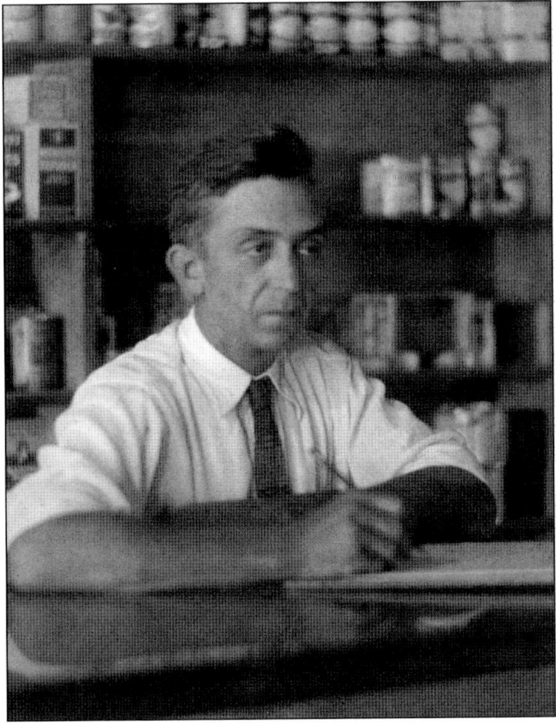

Brasstown storekeeper and community advocate Fred O. Scroggs led the initiative for Olive Dame Campbell and Marguerite Butler to establish a new school in a beloved rural setting. With the help of more than 200 local folks who attended a community interest meeting with Butler, Scroggs and the people of Brasstown convinced both women to bring their dreams to Western North Carolina.

Date 10-17 1925

I, or we, whose names are hereunto subscribed, agree and bind ourselves to donate, in consideration of a school, on the order of the Danish Folk School, being located somewhere near the mouth of Little Brasstown Creek, land, money, timber, days work, etc., as indicated by us below:

Building stone - Any suitable on my farm will haul rock if health will permit.

Witness: Fred O. Scroggs

Name G.W. Crisp

Address age 73

Name Brasstown

Address

When Olive Dame Campbell visited Brasstown with Marguerite Butler in November 1925, they were met with more than 100 cards from local residents, pledging contributions toward the establishment of the Folk School. Labor, money, firewood, and even plants were promised. Financial pledges ranged from $5 to $50, and workdays from three per year to 20. G.W. Crisp, age 73, promised "any suitable stone on my farm" and vowed that he would haul rock, "if health will permit." S.A. Carringer pledged 20 days of work with his teams per year for three years, three loads of firewood per year for five years, and stones from his farm. It was this kind of dedication that convinced Campbell and Butler to choose Brasstown as the official location for the John C. Campbell Folk School.

Date 10-10 1925

I, or we, whose names are hereunto subscribed, agree and bind ourselves to donate, in consideration of a school, on the order of the Danish Folk School, being located somewhere near the mouth of Little Brasstown Creek, land, money, timber, days work, etc., as indicated by us below:

20 days work, Man + Team each year for 3 yrs. 3 loads fire wood per year for 5 yrs. Any suitable stone on my farm.

Witness: Fred O. Scroggs

Name S.A. Carringer

Address Brasstown

Name

Address

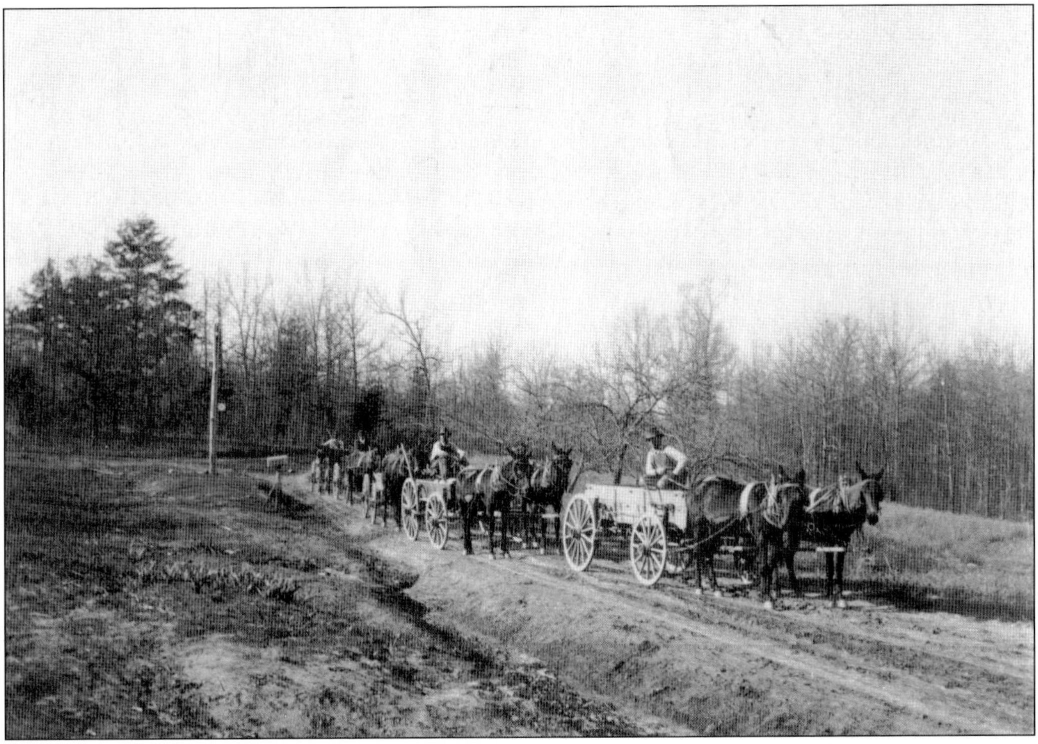

Many pledges were filled within the first few years of the visionary meeting that forever changed Brasstown's story. The back of this late-1920s image reads, "Five wagons coming in with lime, all pledged labor." Lime could be used to dry wet sites and provide stability for building foundations.

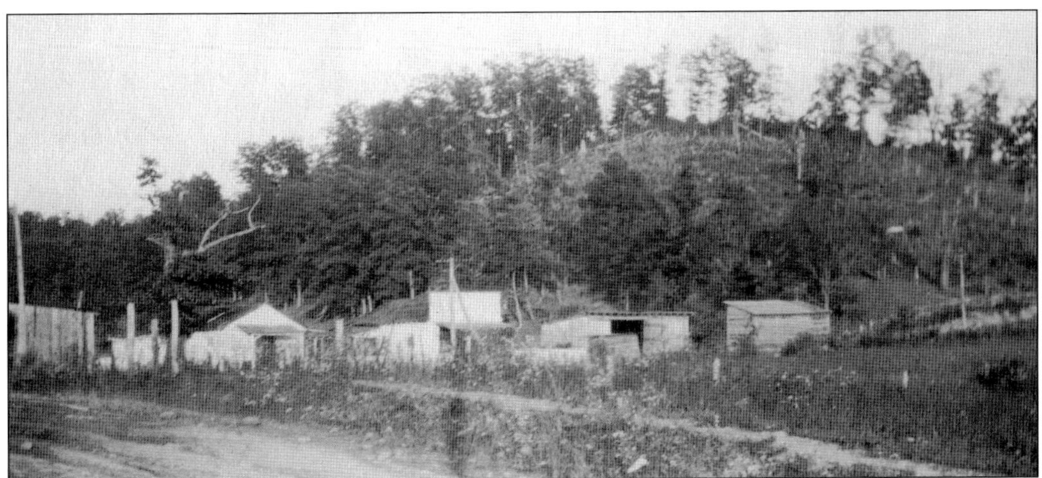

In 1925, downtown Brasstown was small and, as Marguerite Butler and Olive Dame Campbell would discover, inviting. The wooden building on the far left was the post office, and Scroggs' General Store stood in the center of the scene. Surrounded by the mountains, the unincorporated community sits in both Clay and Cherokee Counties in Western North Carolina.

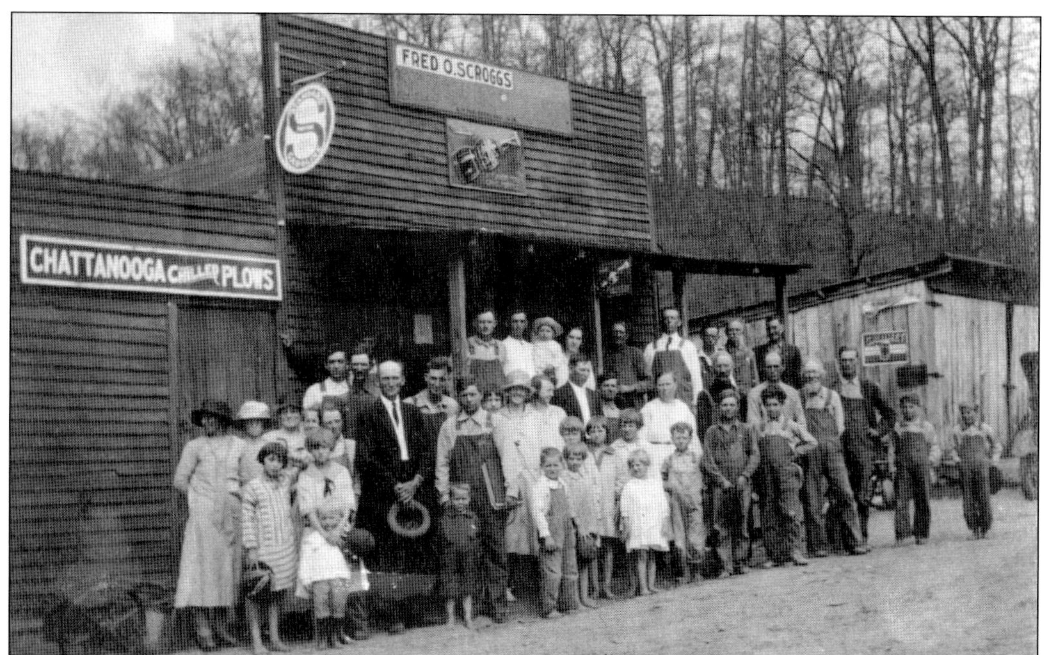

A crowd gathered outside Scroggs' General Store, described as a credit union meeting, reflects the early role Olive Dame Campbell played in the life of Brasstown. In the late 1920s and early 1930s, Campbell helped form several organizations that provided direct support to the community. She is pictured in the row behind the children, to the left of an unidentified man holding a book and dressed in overalls.

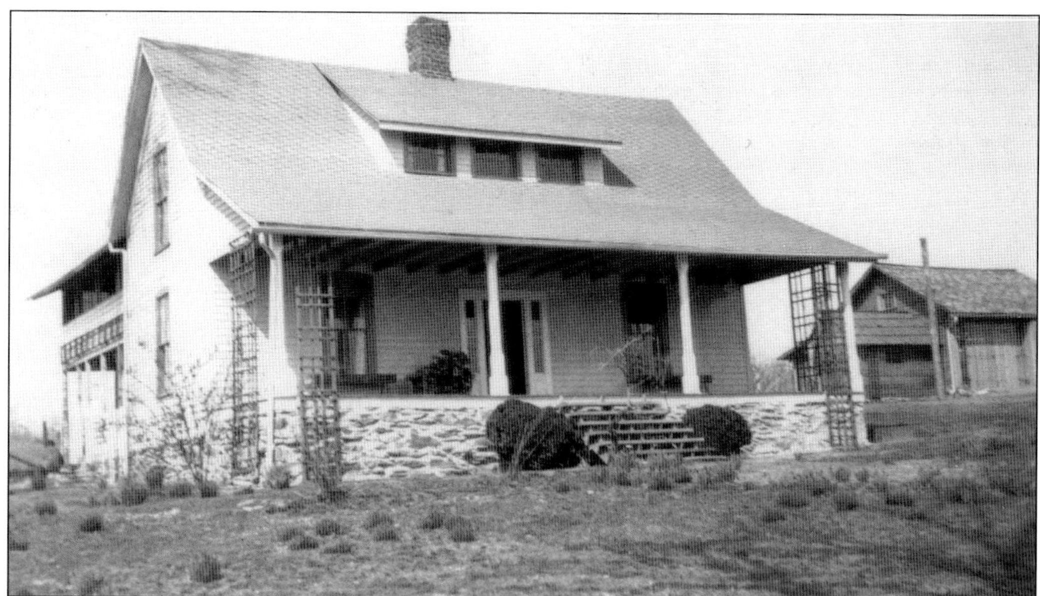

Farm House, seen in this c. 1926 photograph, was the original homestead on the Folk School property and was located on the parcel donated by the Scroggs family. Cofounders Olive Dame Campbell and Marguerite Butler lived there while the school was being established, and it served as the center of the school in its first few years. Students often traveled from within walking distance because no lodging was available.

Georg Bidstrup relocated from Denmark in 1926, bringing his own experience in the Danish folk school movement to Brasstown. Bidstrup helped transform a portion of the school's property into a working farm, which he managed. He also taught gymnastics and folk dancing, and in 1936, he married Marguerite Butler. In this 1927 photograph, he is ringing a bell crafted in Denmark and gifted to the Folk School.

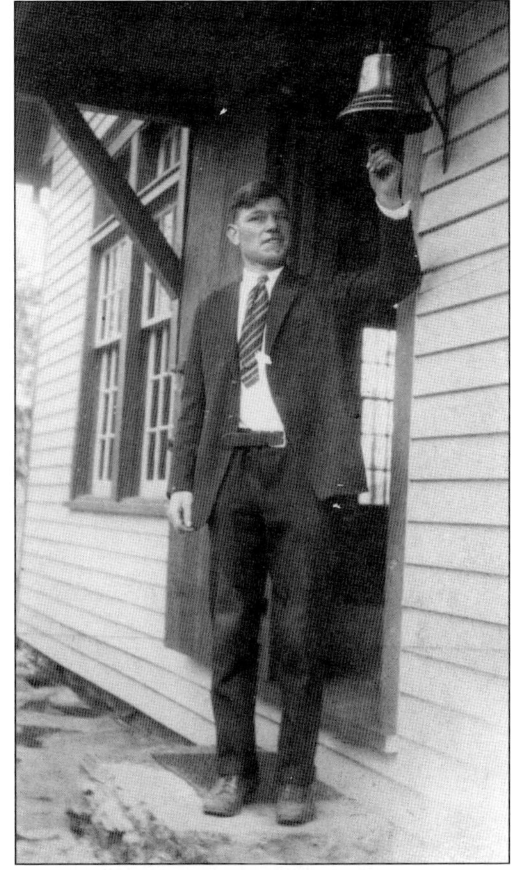

From the beginning, the Folk School set a precedent of no exams, no grades, and no credits. Early classes included discussions on history, public health, and archaeology. By 1927, students were enrolling in a regular session that spanned from December to early spring. Young women and men, like those in this image, studied history, geography, reading, writing, and the Bible.

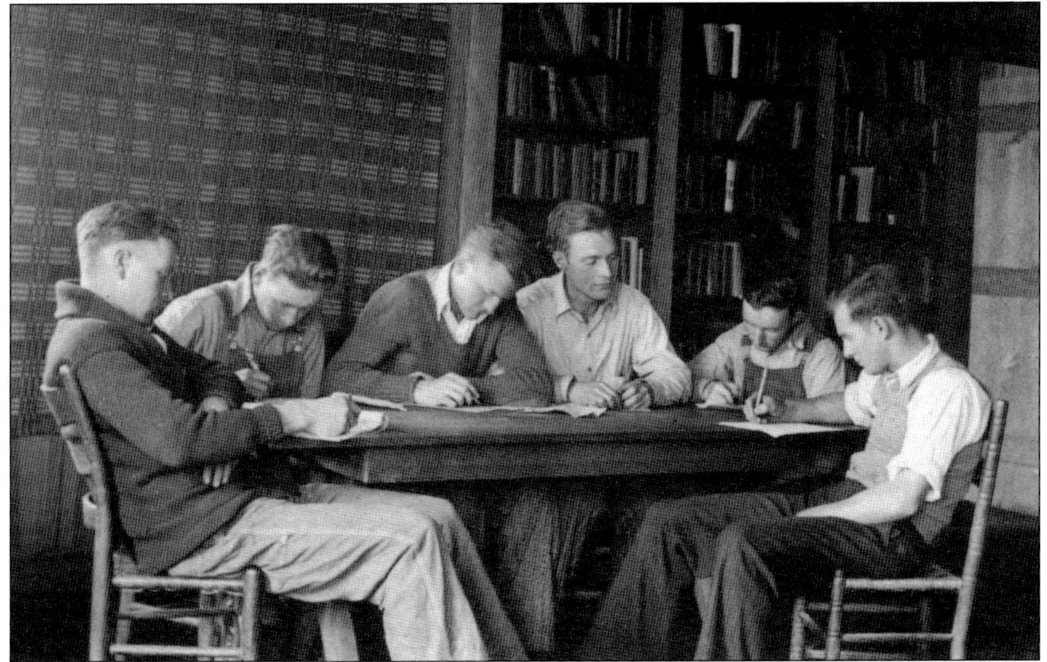

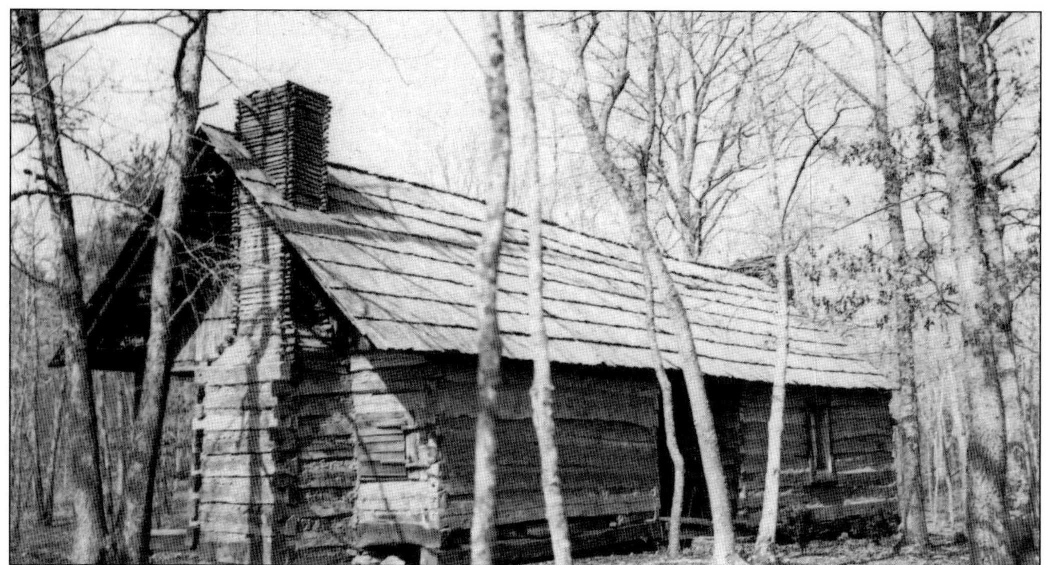

Olive Dame Campbell and Marguerite Butler embraced and preserved traditional Appalachian life and ways. This included the relocation of two log cabins from neighboring counties to Brasstown. The cabins were then reassembled and joined by a dogtrot. All of the work was completed by a group of men ranging in age from 18 to 78. This 1926 photograph of the finished structure includes a note from Butler that reads, "Started Christmas, finished 4th July 1926." In celebration, the Folk School held the first Olde Folks' Party. Almost 100 years later, the log cabin still stands, and the Olde Folks' Party, now held during the holiday season, still welcomes community members annually for a meal and fellowship. Many attendees have shared their Folk School stories at these gatherings, including memories of Campbell and Butler.

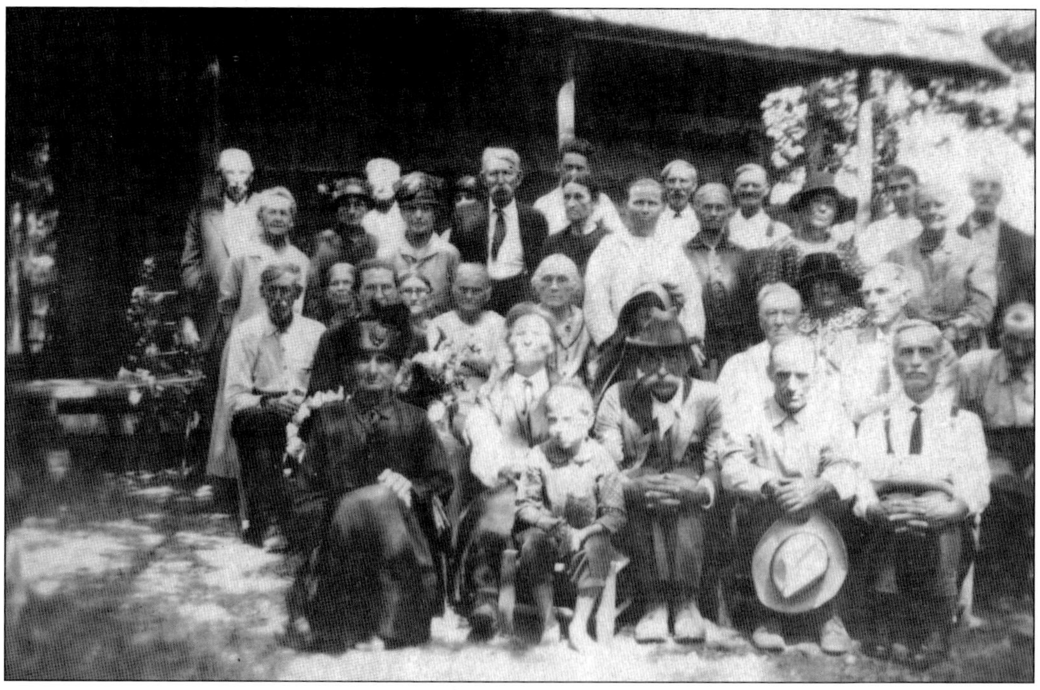

The Community Room of Keith House was dedicated on September 3, 1927, and filled with split-bottomed chairs that were made by local folks. Since its dedication, it has remained a cornerstone of the campus where dances, concerts, readings, auctions, and the Danish traditions of singing, folklore, and camaraderie—also known as Morningsong—have been held for close to a century.

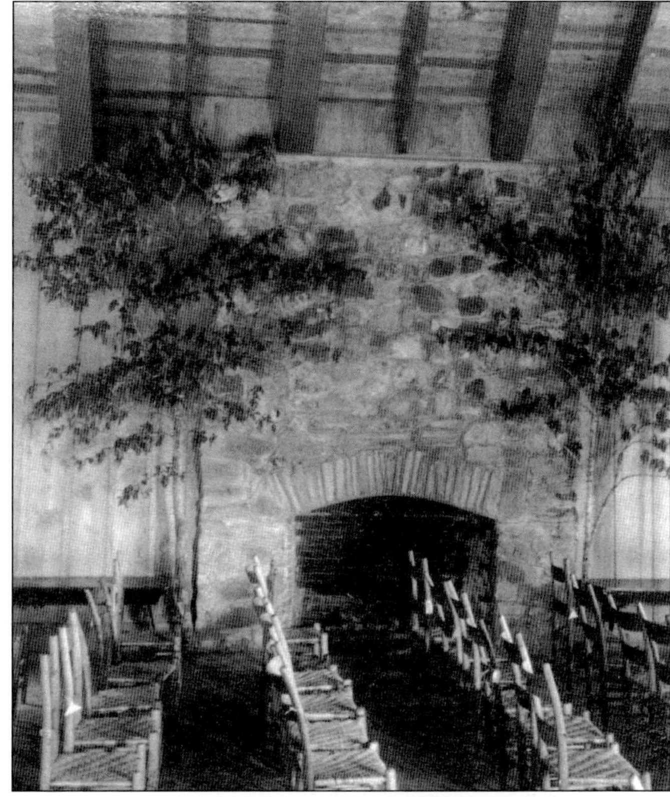

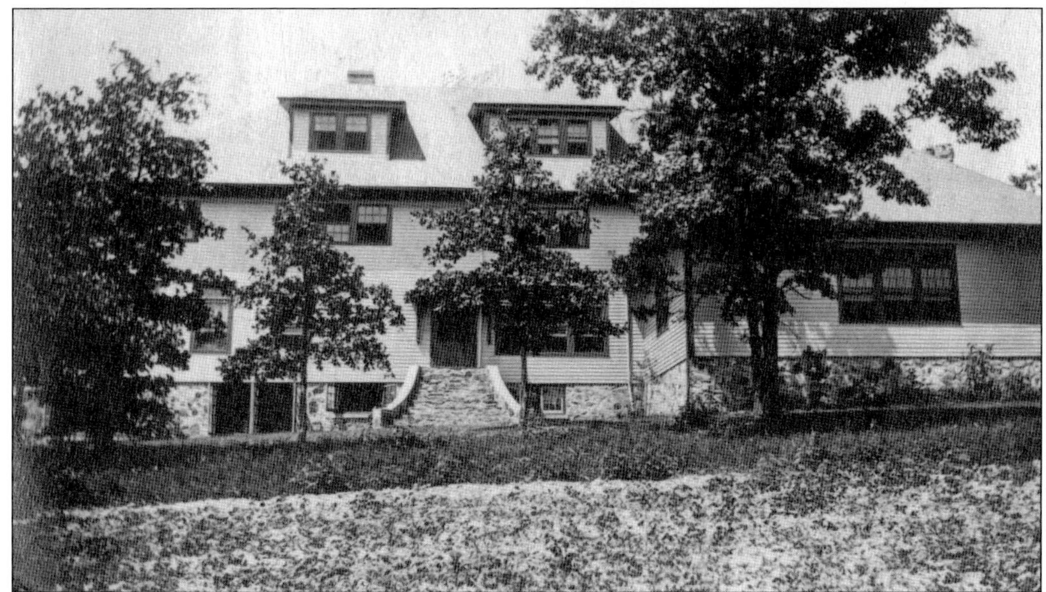

Keith House, originally called Community House, was designed by Olive Dame Campbell's niece Dorothy Bacon. It was an addition to the Community Room and housed the kitchen, dining room, weaving room, office, a classroom, and the girls' room. The building still serves as the center of the school, bringing students and instructors together for events, including Folk School orientation and the student showcase held at the end of weeklong classes.

No. 1 **JOHN C. CAMPBELL FOLK SCHOOL** March 1926

CHEROKEE COUNTY
BRASSTOWN, N. C.

THE John C. Campbell Folk School is an attempt to apply the principles underlying the folk high school of Denmark to the rural problems of the Southern Highland Region. It is an experiment in adult education, named in memory of John C. Campbell, who, after twenty-five years of study and service in the Southern Highlands, felt the need of vitalizing and dignifying the whole content of our rural civilization. In a type of education based on the folk high school of Denmark, he saw a hope of preserving what is best in Highland culture and of opening the way to a deeper and richer life.

For those who are interested I have prepared a brief statement of the theory of the Danish folk high school. It is enough here to say that it is a school primarily for young adults, eighteen to thirty years of age; that it sets no requirements; gives no examinations; offers no credits; that its primary purpose is, through the influence of personality and oral teaching, to arouse the individual so that "he will never stop growing." It distinguishes, in other words, between acquiring and developing. It does not try to assume responsibility for local changes, but to awaken that desire for a better life which is the only sound basis for change.

Principles which have taken form in one country will doubtless take a somewhat different form in a new environment. We emphasize the experimental character of the John C. Campbell Folk School. It must find a new approach to old subjects; it must develop a new technique of teaching. Furthermore, if the teaching is to enrich rural life, it must be rooted in a deep belief in the country; not perhaps as it is, but as it may be: its power to satisfy; to offer a full life.

Not the most difficult, but the most favorable conditions should be the ground for such initial adaptations. We have felt that the first mountain folk school should be placed in a region plainly possible of agricultural development, a natural center not too far from the railroad, and among a substantial, land-owning population who really desire it. In selecting Brasstown, North Carolina, we believe we have found this favorable combination of circumstances. A section poor, but capable of agricultural development, a natural center for an area of some fifty square miles, it is on a good highway within eight and a half miles of Murphy, the terminus of two railroads (the Southern and the Louisville and Nashville), and about one hundred miles from the markets of Asheville, Knoxville and Atlanta. Its greatest asset is its citizenship, a strong group of small farmers with a high reputation for integrity. Ninety-seven per cent are land-owners. Their desire for a "school which will help the country" is partially indicated by the following summary of pledges, representing 116 citizens, and made entirely on their own initiative as an earnest of co-operation. The form of these pledges was drawn up by a local lawyer so as to be binding:

Over $800 in cash.
Locust posts.
Telephone poles.
Building logs.
Building stone.
Firewood.
Native shrubs, trees and bulbs.
In the first three years of the School, 1,495 days of labor, 397 with team.
Yearly, 388 days' labor are pledged without time limit.

In addition to the above list, about thirty acres of excellent land, partly in woodland and in the center of the community fronting on the high road, were given by a leading citizen and his family. An adjacent farm of seventy-five acres, with a farm house, has been purchased to provide for future development. A further twenty-five acres of distant woodland have been promised.

The John C. Campbell Folk School begins its life as a home and farm in the Brasstown community, a home and farm in which the citizens of the region have a real share and stake. Those who live and work in it are members of the community, with a share and stake in the community life. Their life is different only in that its main purpose is not the welfare of one family but the welfare of all. They seek to understand and to serve the best interests of the neighborhood. This end will govern as far as possible every step in the School's development, whether agricultural, social, or educational in a limited sense. In other words, the ultimate form which the John C. Campbell Folk School is to take must grow out of community need and the consciousness of that need. Such a growth will, of necessity, be slow, its direction uncharted and conceivably unexpected, but we who have seen abroad the vitality of the principles upon which the folk school rests and are satisfied as to their fundamental rightness, have faith to believe that a school based on the Danish theory and adapted to local conditions will result.

We look forward to a small boarding family, not exceeding one hundred boys and girls in all, who will come to live with

The first Folk School newsletter was written by Olive Dame Campbell and published in March 1926. She described the Folk School as an experiment in adult education and emphasized that her husband and namesake of the school, John C. Campbell, "saw a hope of preserving what is best in Highland culture and opening the way to a deeper and richer life."

us—a new group every year—for the five or six winter months when farm work is at its minimum. We picture these boys and girls sharing in the tasks and in the pleasures of our farm home; we see them gathered in the big community room for vivid personal lectures on history, geography, literature, sociology, civics and nature study; we follow them into the class rooms where they learn to think through arithmetic which deals with daily problems, where they express themselves in reading and writing, where they discuss what they are learning. We listen to sound of hammer, saw and plane in the carpentry room, to the thud of loom and whirr of spinning wheel in the weaving and sewing room; we watch them at their daily physical training in the gymnasium; we hear them singing—for it is song that welds the group together. Nor is their singing, discussing or learning a thing apart from the community. The doors of the lecture hall swing open to those of the community who care to enter. Many come to share, day by day, in the program of the School; they take part in its festivities and its pageants; they help to work out its problems. If they wish for certain practical short courses, we shall from time to time call in those who can supply this need.

Such, in brief, is the ideal toward which we work. Such is the way we hope, slowly, step by step, year by year, to increase the number of thinking, aspiring young people who will see the promise of the country, who will strive to make country life what it may be. How well and how soon we can realize this ideal depends upon a number of things,—especially upon the continued co-operation of the community, and the help, moral and financial, of those who believe in what we are trying to do.

The immediate program of the School calls for the repairing of the farm house and outbuildings. For this purpose a few trained carpenters, who have worked out their pledges, are being employed. The rest of the labor is largely pledged. So far the hauling has been done free of cost. Two of the citizens have given the old, hand-hewn log houses which are being set up on the place as nearly as possible in pioneer fashion, to serve as a museum for the fast-vanishing relics of early days in this country. Logs and poles to replace those decayed and new puncheon floors are being supplied by other citizens, and again all labor freely and gladly given. Spring will mean the putting in of a crop to build up the soil. The pruning of trees, vines, etc., has already been done under the direction of a State expert with the assistance of the two nearest County Agents.

This program for 1926 we have begun on the small budget of $7,000.00, a budget which has been secured by the support of three Church Boards—Presbyterian, U.S.A., Congregational and Episcopalian—and by a grant from the Carnegie Corporation, through its interest in adult education. Naturally, such a budget cannot cover the Community House, which must soon be built to serve as lecture hall and center for community gatherings, and which will include carpentry, weaving and sewing rooms as well as class rooms. Some satisfactory water system should be arranged for at once. Electric lights will simplify living and reduce fire risks. Our agricultural program in the near future calls for barn, stock, poultry and other equipment. These must precede any attempt to make a self-supporting demonstration farm for this section.

Slowly and carefully as these plans may be developed, economically as they may be managed, they call for financial support far beyond the abilities of local citizenship. We earnestly ask that individuals and organizations who have at heart the future of the mountain country, or who for one reason or another are interested in a new approach to rural problems, will rally to the support of this experiment, which has, we believe, a far more than local significance.

OLIVE D. CAMPBELL
Director

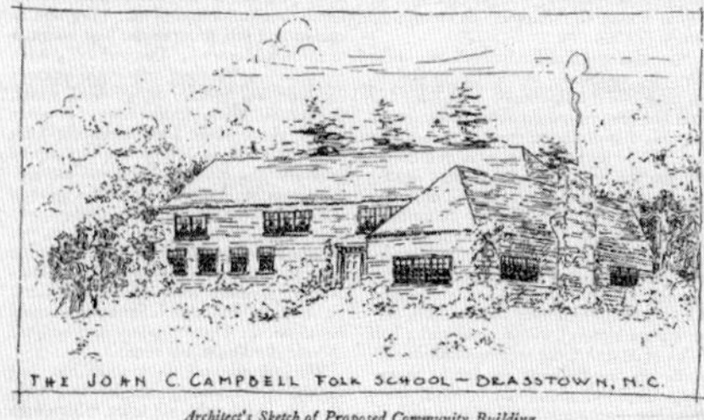

Architect's Sketch of Proposed Community Building

When speaking to the relationship between the local population and the school, Campbell said, "Many come to share, day by day, in the program of the School; they take part in its festivities and its pageants; they help work out its problems. If they wish for certain practical short courses, we shall from time to time call in those who can supply this need." Her observations and sentiment remain relevant today.

Two

1930s

Young Men and Maids

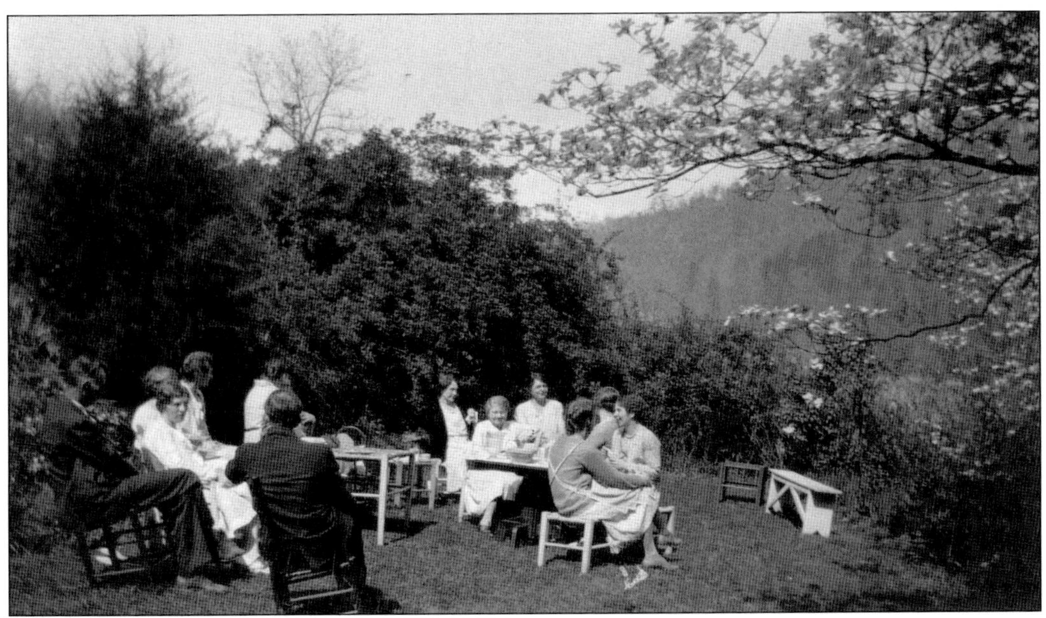

The 1930s were formative years for the Folk School. Agriculture took the main stage. Class offerings expanded, and community organizations were formed to help residents. In its early days, the craft of wood carving received recognition from the White House. Historic buildings were constructed, and the model of student participation in the full life of the school began. It was a promising decade in Brasstown.

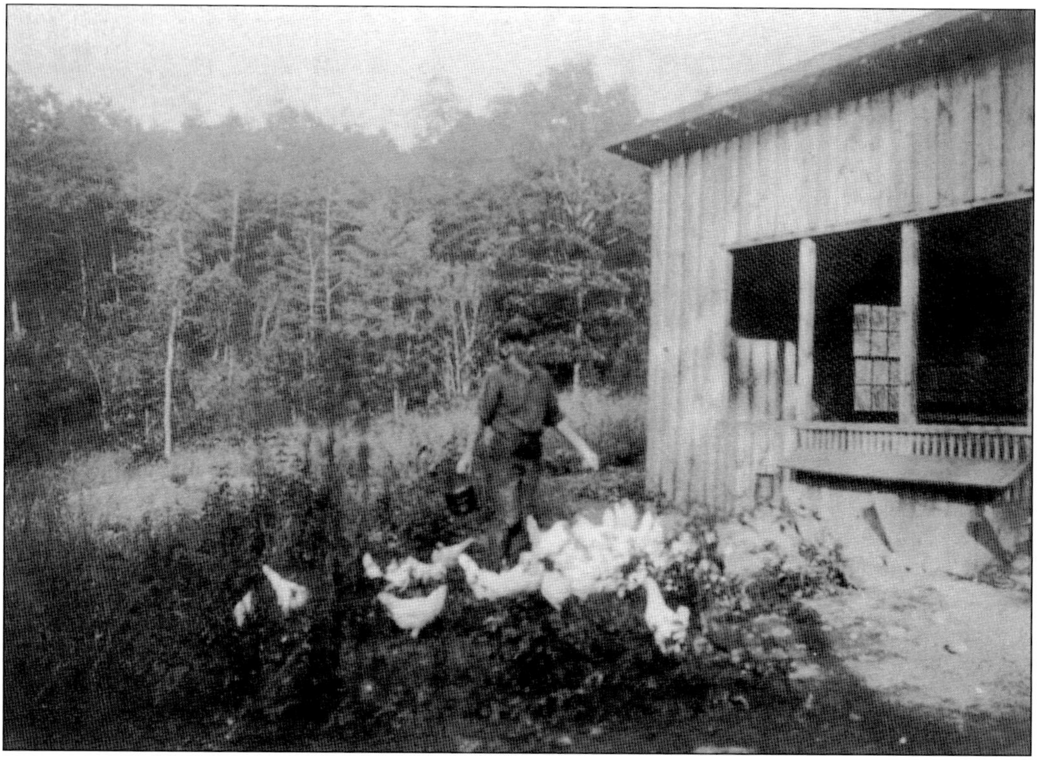

By the 1930s, agriculture played a pivotal role in the school's continued growth, honoring the hopes Fred Scroggs and his father, Lucius, originally shared with Marguerite Butler Bidstrup. A demonstration farm, led by Georg Bidstrup, included a diversity of crops, featured large poultry and dairy operations, and taught local farmers progressive farming techniques. Operations were vital to the school's success and supplied much of the food for students and staff. Fields and structures across campus hosted a bounty of livestock for milk, meat, and eggs; vegetables for cooking and preserving; and grains for baking. From raising chickens to threshing wheat, farm-to-table was fundamentally and economically beneficial.

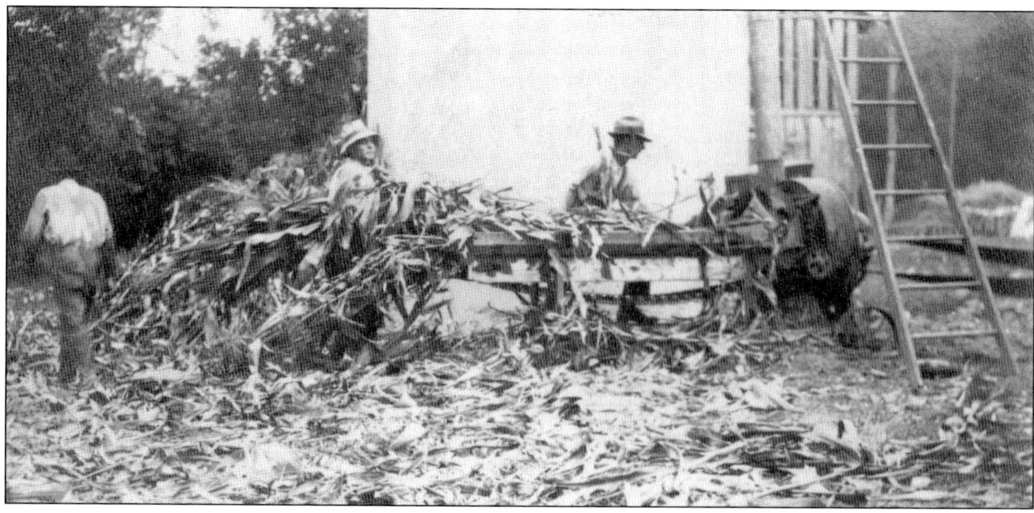

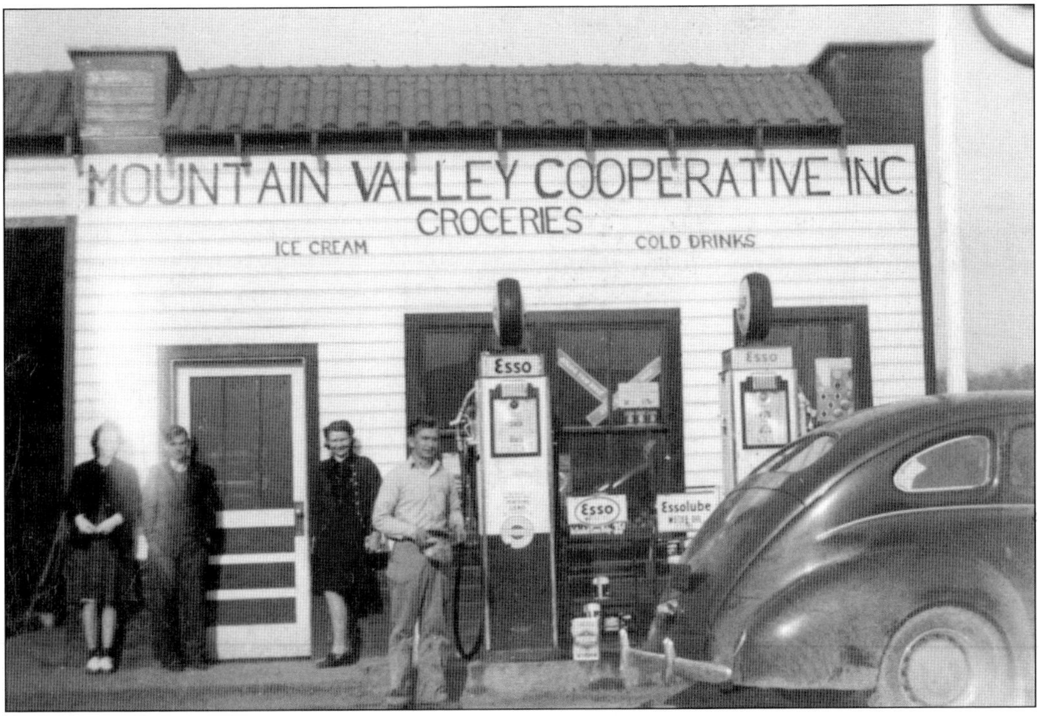

Agricultural efforts expanded to include cooperatives, which provided financial support to local farms and the school. It was one of Olive Dame Campbell's initiatives to preserve the tradition of farming and uplift the local community. Starting in the late 1920s and into the early 1930s, Campbell established community cooperatives, including the Brasstown Savings and Loan Association and the Mountain Valley Creamery. Groceries and supplies were made available to nearby residents and shared through distribution in larger areas. The creamery truck parked near Fred O. Scroggs's general store was recorded as returning from Atlanta with 30 bags of meal, 63 empty egg cases, 3 empty creamer cans, and lard.

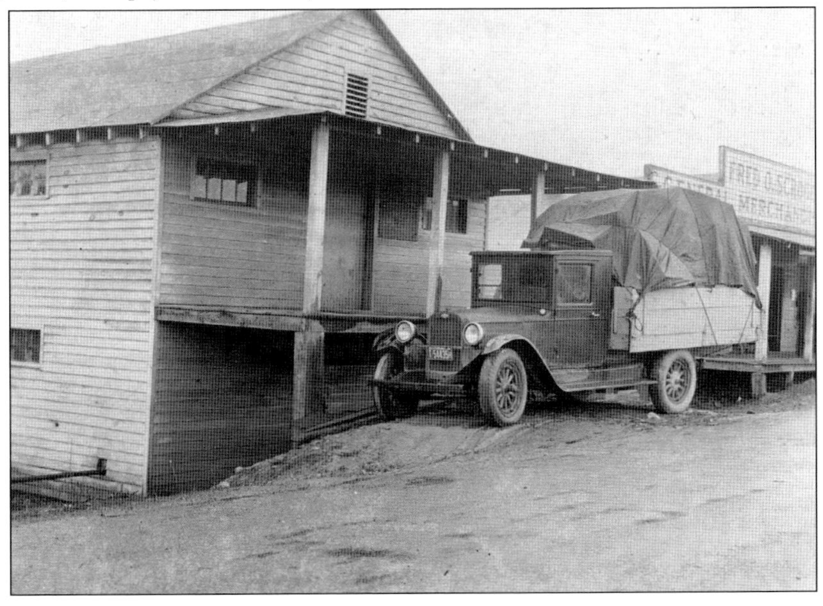

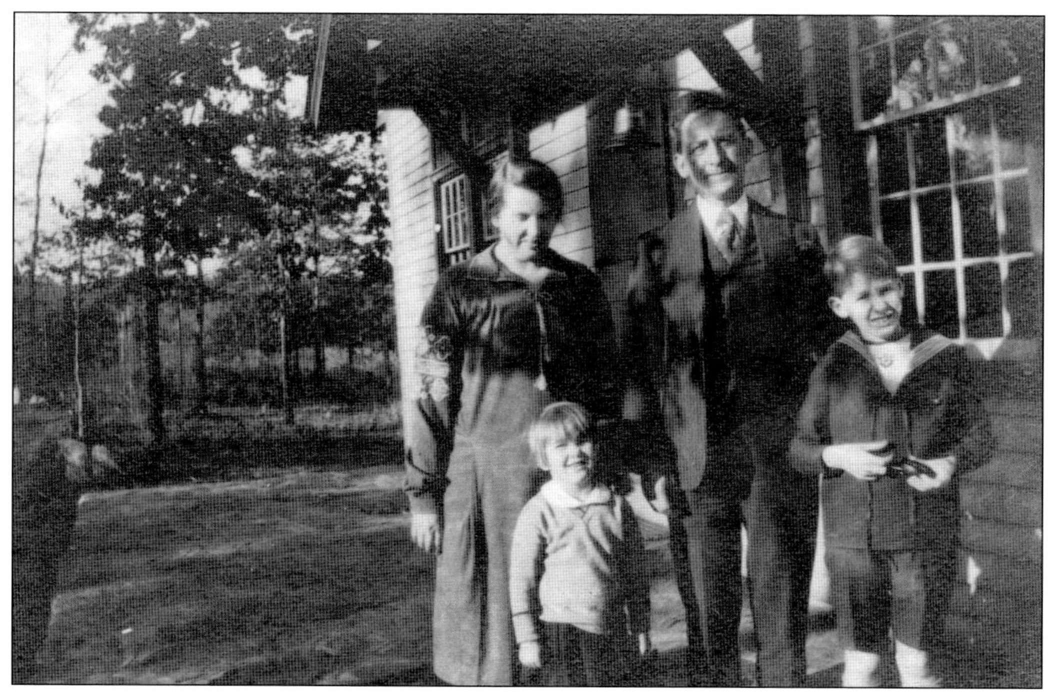

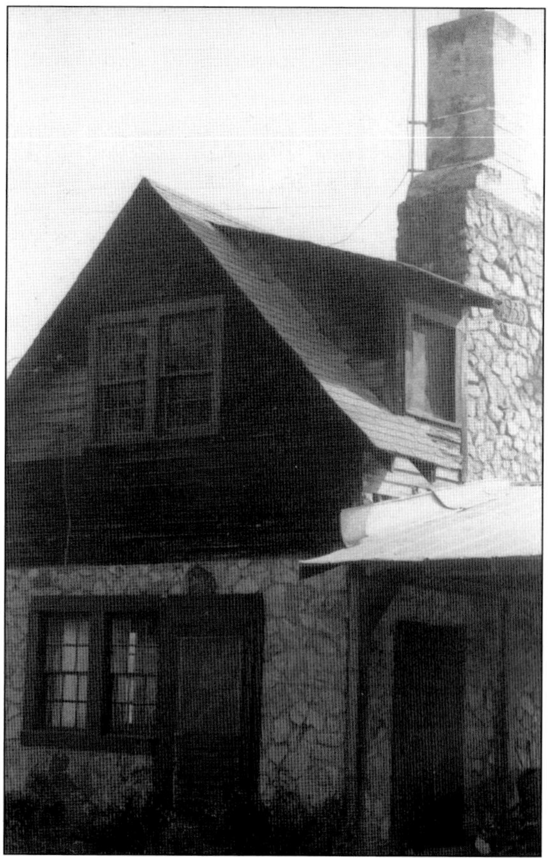

Originally from Belgium, Leon Deschamps moved to Brasstown in the late 1920s and quickly settled into Folk School life. He was described as a construction manager, engineer, forester, surveyor, electrician, and plumber. Deschamps is known for the buildings he designed, and many of those structures were finished in the 1930s. He is pictured here with his wife, May, and their two oldest children, Clotilde and Alfred.

In the agricultural era of the school, Tower House provided living quarters for the school's chief herdsman on the top floor. The structure replicated the rural style of Leon Deschamps's native Belgium, and the blacksmith shop on the first floor followed the European practice of conserving space and using heat to warm upper floors.

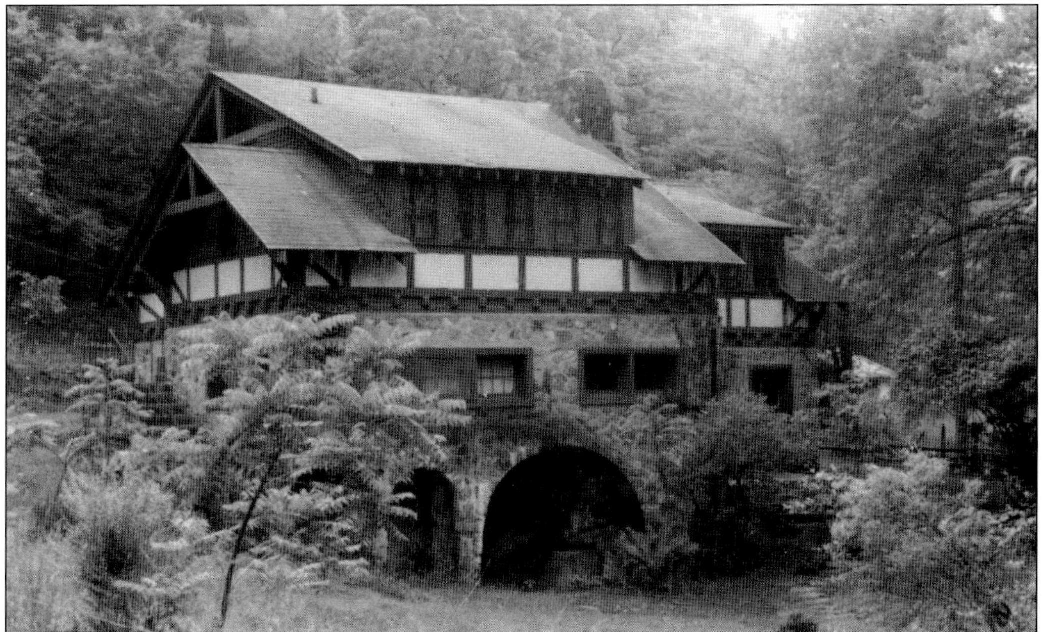

Mill House was a half-timber creation that required skill and creativity from Leon Deschamps. With the absence of electricity, he designed and built a system in the nearby creek with an upstream reservoir, connective piping, and a wheel that provided power for the first-floor workshop. The second floor served as the boys' dorm and was the maximum distance from the girls' dorm on the second floor of Keith House.

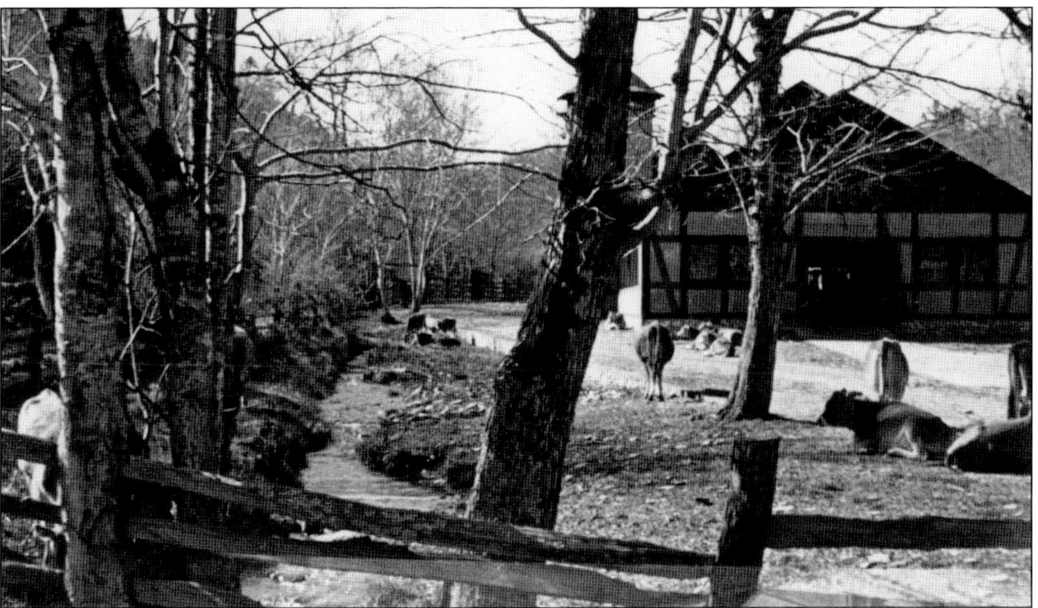

The milking barn, completed in 1931, was another of Leon Deschamps's half-timber structures. The prominent building served as the dairy barn for more than 40 years, until the school's dairy ceased operations. In keeping with his attention to detail, Deschamps carved ornaments in the timbers between the windows and over the side door. The building was later repurposed to become the Francis Whitaker Blacksmith Shop.

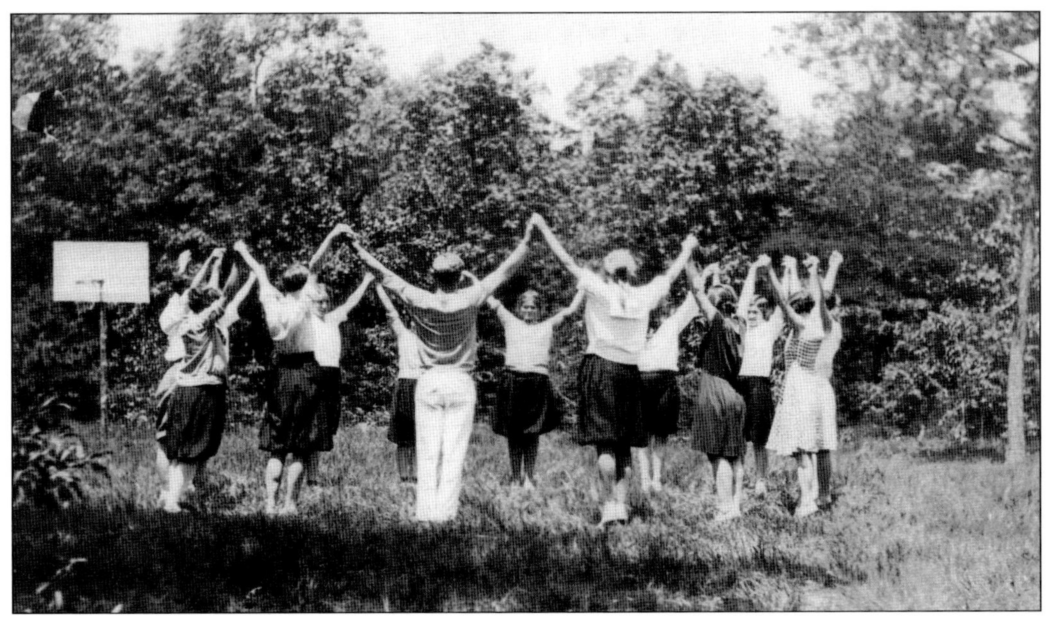

Music and dance played an important role in maintaining tradition and encouraging socialization from the Folk School's early days. A note on the back of the above photograph reads, "Rosalille and her mother sat talking one day," a rough translation of a line from the Danish folk song "Roselil og hendes moder." Another group of students gathered outside Keith House and joined their instruments together in song. Banjos and a triangle are included among the instruments. Group jams are still a regular occurrence on campus.

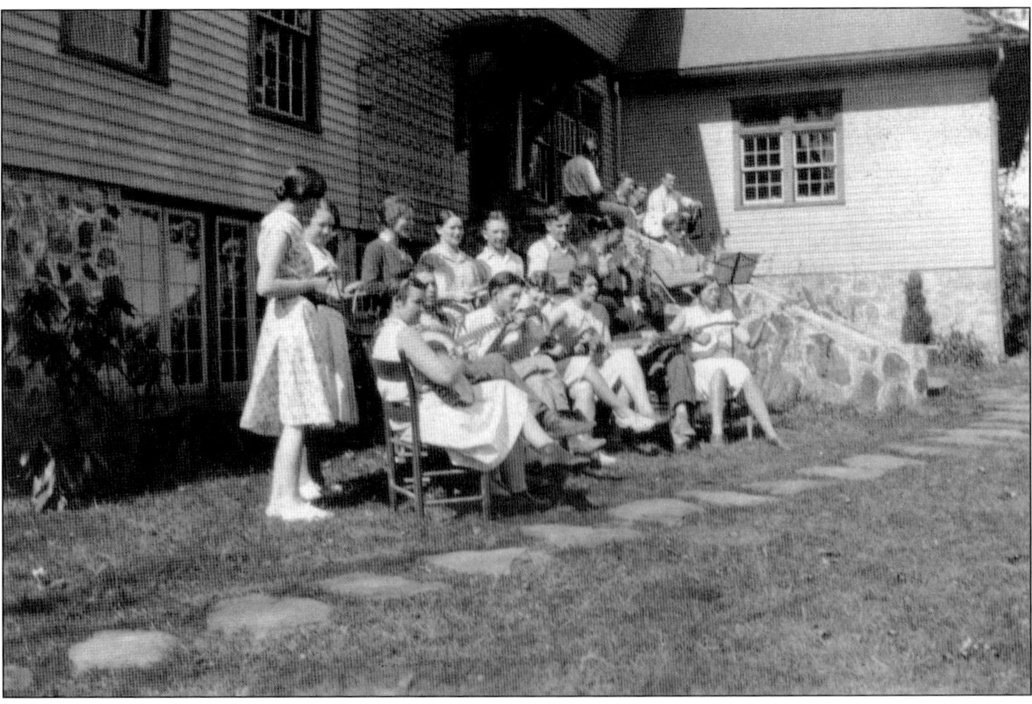

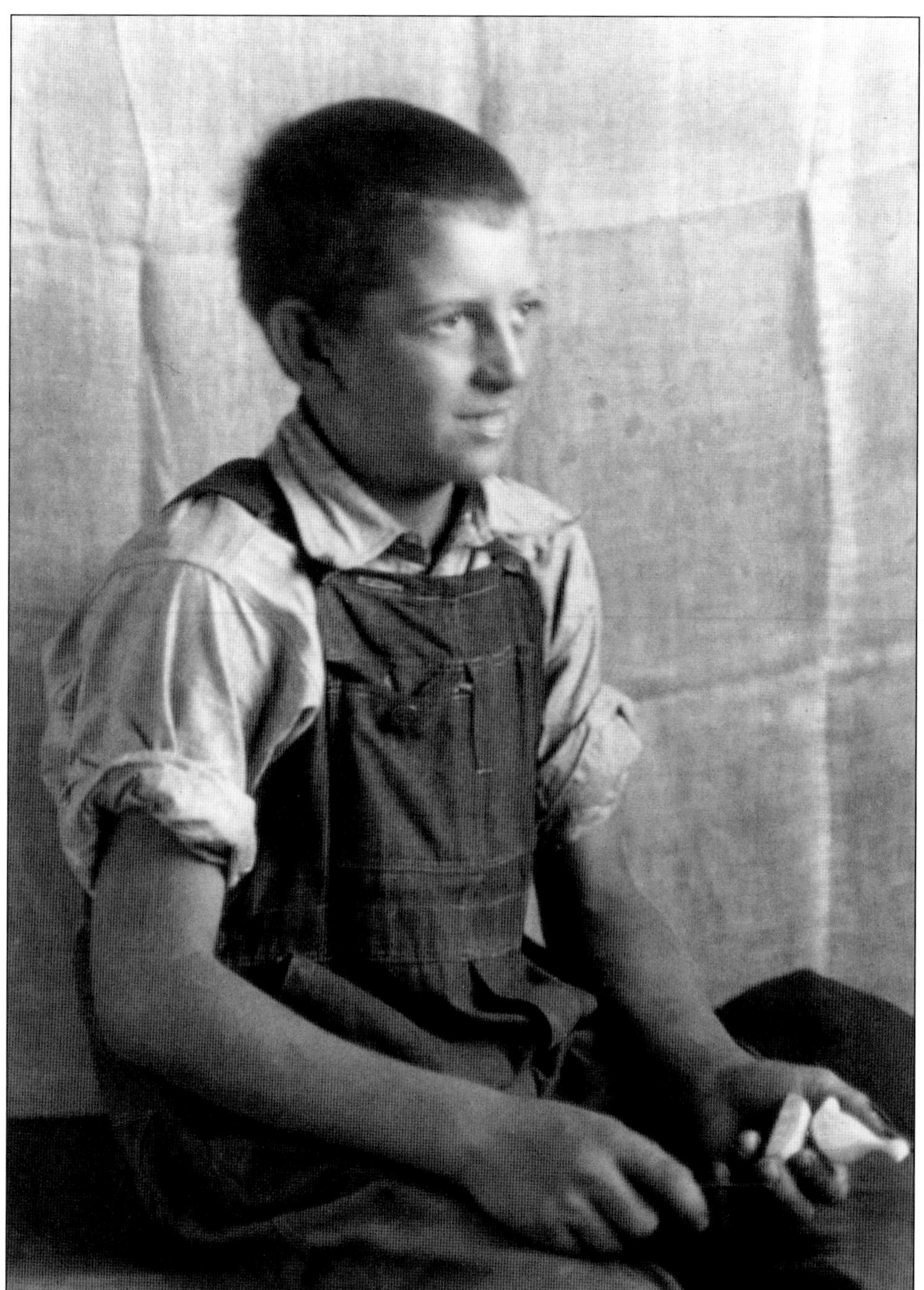

By the 1930s, wood carving was a successful program at the Folk School. While it paved the way for many men and women to provide financial stability for their families, it also offered younger folks the opportunity to follow the same path. Quentin Clayton, pictured here with one of his works-in-progress, was one of those young boys. Clayton took to the craft naturally, and by the age of 10, one of his mules could be found in the home of Pres. Franklin Delano Roosevelt and Eleanor Roosevelt. Eleanor's secretary, Malvina Thompson Scheider, reached out on her behalf to recognize Clayton's talent and encourage his continued craftsmanship.

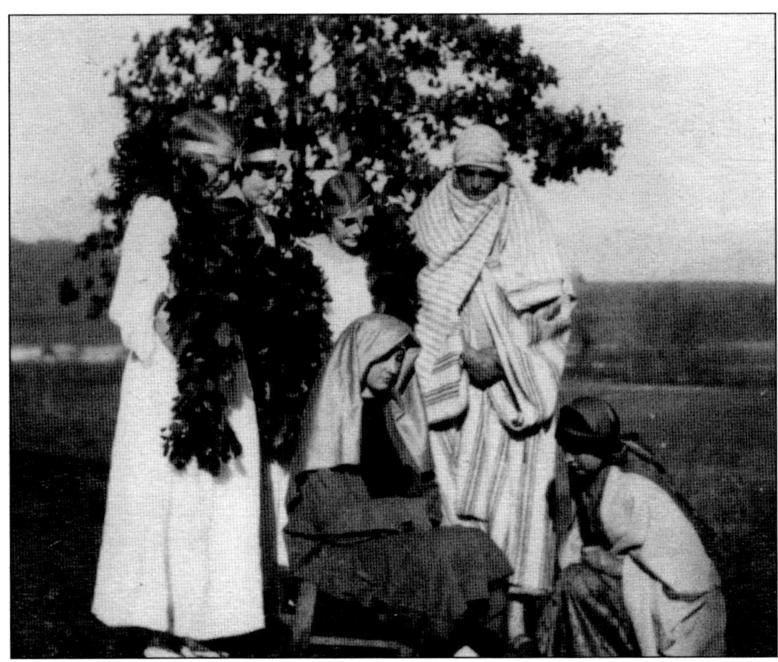

Women and men who were studying on campus during the holidays also participated in the annual Christmas play. This 1930s image includes students dressed as Mary, Joseph, and a host of angels. Performances were held inside the gathering space of the Community Room, welcoming friends and family to join in the seasonal celebration.

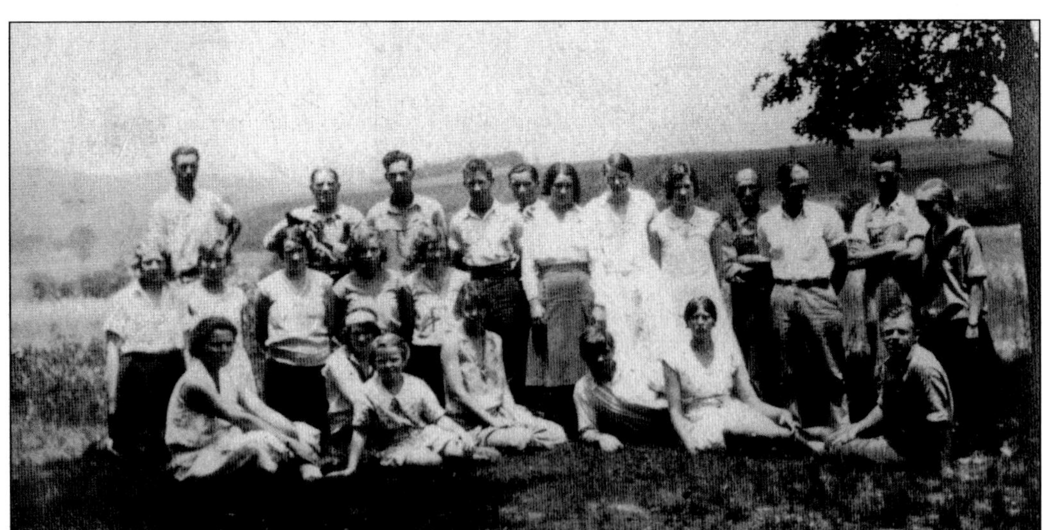

Students who enrolled in educational offerings, including this 1931 short course, also held responsibilities for upkeep and maintenance to support their Folk School experience. Women worked in the laundry, men were on the farm, and both cooked and served family-style dinners. The model has been carried forward through the current host and work-study programs, which provide residential opportunities for students to take classes in exchange for labor.

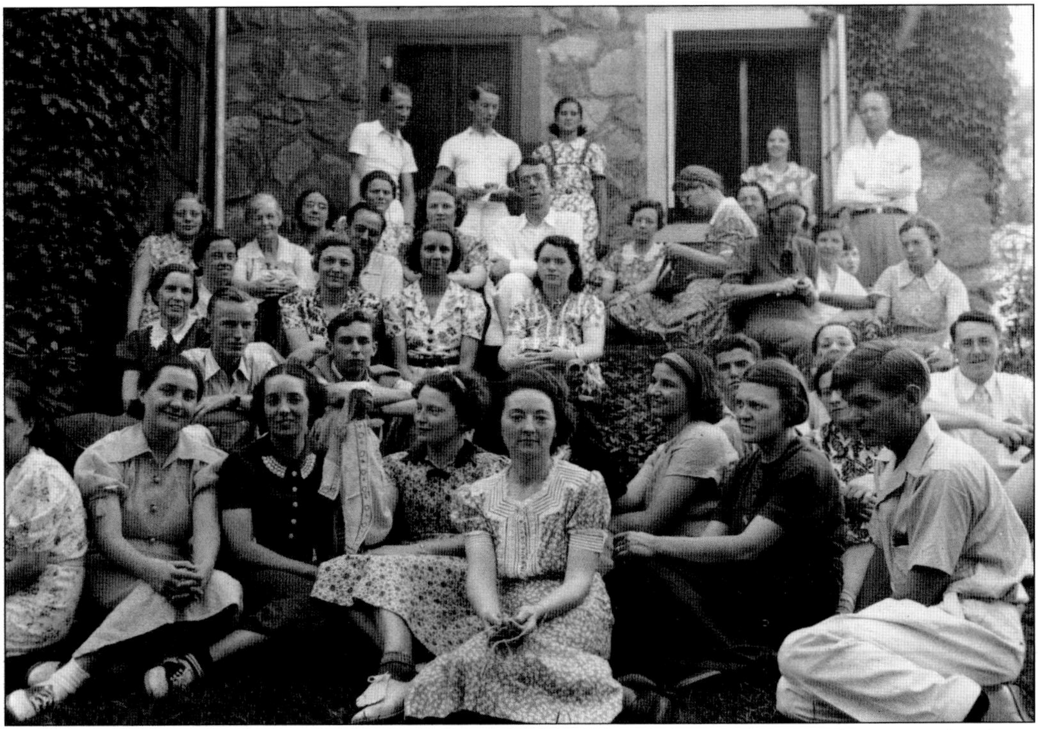

Victor Obenhaus (top right, standing) attended a short course in June 1938. At the time, Obenhaus was principal of Pleasant Hill Academy in Tennessee. The academy also managed a large farm and craft shop, and his visit to the Folk School let him observe how the staff managed operations and student engagement. His classmates are not identified in the photograph on the stairs, though Olive Dame Campbell (fifth row, second from left) and George Bidstrup (first row, far right) are included. His images from the short course also included an outdoor gathering led by Campbell. Louise Pitman, who served as craft director during Obenhaus's visit, once described Campbell as being at her best when engaged in informal meetings with her students.

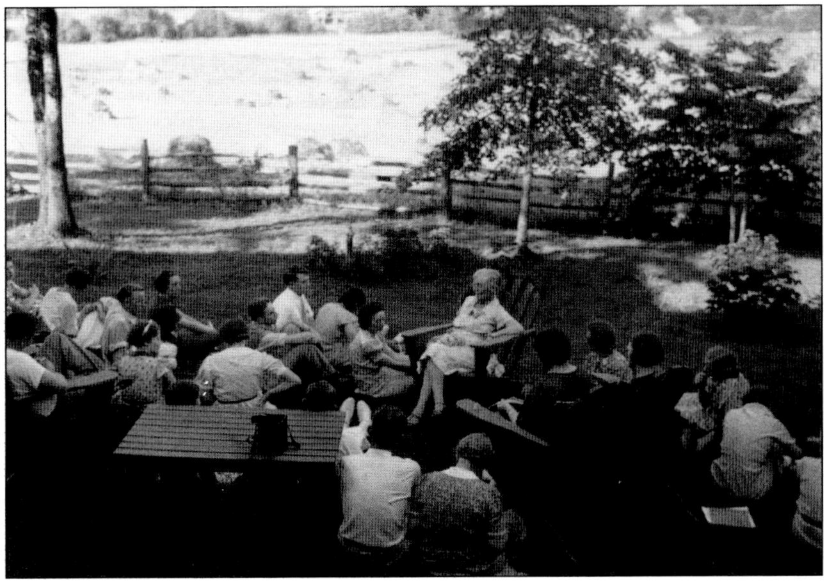

Thurs., April 11, 1935.

A TRIBUTE TO MR. L. L. SCROGGS
By Olive D. Campbell
For the
JOHN C. CAMPBELL FOLK SCHOOL

For ten years, workers, students, and visitors at The John C. Campbell Folk School have enjoyed the friendship of "Uncle Lucius Scroggs". His death, on March 31, is keenly felt by his many Folk School friends. His eagerness to have the school established at Brasstown, the gift of land by himself and Mrs. Scroggs, his work on the Museum his unflagging interest in the clubs and cooperatives, his unfailing courtesy and friendliness to all, will never be forgotten. We are told that a few days before his death, he explained the Folk School to his nurses in the Knoxville hospital, and made them feel that they wished to visit us.

We have often quoted his remark that he wished the Folk School had come twenty-five years earlier. We say, from our hearts, that we wish "Uncle Lucius" could have been with us twenty-five years longer. However, he will live on far longer that that, through the school, and all that he has done for it, and meant to us.

In 1935, Brasstown lost Lucius Scroggs. It was the generosity of his family that provided the land for the Folk School to take root and grow. It was the leadership of his son Fred that brought a community together to advocate for themselves. In her tribute to Scroggs, Olive Dame Campbell said, "We have often quoted his remark that he wished the Folk School had come twenty-five years earlier. We say, from our hearts, that we wish 'Uncle Lucius' could have been with us twenty-five years longer. However, he will live on far longer than that, through the school, and all that he has done for it, and meant to us."

Three

Doris Ulmann

Dear Companion

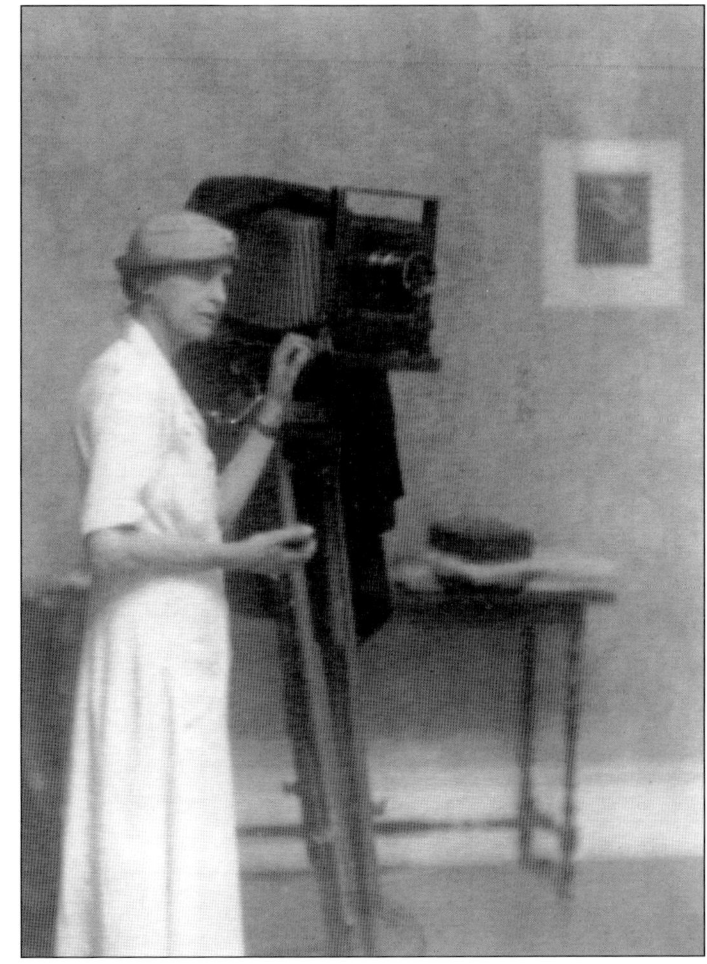

Doris Ulmann was an influential photographer who traveled to Brasstown in 1933–1934 and made images of Folk School life and the local community. Her photography captured the depth of stories illustrated in facial features and informal imagery. Ulmann died in 1934 and gifted an extensive collection of her work to the Folk School. (Courtesy of John Jacob Niles Collection, Special Collections and Archives, University of Kentucky Libraries.)

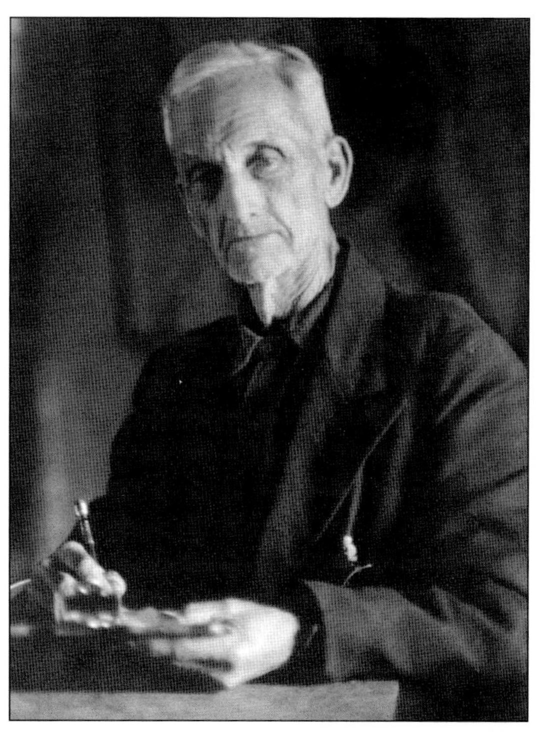

Lucius Leander Scroggs (left) was often called "the host of our community" by Brasstown folks. He and his wife donated acres of land for the Folk School's establishment. He was also involved with the Log Cabin Museum on campus that preserved the history of the mountain life he knew. Lillie Strange Scroggs (below), wife of Lucius and mother to Fred, inherited the land that would become the John C. Campbell Folk School. On her 1925 pledge card, she also promised 500 narcissus bulbs in all varieties, three different colors of peonies, and any wild shrubs from her farm. While Fred O. Scroggs did much of the work to advocate for his neighbors, his parents provided the property where countless others have continued to create community for 100 years.

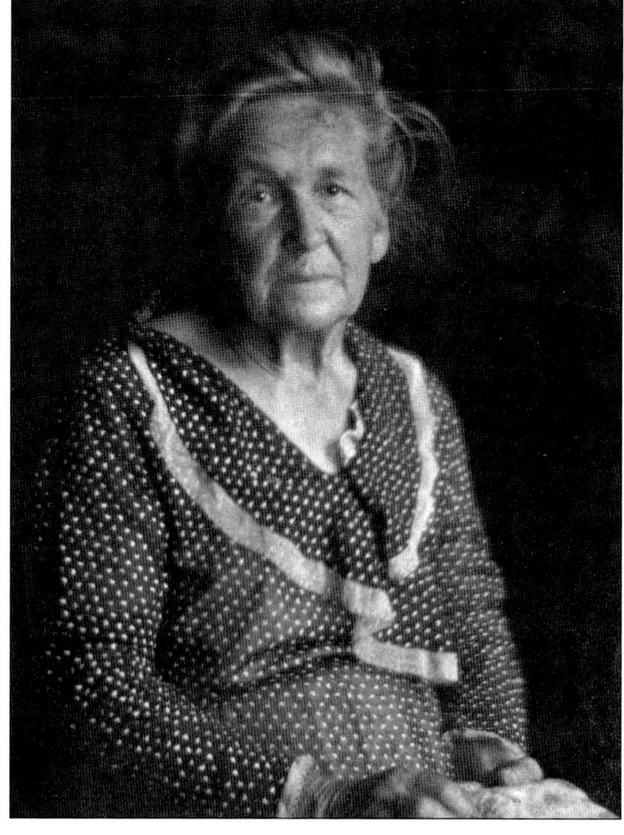

It was on the porch of Fred O. Scroggs's store that Olive Dame Campbell originally found a group of young men "idly whittlin" with their pocketknives. When no spare wood was available, these self-proclaimed "sons of rest" took their knives to the bench where they sat. Scroggs (right, standing) drove nails into the bench, which the carvers then worked around. Campbell saw potential, leading to the birth of the Brasstown Carvers.

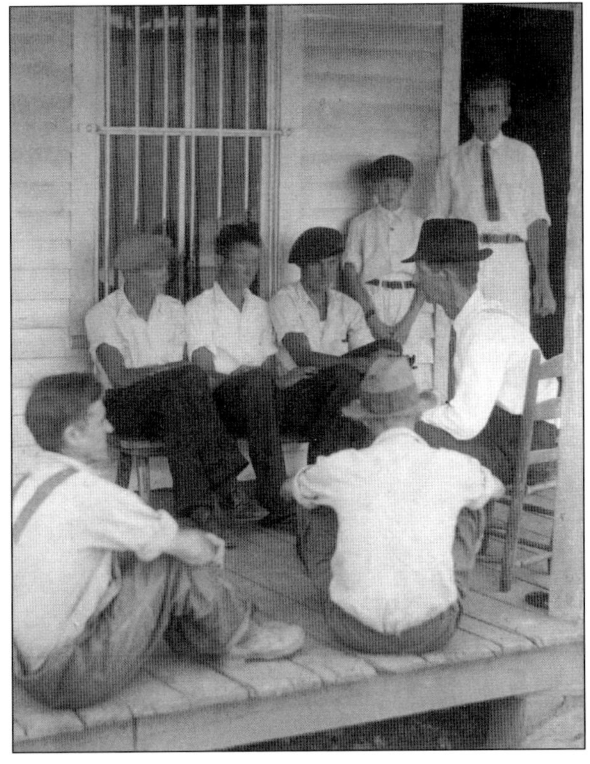

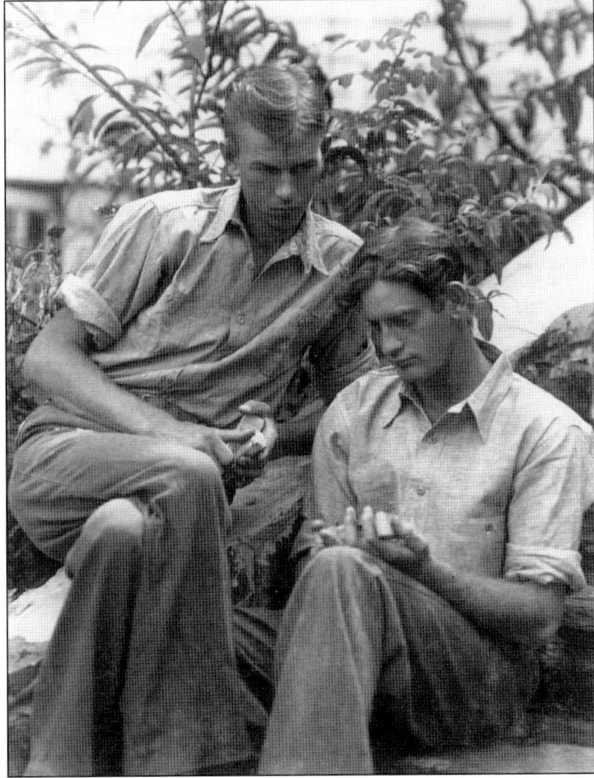

Some Brasstown Carvers had connections with the Folk School outside of their craft. Gwen Cornwell (left) was both a carver and, in 1938, the school's poultry manager. He and William "Gyp" Johnson (right) were students during Ulmann's visit, and both studied under Park Fisher, a friend of John C. Campbell who also served as one of the first Folk School carving instructors.

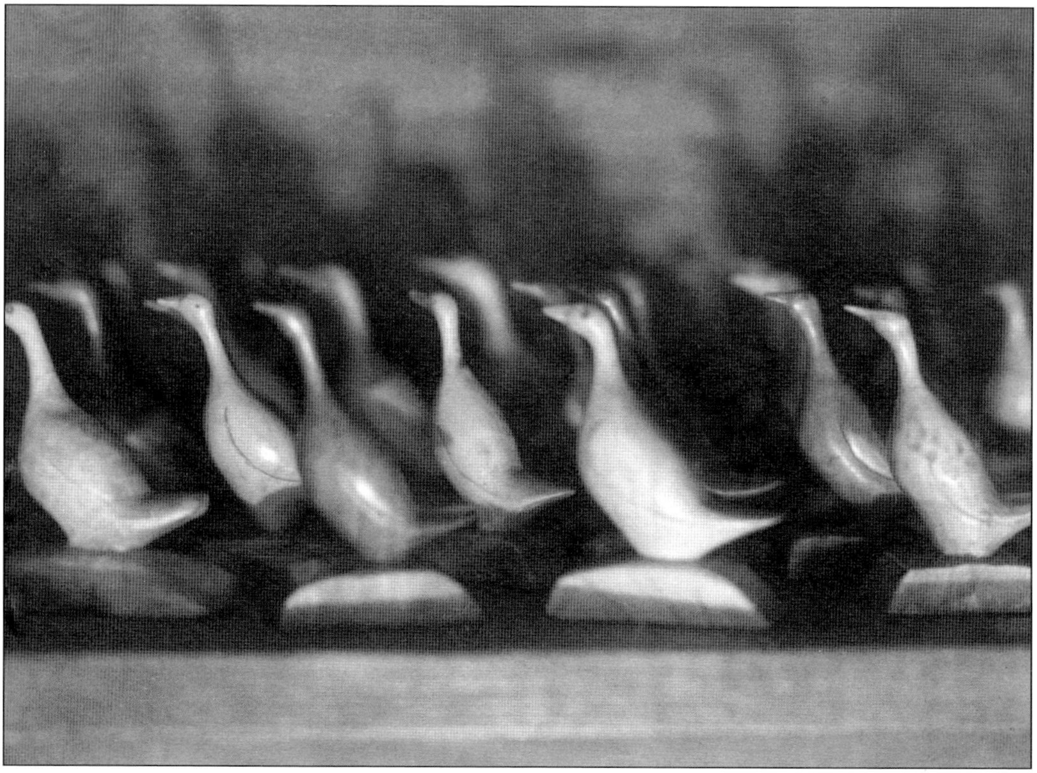

The Brasstown Carvers flourished in the 1930s and 1940s, with carvers and their wares included in regional and national shows and a Rockefeller Center shop. In the early days, carvers would pick up rough-sawn blocks of wood, take them home to carve, and bring them back to the school for final polishing, approval, and sales. Both images represent only a small fraction of the work that was created by women and men who transformed wooden blocks into stunning figures. The carvers often reproduced the livestock or farm animals they saw in their daily lives, including pigs, horses, geese, donkeys, and rabbits.

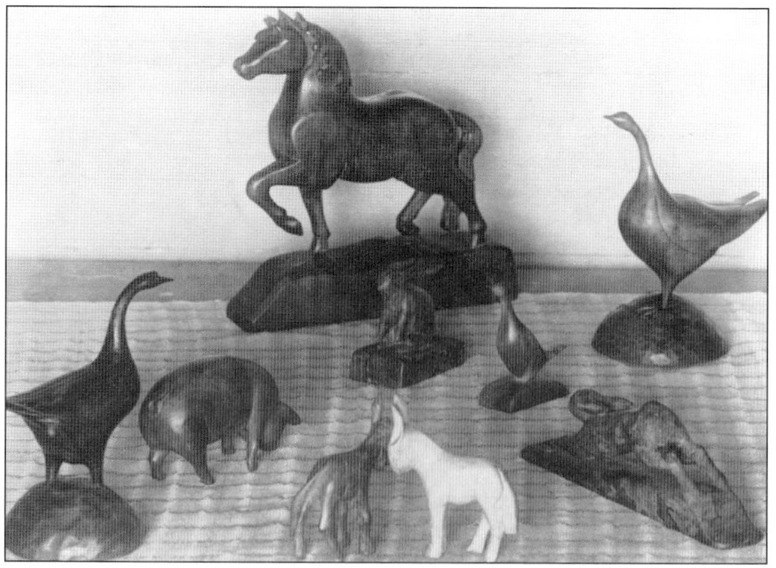

As a photographer, Doris Ulmann was drawn to overlooked or marginalized people. Her work outside of Appalachia included the Gullah community of South Carolina, African Americans who lived in the Lowcountry region. Ulmann gravitated toward the beauty and intensity found in aged faces and the simplicity of daily activities. In Brasstown, she captured striking images of community members like Arminda Curtis, also known as "Aunt Mindy," peeling apples. Ulmann's photographs also include Curtis with her spinning wheel. Curtis and her husband, Amos, lived in the Green Cove community, just down the road from the Folk School. Amos Curtis is pictured below holding a worn Bible.

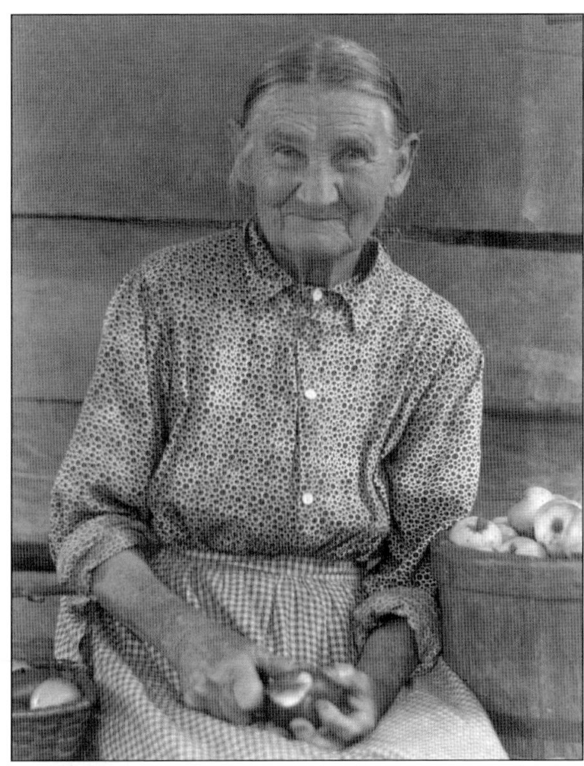

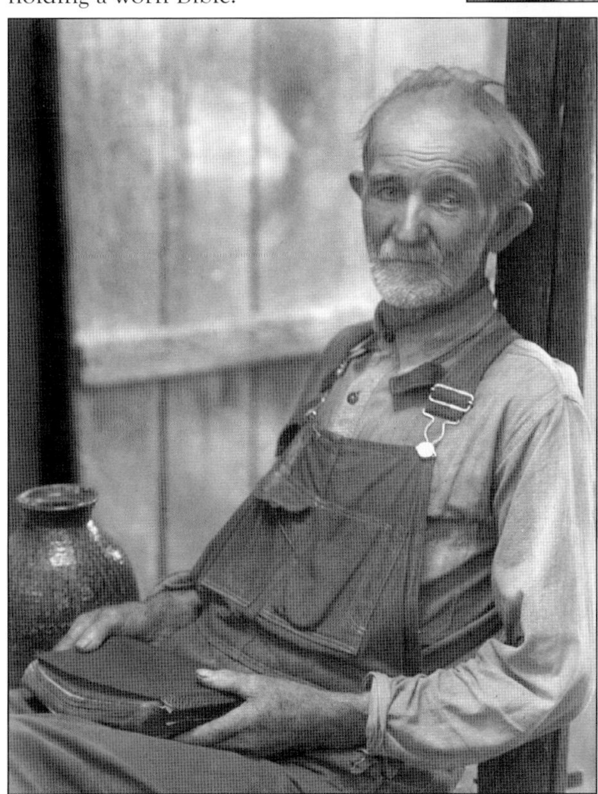

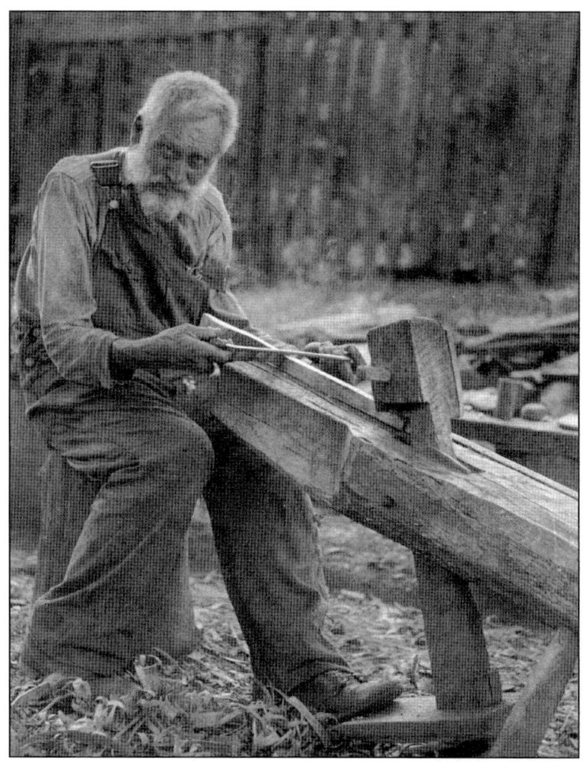

Jason Reed was a chair maker and a native of Blairsville, Georgia. He was one of the local crafters who made chairs for the 1927 dedication day of the Keith House Community Room at the Folk School. Ulmann made many photographs of Reed, one of which later appeared in Allen Eaton's 1937 book *Handicrafts of the Southern Highlands.*

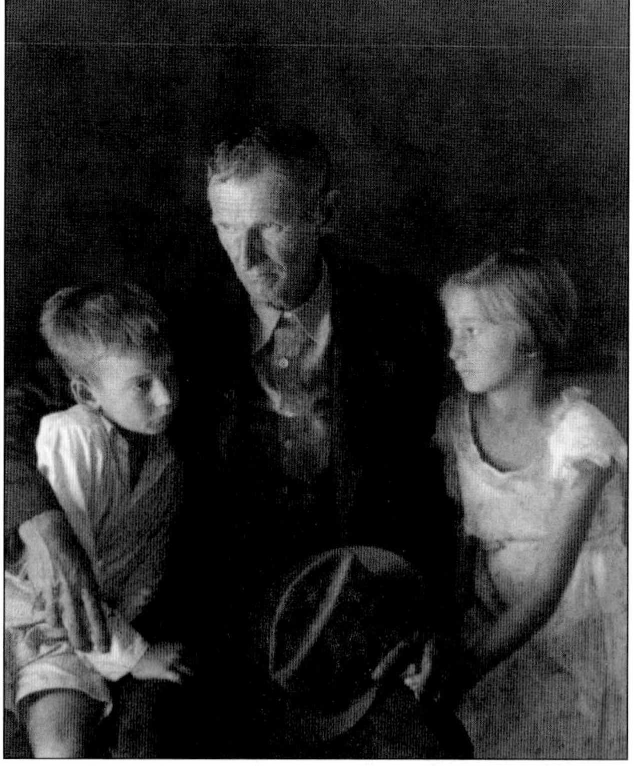

The Carringers were one of several Brasstown families who offered their time and talents to bring the John C. Campbell Folk School into existence. Sam Carringer, captured here with his grandchildren Jack and Roberta, lived near the school in Carringer Cove. They regularly took part in Folk School classes and activities, including dances.

Frank Henderson was known as "the Jenny Man." Jennies (female donkeys) and jacks (male donkeys) were a valuable resource for farmers. Their strength was especially beneficial for carrying heavy loads and transporting goods. They were also utilized to plow fields, and their natural instinct to protect livestock offered a level of security that was practically and financially beneficial.

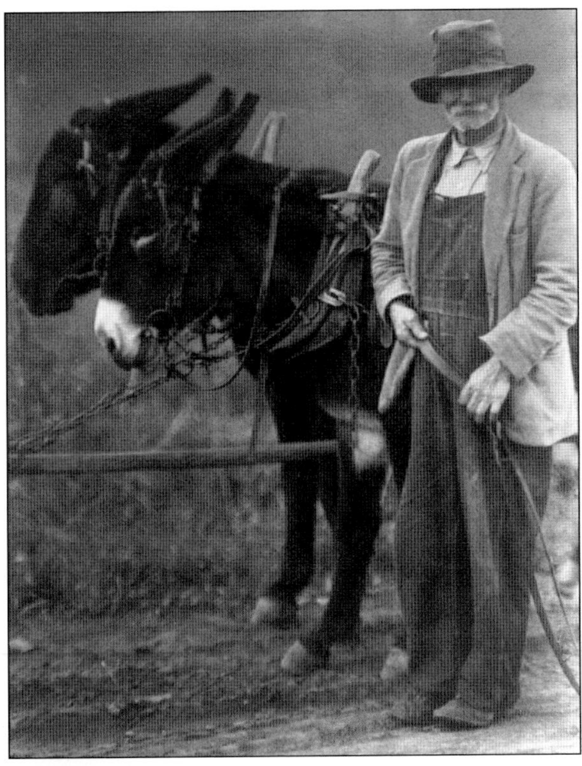

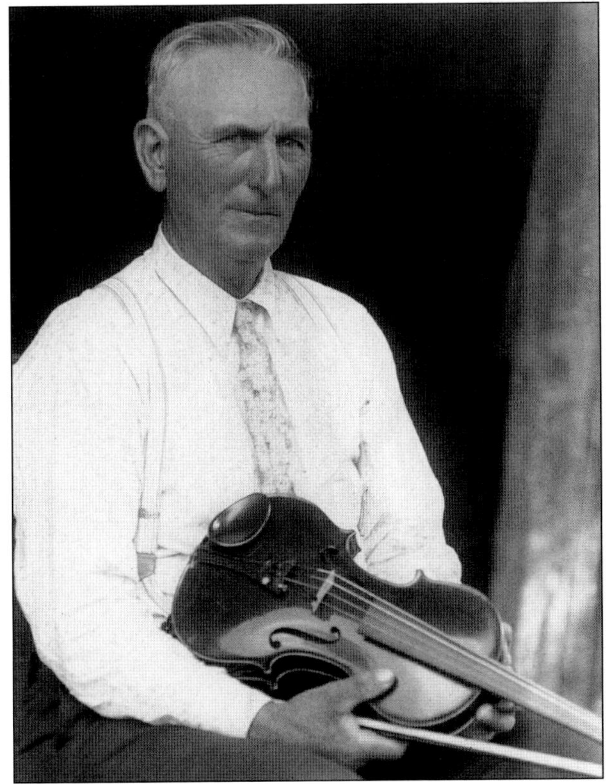

Tom Barnett was a fiddler and folk singer from the Peachtree, North Carolina, community. In old-time music, fiddles often carry the melody or tune of a song while other instruments, including the guitar and banjo, provide accompaniment. Barnett was especially remembered for "The Seven Joys of Mary," a song that was shared at the annual Christmas play held during the Folk School's early years.

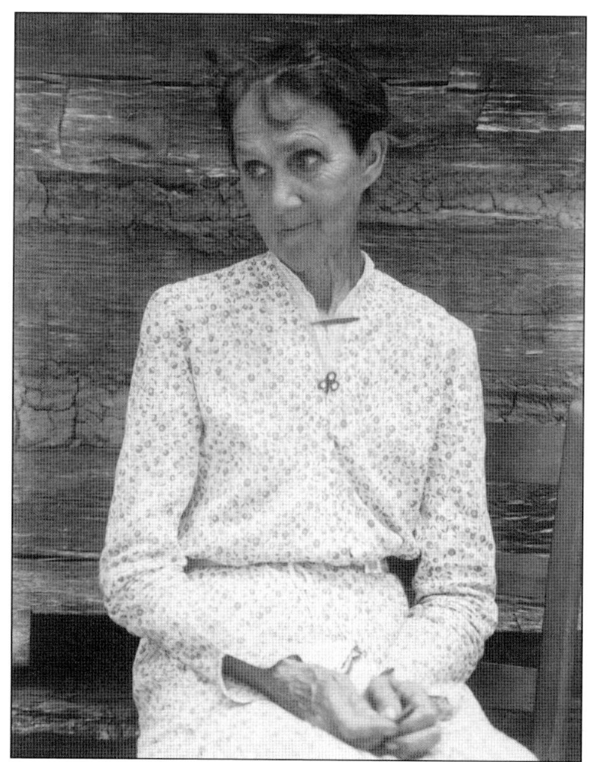

Bird Patten Adams was an active member of the Women's Community Club in Brasstown. Within its first year, the Folk School formed the club as a means of connecting with local people. Members met monthly for dinner and conversation, "recalling the life of bygone years." The club provided the school and the community with another opportunity to preserve traditions.

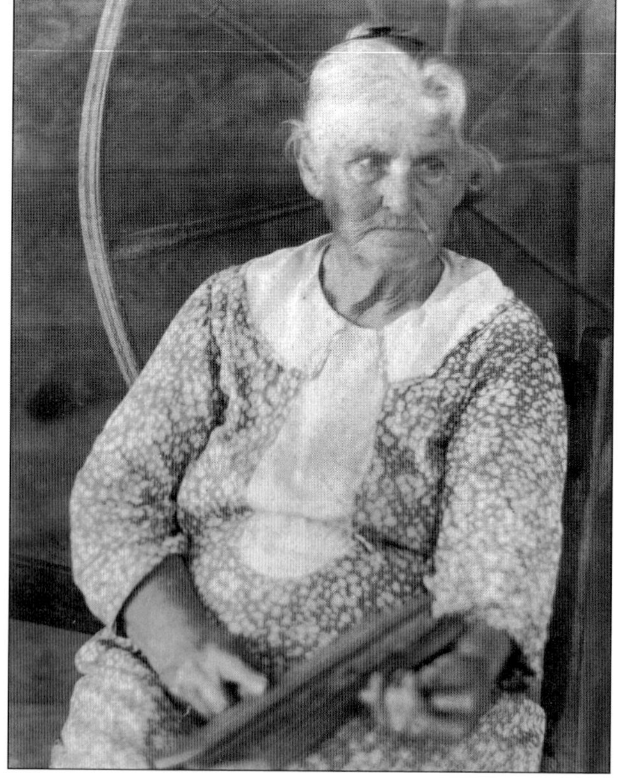

Sarah Sanoma Hatchett, known as "Granny Hatchett," was a spinner and weaver from the Bellview community. She is holding hand carders, tools used to prepare sheared wool for spinning into yarn. It is a practice still used today, starting with a section of wool being placed on one carder, then brushed upward with the second. The process is repeated until the wool is well-separated and ready for spinning.

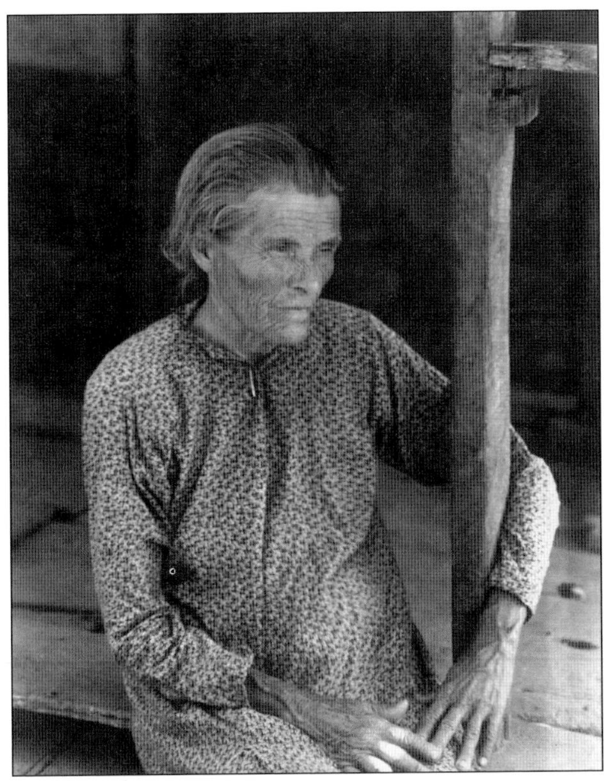

Sara(h) Jane Johnson was the mother of early carver William "Gyp" Johnson. Her family was one of many in the area who supported the school's establishment and participated in many of the school's activities. Johnson was remembered as a singer, known especially for "Farewell, Sweet Jane." The ballad was later sung by Aunt Molly Jackson and recorded by Alan Lomax.

Church life played an important role in the life of the Brasstown community. It was inside a local church where more than 200 community members greeted Marguerite Butler with their support for the Folk School's founding. This Sunday school class included community members, from left to right, (first row) Jim Clayton, Evie Clayton, and Bill Clayton; (second row) Bert Hogan, Sam Carringer, and Henry Carringer; (standing) Virge Coker and Lee Coker.

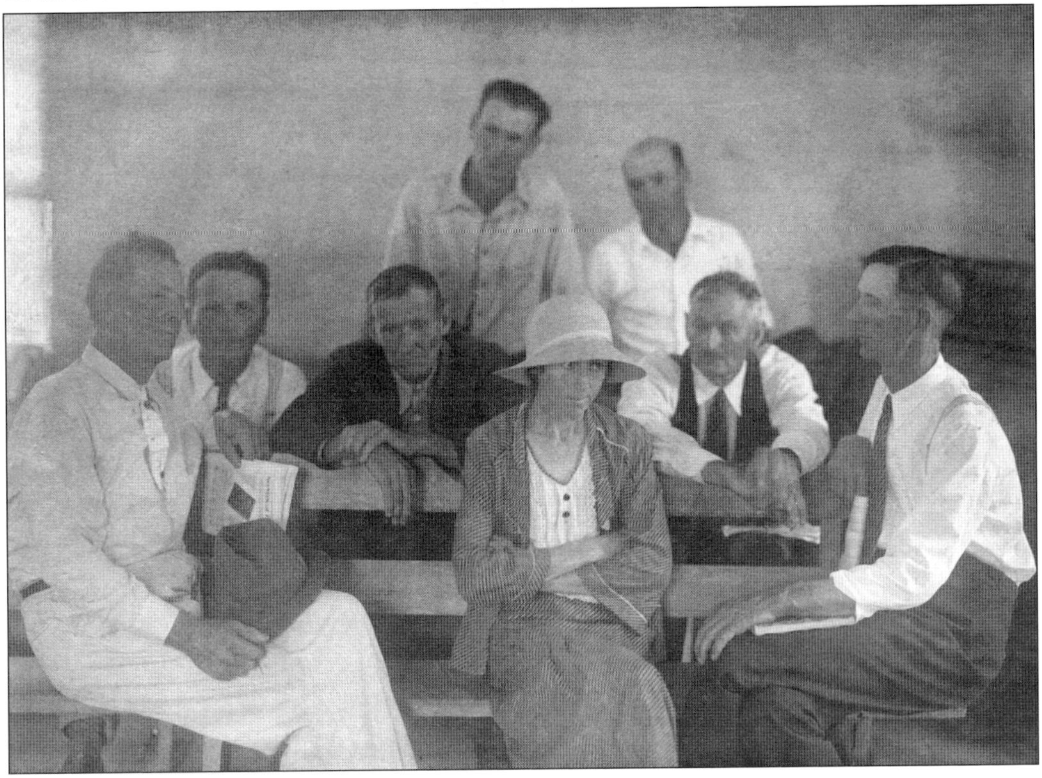

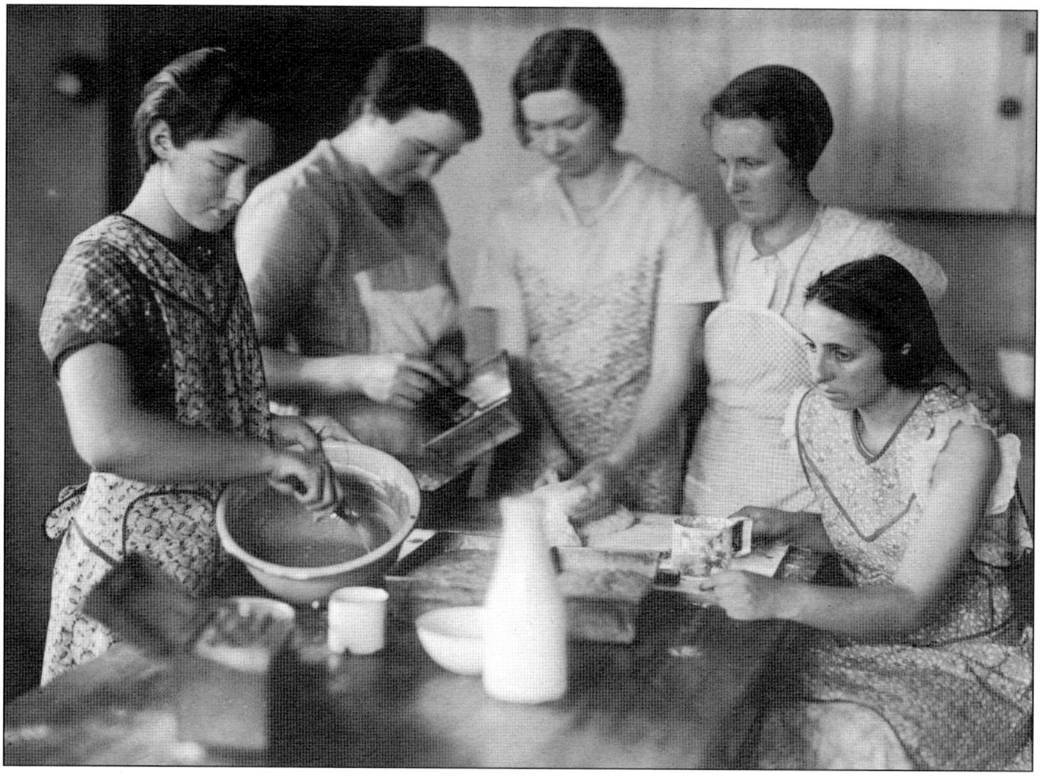

In the early years of the Folk School, students participated fully in daily activities. Recreation and responsibilities were both communal, including preparations for breakfast, lunch, and supper. In the Keith House kitchen, from left to right, Vessie McIntyre, Maud Cox, Nina Bryan (dietitian), Inez Bailey, and Meg Hunt created a homemade meal that was as much about sustenance as it was about cooperation and fellowship.

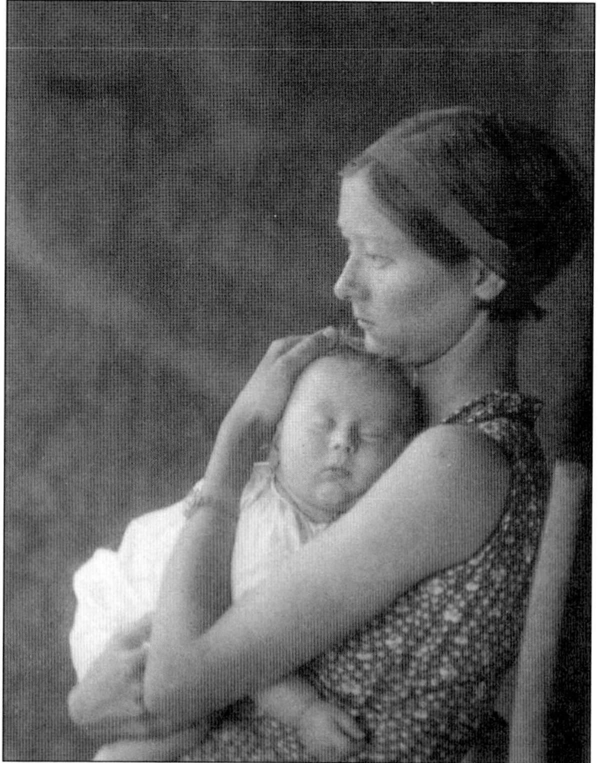

Bonnie Logan (holding her son John) attended the 1927 winter session at the John C. Campbell Folk School and met Hayden Hensley, who would become her husband. While on campus, she lived in the Farm House with Olive Dame Campbell and Marguerite Butler and later worked in the school kitchen. She and Hensley married in 1931, became prolific wood-carvers, and raised their family in "the house that carving built."

The annual Folk School tradition of the Olde Folks' Party, first celebrated in 1926, was originally held outside by the Log Cabin Museum. The historic building, with its preservation of traditional artifacts, provided a meaningful event location. At the 1934 party, Ulmann captured this image of Nancy Sue Waldroup leaning out of one of the log cabin windows.

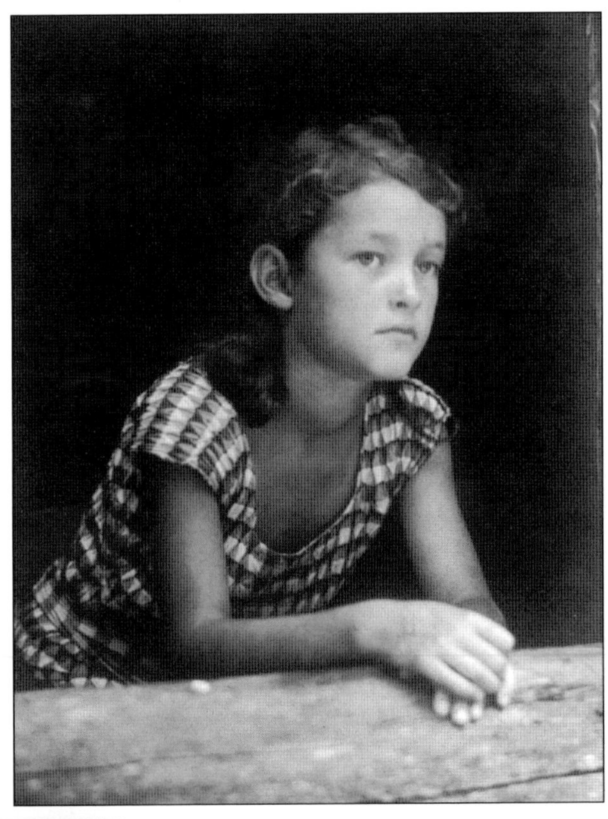

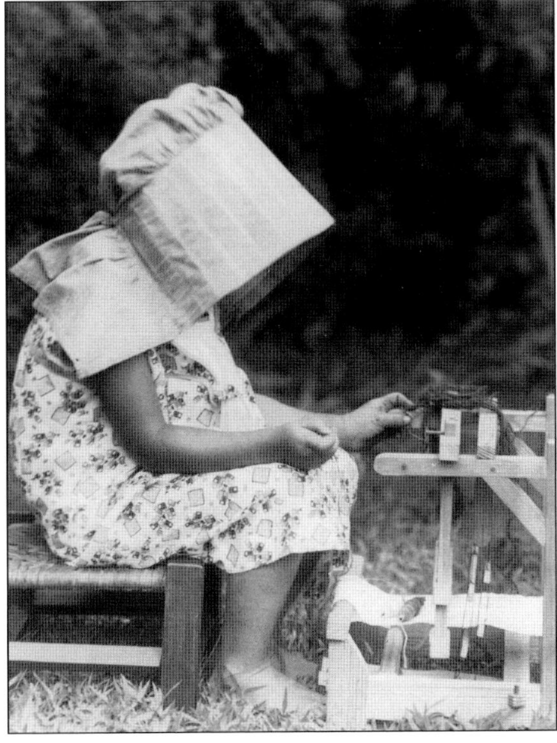

Doris Ulmann sometimes posed her subjects in outfits or accessories that recalled an earlier time. This side view of Wanda Scroggs, dressed in a bonnet and sitting with a small loom, connected the generations in her family that were directly connected to the Folk School. Scroggs was the daughter of storekeeper Fred O. Scroggs and granddaughter of community leaders Lucius and Lillie Scroggs.

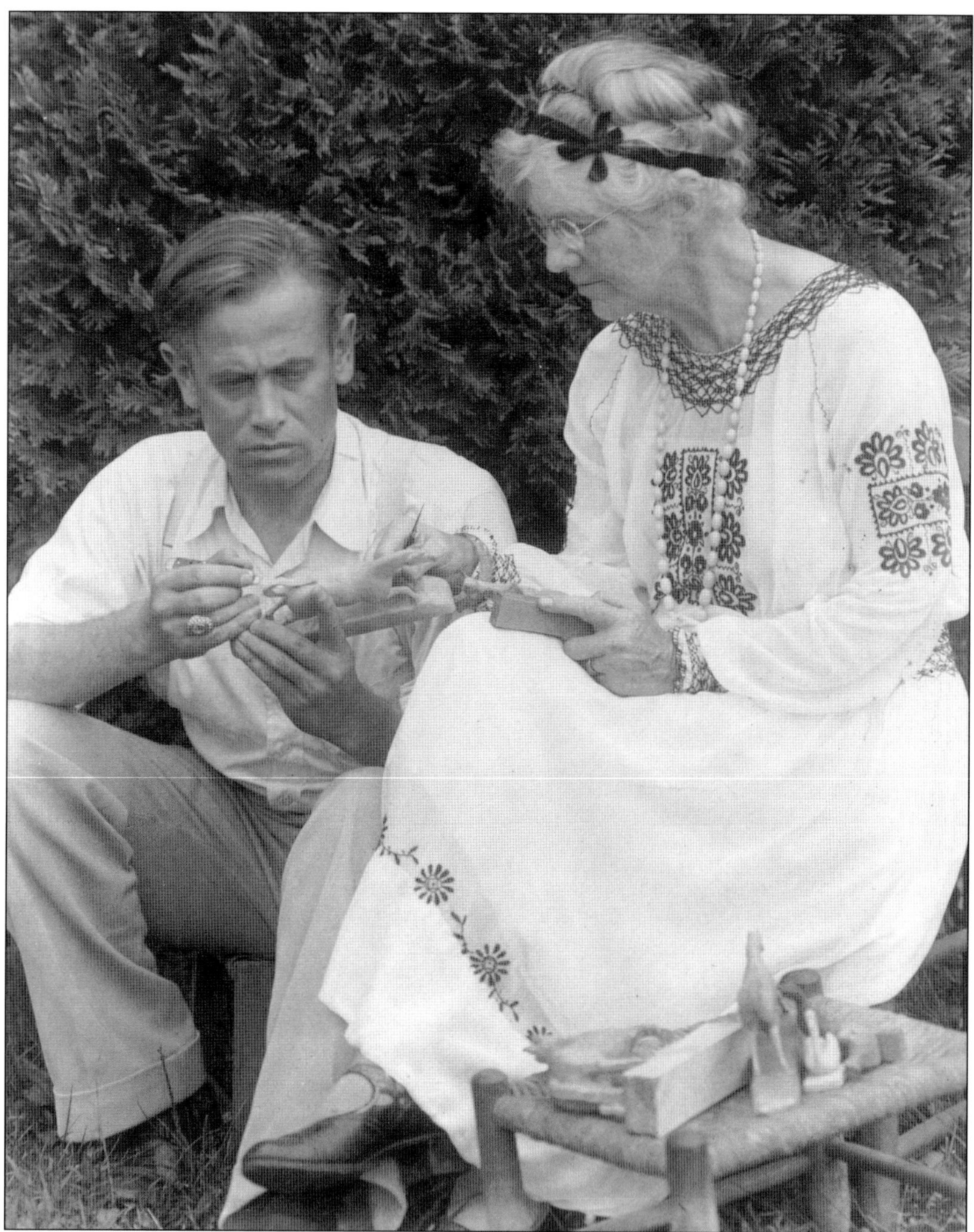

John Jacob Niles (left) was a folk musician and ballad collector who traveled with Doris Ulmann and served as her assistant during photographic expeditions throughout Appalachia. In this image, Niles and Olive Dame Campbell examine animal figures from the Brasstown Carvers. He later published 63 of Ulmann's images in *The Appalachian Photographs of Doris Ulmann*. Niles also returned to the Folk School in 1935 to serve as the music director. In the beginning, Campbell provided a place for the Brasstown Carvers to turn their hobby into a craft. Later, she became a carver herself. The Folk School still retains some of her finished work, including an angel, a cat, and a goose.

Four

1940s–1950s
The Rugged Soldier

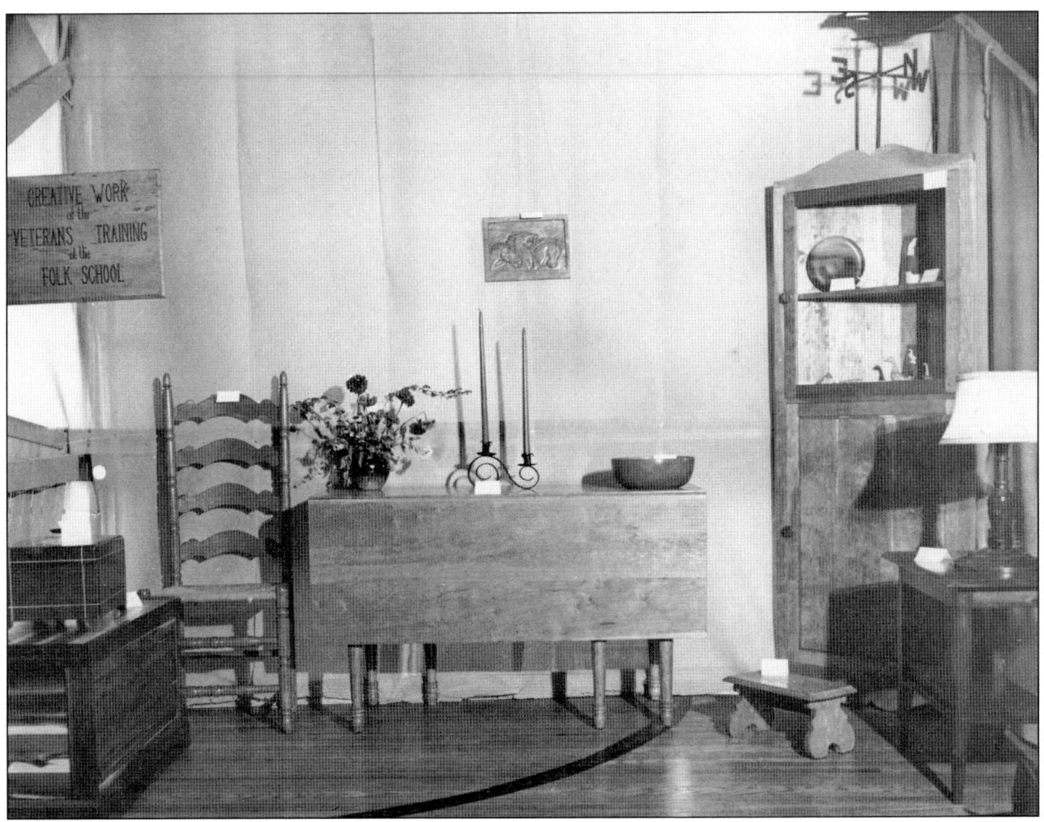

The effects of World War II were keenly felt in Brasstown. As men were sent to battle, women began to whittle. Some became prolific members of the Brasstown Carvers cooperative. Postwar, the Folk School became an approved training site for veterans. Crafts also continued to expand. George Bidstrup became director in 1952, growing the farm operations and establishing Danish gymnastics and dancing as core activities.

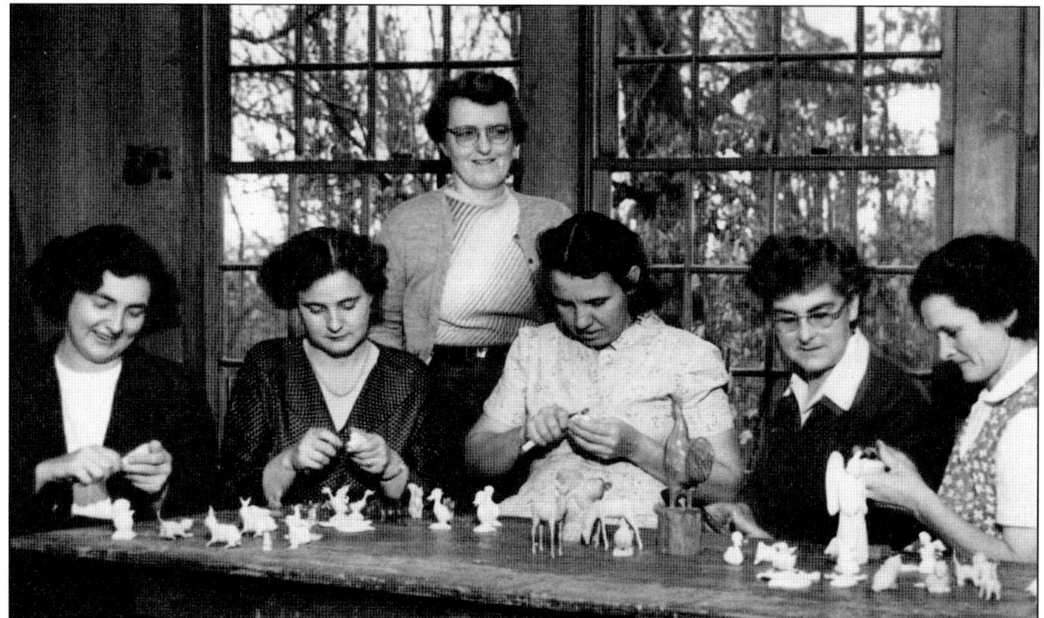

Murrial Decker Martin (standing), better known as Murray, was hired as a craft teacher in 1935. During World War II, Martin's leadership of the Brasstown Carvers included a growing number of women. Traditionally, wives would participate in sanding and finishing carvings, but increasingly stressful economic conditions brought more women to the table. Here, she watches over, from left to right, carvers Ethel Hogsed, Pearl Massey, Janita Deputy, Sue McClure, and Hope Brown.

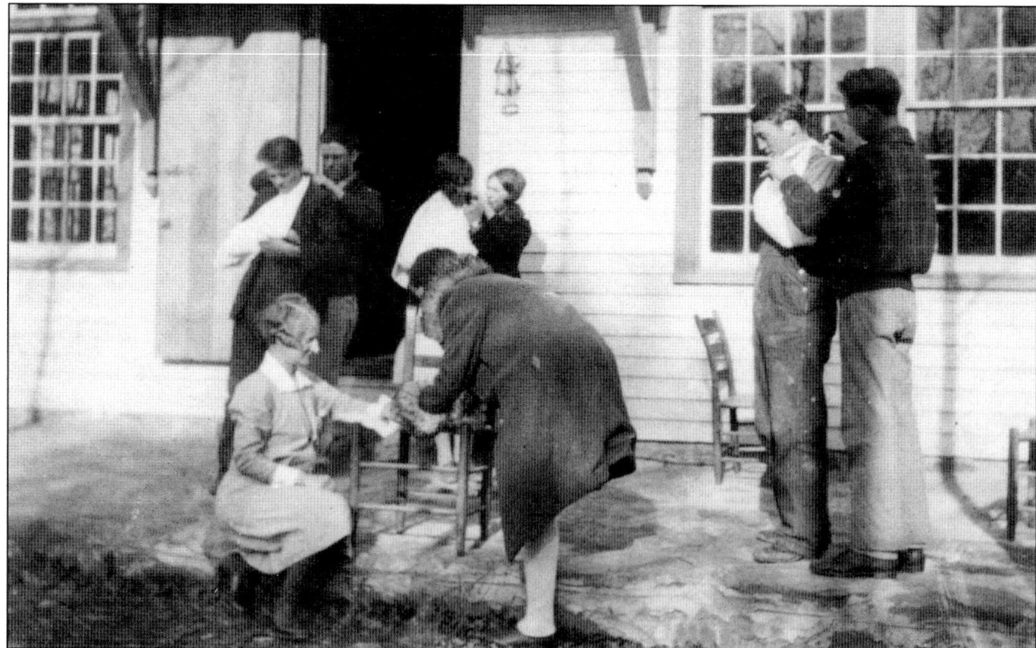

As the Folk School adjusted to the changing wants and needs that existed during wartime and postwar settings, it added first aid instruction to the evolving curriculum. This simulation exercise, held outside the Community Room in Keith House and captured by Marguerite Butler Bidstrup, illustrates how students learned basic emergency assistance.

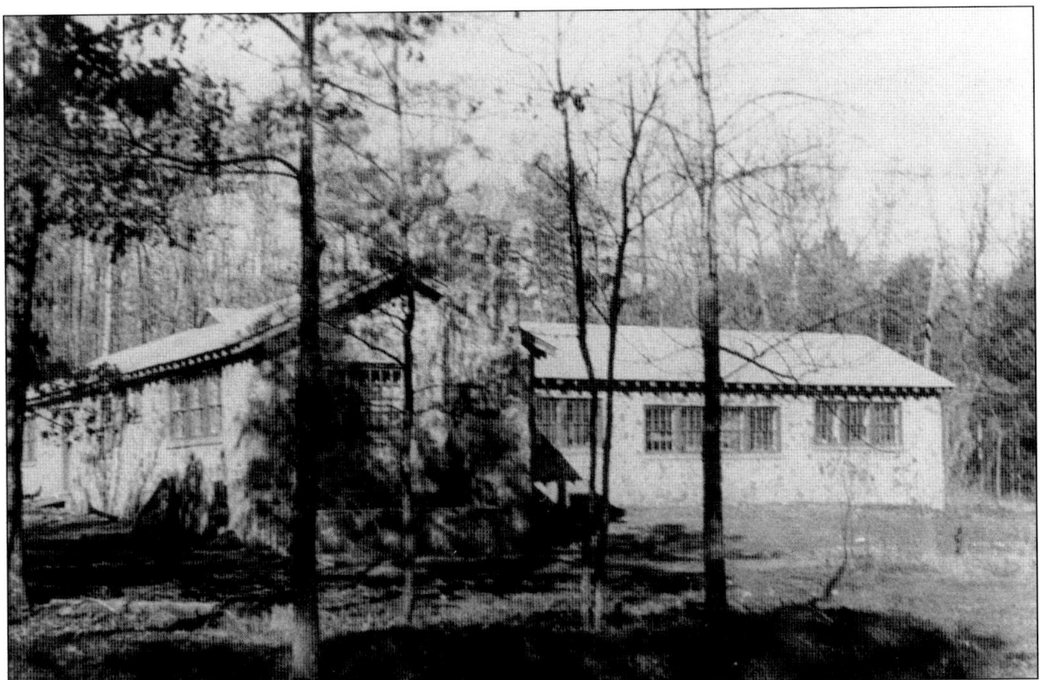

In the summer of 1945, a group of young people from the American Friends Service Committee helped install the walls of the new woodworking shop (above) after a fire destroyed it in 1944. The following summer, a different group returned to help with threshing and haying, painting and staining, and, in the last few weeks of their program, building the stone structure that became the Oscar Cantrell Blacksmith Shop. A feature in the October 1947 Folk School newsletter stated, "The American Friends Service Committee believes that it is a valuable experience for young people to give of their labor and time to some worthy project, and in this way to learn to know another community."

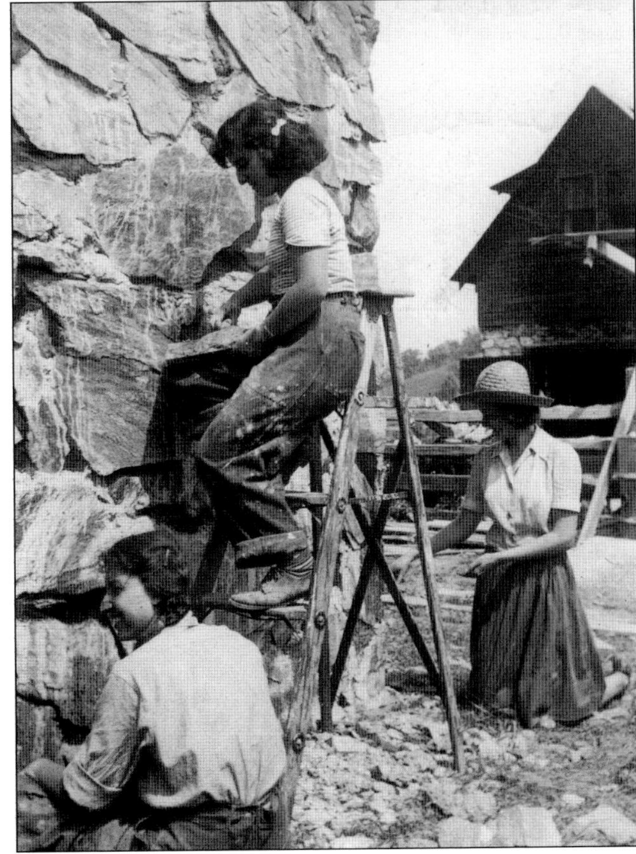

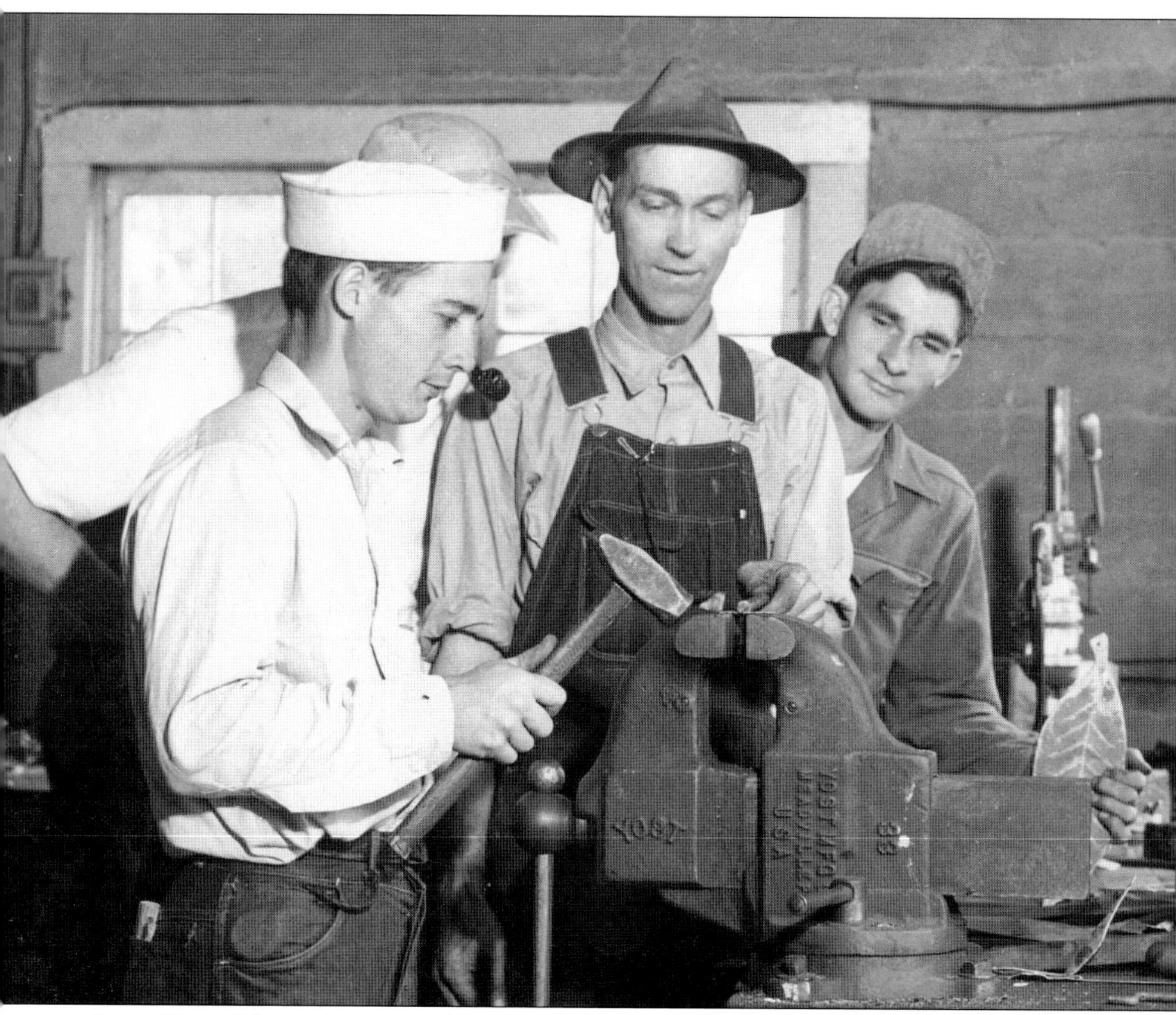

Oscar Cantrell (center) was one of the many community members who pledged labor to establish the Folk School in Brasstown. When the school received approval to serve as a site for veterans who wanted to take advantage of the GI Bill, Cantrell's role as the school's blacksmith expanded into training those who served in World War II in the craft of blacksmithing. Woodworking, including cabinet making, was also open for study through the program. A 1950 letter from George Bidstrup to Olive Dame Campbell and the Folk School Board of Directors highlighted the success of the veterans' training program. "We have taken five new veterans from our local area," he wrote, "and have promised the VA supervisors to take two from outside the area." Long waiting lists for other veterans reflected the level of interest in the training program as well as its growing reputation.

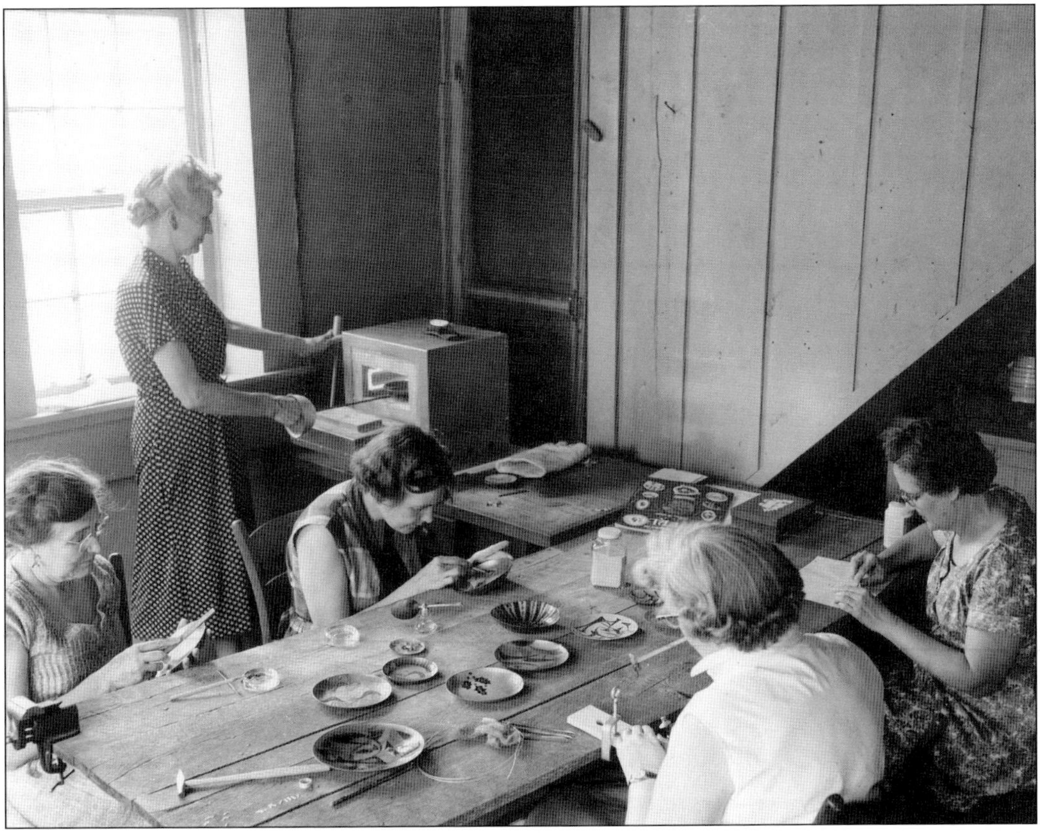

Before the current Enameling Studio was created, enameling classes were held in Tower House. This 1950 class, focused on copper enameling, used high heat to fuse powdered glass to copper, creating a surface that is both smooth and colorful. Finished products can range from decorative pieces to ornate jewelry.

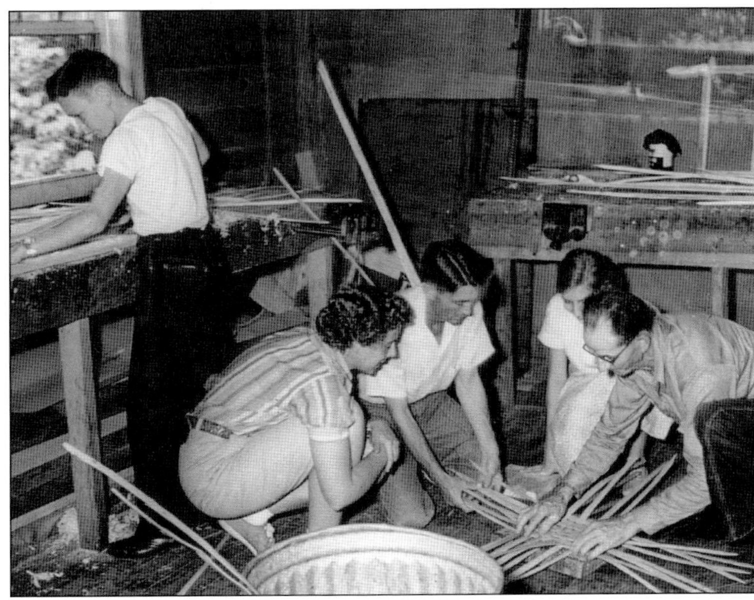

As program areas continued to expand throughout the 1940s and 1950s, the art of chair seats met both functional and decorative purposes. The craft creates durable furniture and brings new life to family heirlooms or secondhand treasures. Here, an unidentified instructor (right) demonstrates weaving techniques for chair seats while another student prepares materials.

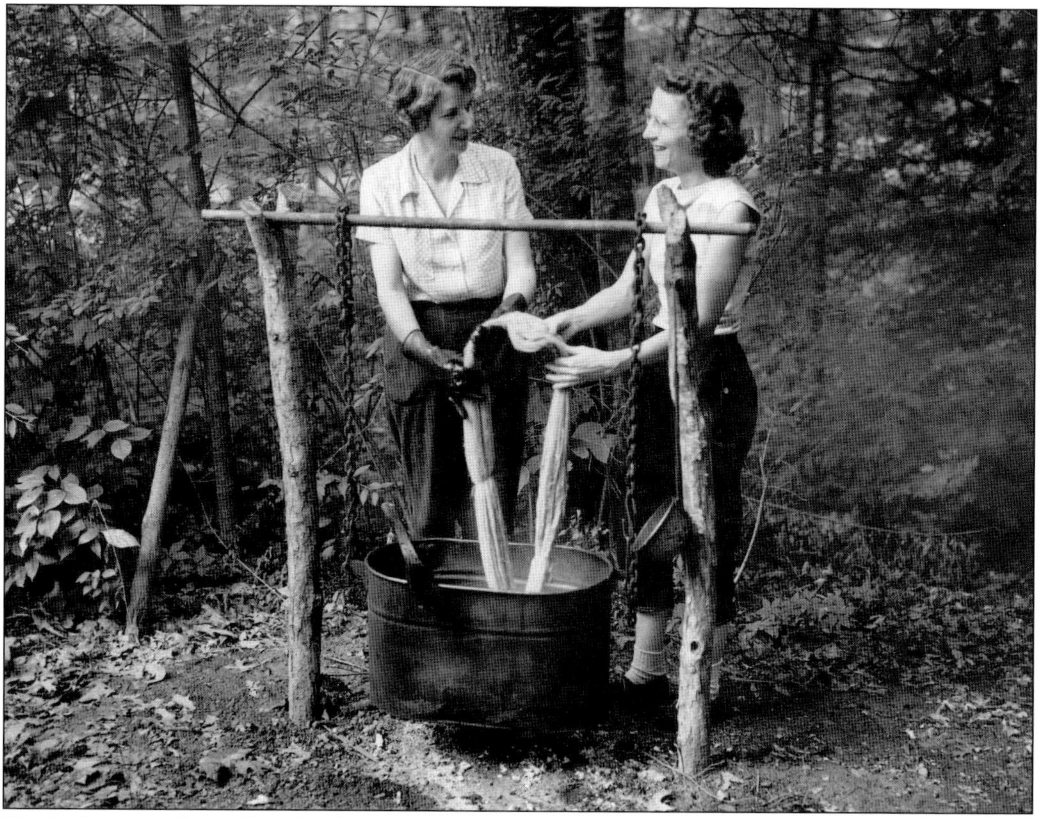

Kettle dyeing at the Folk School dates to the early years when high-quality, dyed yarn was needed to supply the school's weaving program. The method uses the heat of a campfire and the generous space of a large kettle to create colors that range from soft to bold, often with the use of natural ingredients like flowers and vegetables. While the first kettle-dyed yarns supported weaving classes at the Folk School, the finished product can also be used for knitting, crochet, and other textile arts. The school's natural dyeing classes now include an endowed dye garden that grows French marigolds, chamomile, indigo, and more.

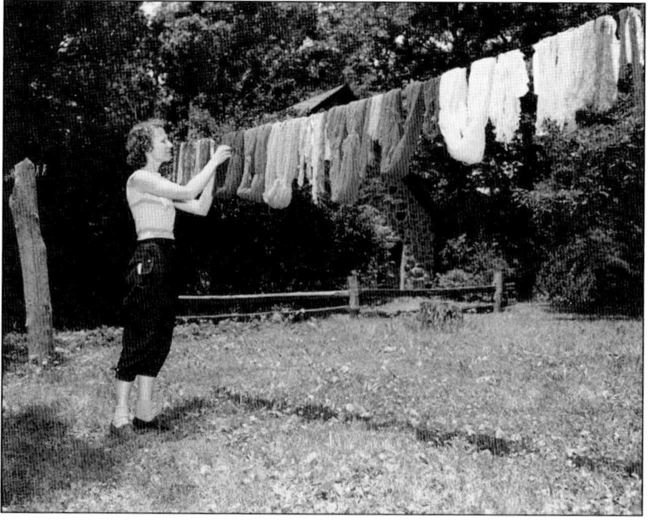

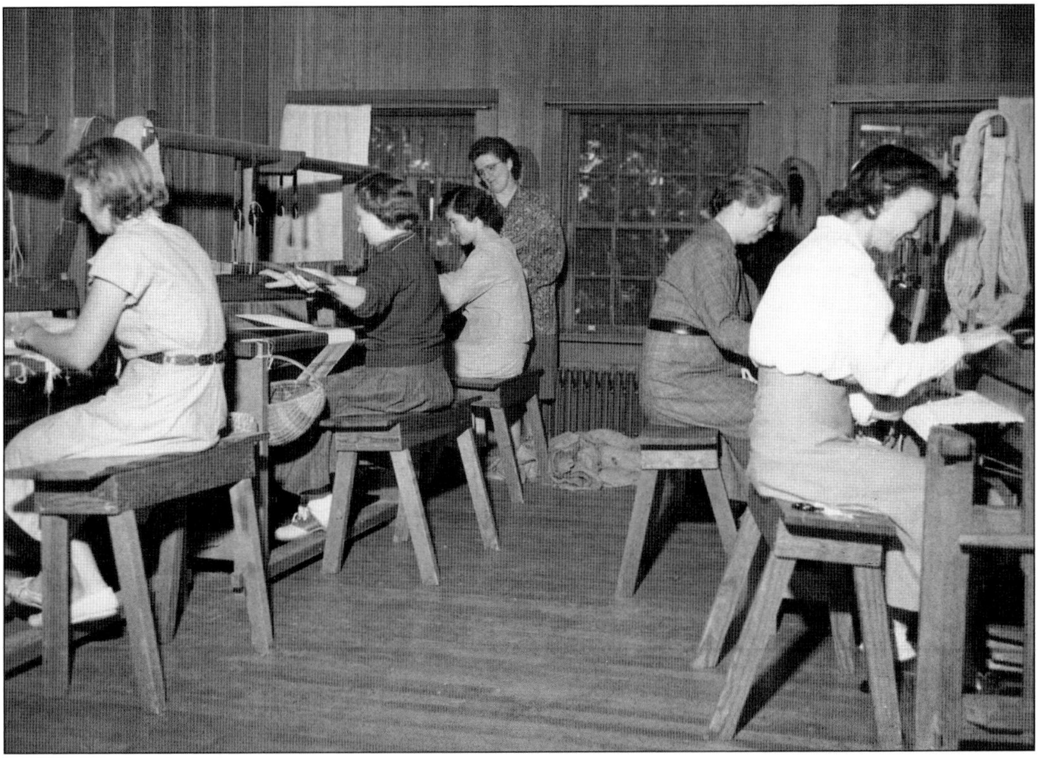

Early weaving classes were held in Keith House, then in the Leon Deschamps building that now houses the History Center. Murray Martin (standing), who managed numerous roles at the Folk School, also served as a weaving instructor. The traditional Appalachian craft played a vital role in family and community life by providing material for clothing and blankets. From the early days, weaving classes at the Folk School taught students to create works-in-progress as well as final pieces. These examples from a 1950s class include many items that are still taught today. Over the years, the program has expanded into rugs, instrument straps, bags, and tapestries.

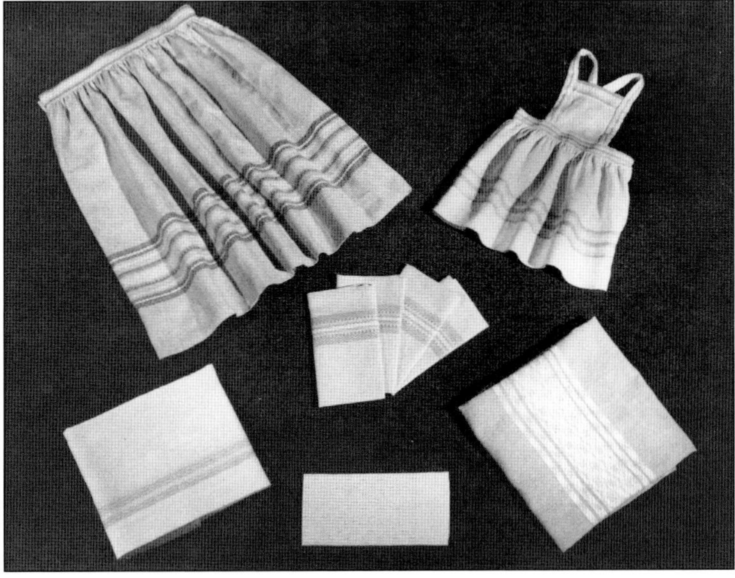

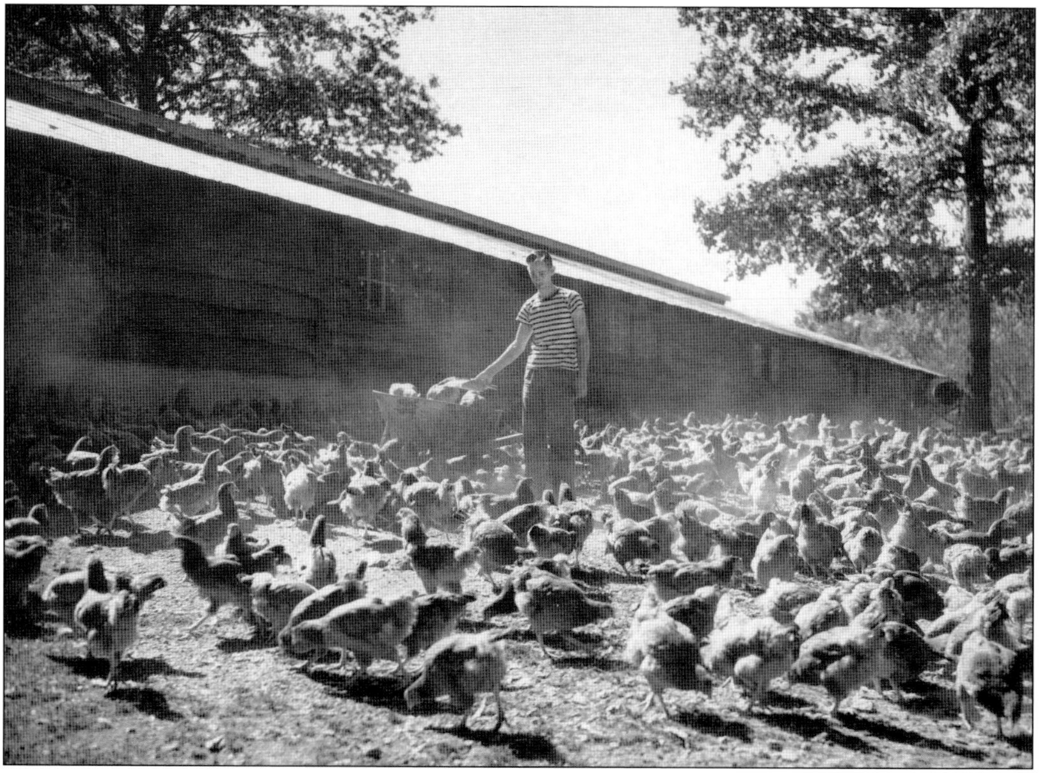

During and after the war, the school's focus on agriculture continued to flourish. George Bidstrup, who served as the farm manager until his appointment as director in 1952, expanded farm operations during his tenure. The structure that served as the chicken house in agricultural days, pictured behind a young man distributing food, now serves as the site of the Louise Pitman Fiber Arts Studio.

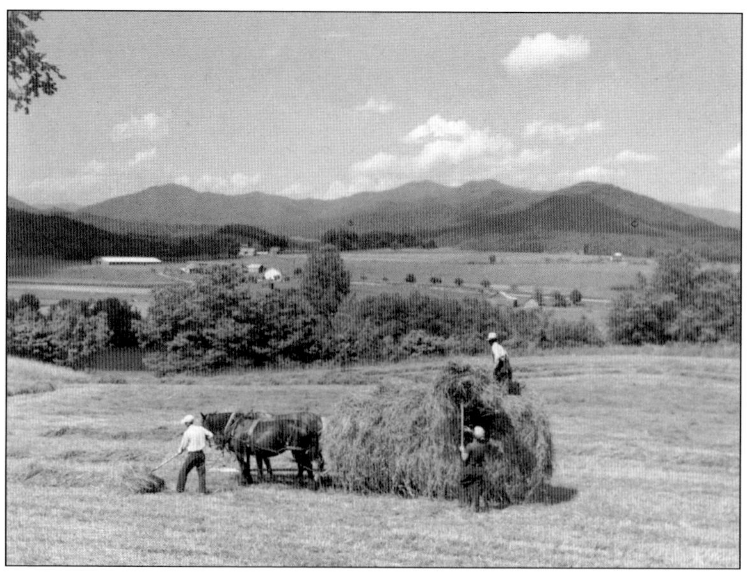

Hay fields served numerous purposes for the school's farming focus, from providing food for livestock, especially in the winter months, to creating walkways and seating areas. The latter is a tradition still seen on campus today, especially during the Fall Festival celebration in October. The work of gathering hay required tremendous physical labor from the horses and the men who guided them.

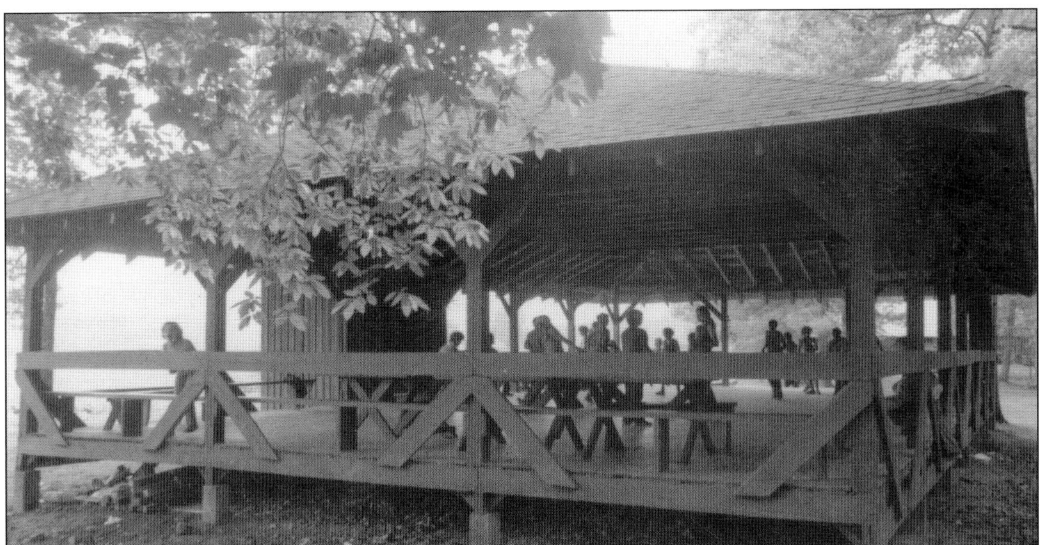

Open House, a shaded, outdoor pavilion completed in the late 1940s, originally served and continues to serve as a gathering space for community events and educational activities. As the original site of the annual Fall Festival, held in 1974, it has also been the scene for weddings, memorial gatherings, children's events, and a quiet place to take in the peaceful surroundings of gardens and open fields.

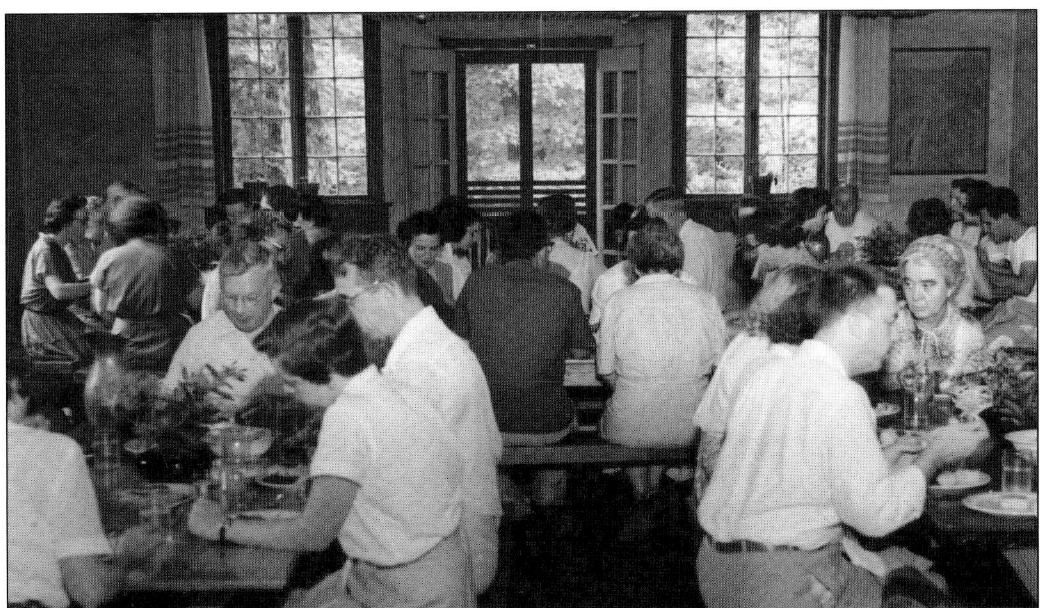

This 1950s image featuring Marguerite Butler Bidstrup (front table, right, with braided hair) captures the family-style dining that continues today. Prior to the construction of the Olive Dame Campbell Dining Hall, meals were served on the lower floor of Keith House. These opportunities for connection, served three times a day, invite students, instructors, and staff to share good food in good company.

John C. Campbell Folk School
Olive Dame Campbell Memorial Service

Hope Brown

Friends of Mrs. Campbell, one of the greatest tributes that I can pay Mrs. Campbell in behalf of the carvers is to say that she understood the mountain people.

She saw their need and loved them; she had a deep desire to help them. In the bench carved and hacked by jack knives she saw a restlessness and sought a way to turn idleness into usefulness and a creative art. It became a dream to make craftsmen out of them and I believe that she was more than satisfied with the outcome.

To us who knew her and worked with her, Mrs. Campbell is one of the great women; she was gracious, kindand considerate.

She brought to us Murrial Martin. And I am sure had she searched the world over, she could have found no one better qualified to help and guide us.

I feel that the life of each carver has been enriched for having known Mrs. Campbell. Through her efforts many of us have found peach of mind and, shall I say, a diversion from the drudgery that so many of the mountain people know. We have gained self-respect and confidence in our ability to create something. And some of us are known throughout the world for our carvings. This skill would have lain dormant within all of us had it not been for Mrs. Campbell, and now that this creativeness has been brought out, it is with pride that we shall strive to make carving even better.

Contact with her and the School she established has opened up new ways of living for many of us. We have a way to express our feelings and emotions and an outlet for them through carving.

In later years when Mrs. Campbell could no longer be with us at the School, when she wrote to Mrs. Martin she never failed to ask, "How are all the carvers and their families?" The memory of her and all the good she has done for us will remain with each of us and our families for many years to come.

It is with the deepest gratitude that I say we all loved Mrs. Campbell and will strive to keep the high standard which she sought so diligently to help us reach. We all feel deeply our great loss, but our loss is heaven's gain.

Again let me say, our lives have been made richer and fuller through Mrs. Campbell, and may she live long in all our hearts.

From 1925 to 1947, Olive Dame Campbell served as director of the school named in her husband's memory and as an advocate for the people who so eagerly and warmly welcomed her to Brasstown. She retired in 1946 and returned to Medford, Massachusetts, to write her husband's biography, *The Life and Work of John Charles Campbell.* Olive Dame Campbell died in 1954, and a memorial service was held in Keith House. Brasstown Carver Hope Brown shared a heartfelt tribute, saying that Campbell "understood the mountain people. She saw their need and loved them." Recorder music was also played during the service, honoring Campbell's love of the folk instrument.

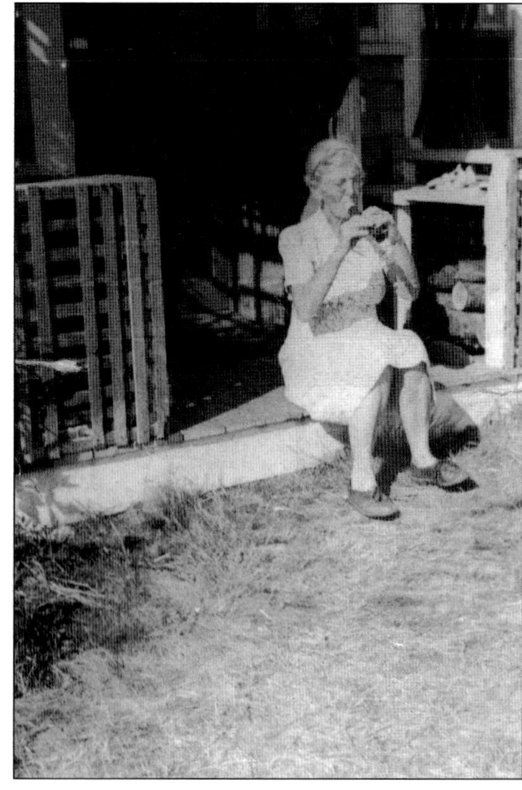

Five

1960s–1970s

Time Enough Yet

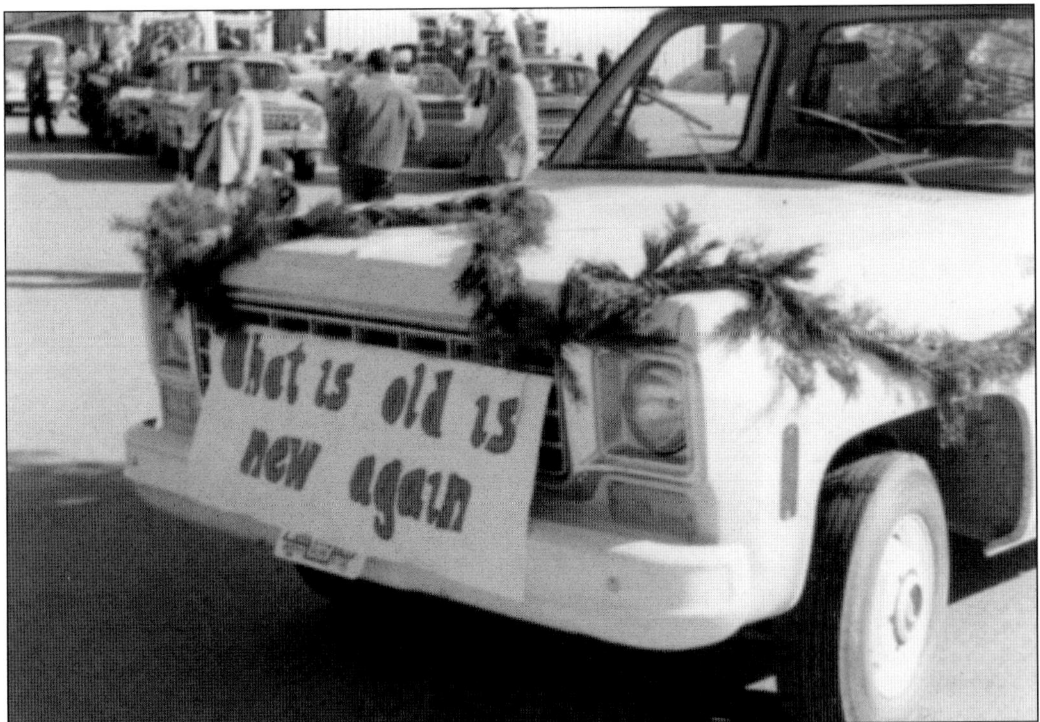

The 1960s and 1970s were an evolutionary period for the Folk School. Little Middle, a program for youth, expanded; a large milking barn for the school's dairy was built; and the school received financial support for programming. Despite this growth, the school faced significant financial challenges and nearly closed. Through two leadership transitions and new events, including Fall Festival, the Folk School found new life.

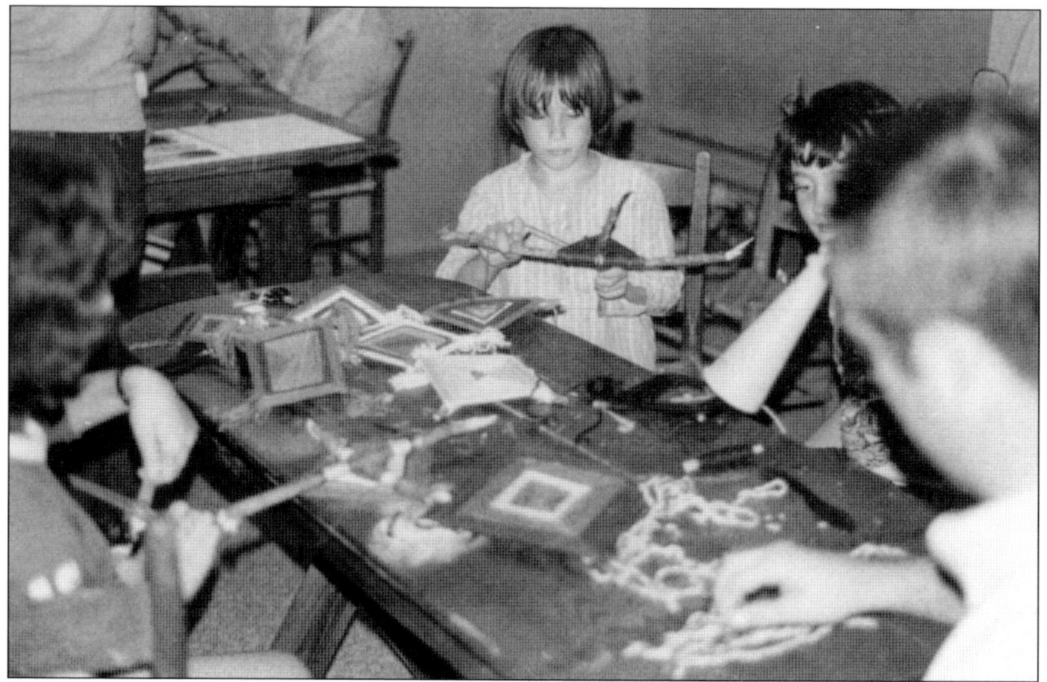

By the 1960s and 1970s, Little Middle Folk School blossomed, bringing with it both new classes and increased enrollment. While arts education throughout the United States began to suffer the consequences of funding cuts, programs like Little Middle provided the creative opportunity many parents desired for their children. The Little Middle class of 1968 included more than 30 participants, representing early elementary to older high school students. In recent years, enrollment has risen to a steady stream of hundreds of youth who immerse themselves in a week of making crafts, making friends, and making memories, all while carrying forward the tradition of hands-on creativity.

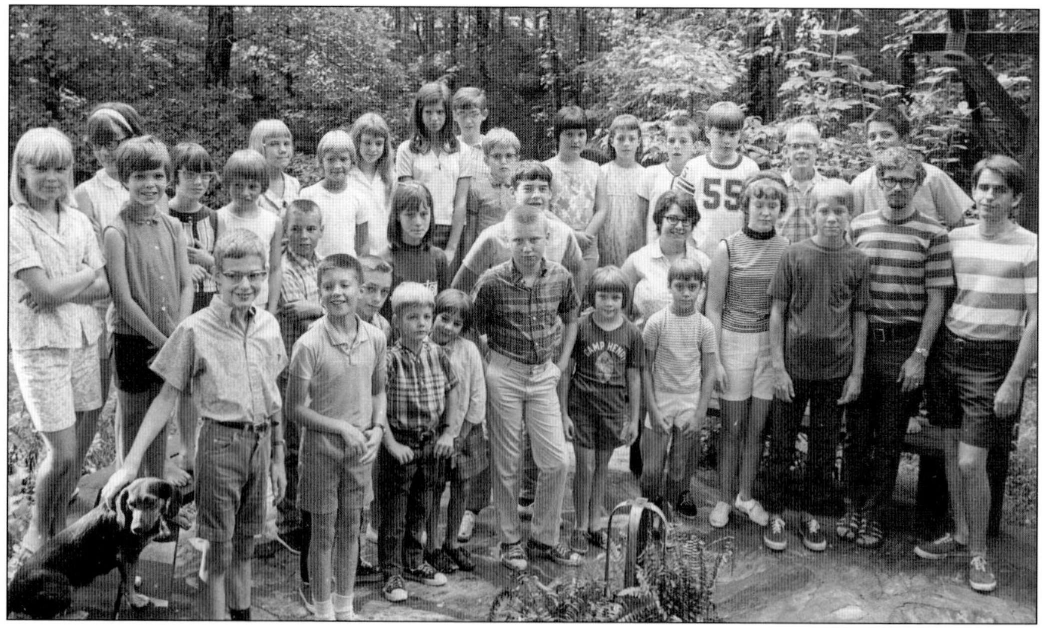

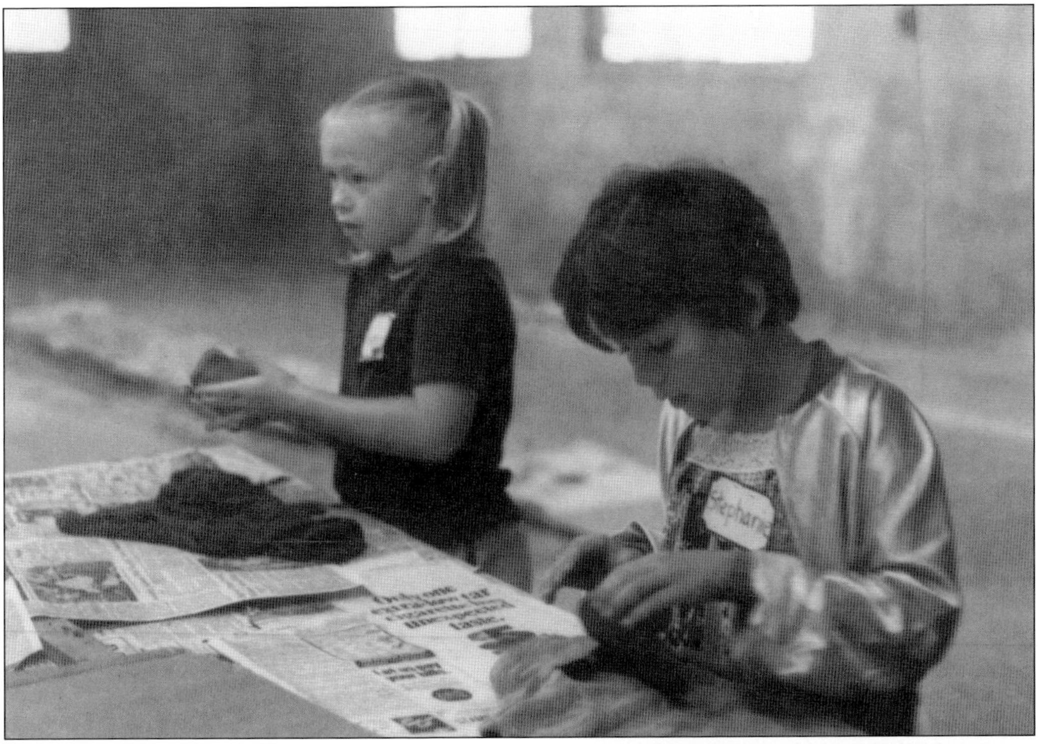

Class offerings for Little Middle students have long included a mix of traditional and nontraditional arts and crafts. In one 1970s class, first-time potters learned the basics of rolling, pinching, and building forms, including animals, people, and small dishes. In another session, an aspiring woodworker carefully navigated a mallet and chisel to shape the areas that needed empty space or rounded edges. While focusing on their final creations, they also learned the significance of and need for patience, guidance, and starting over—lessons that stretch far beyond the studio. Much like the program expansion in its first 40 years, Little Middle offerings have since broadened to include jewelry, puppetry, beading, printmaking, and much more.

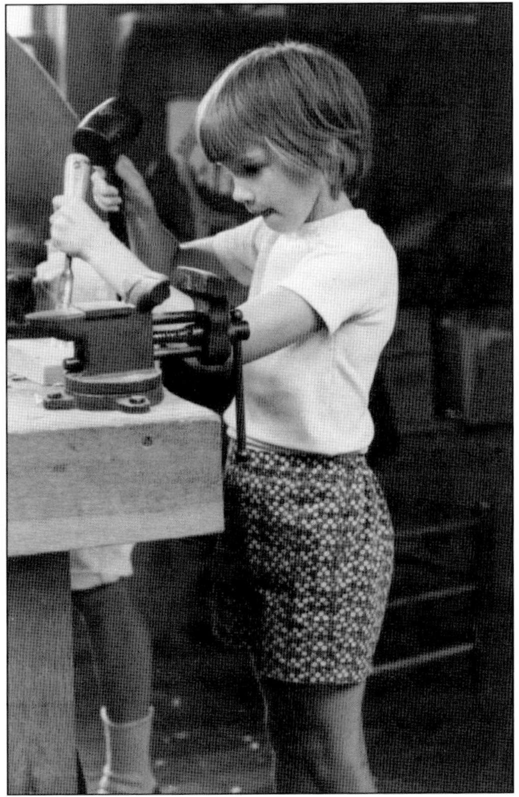

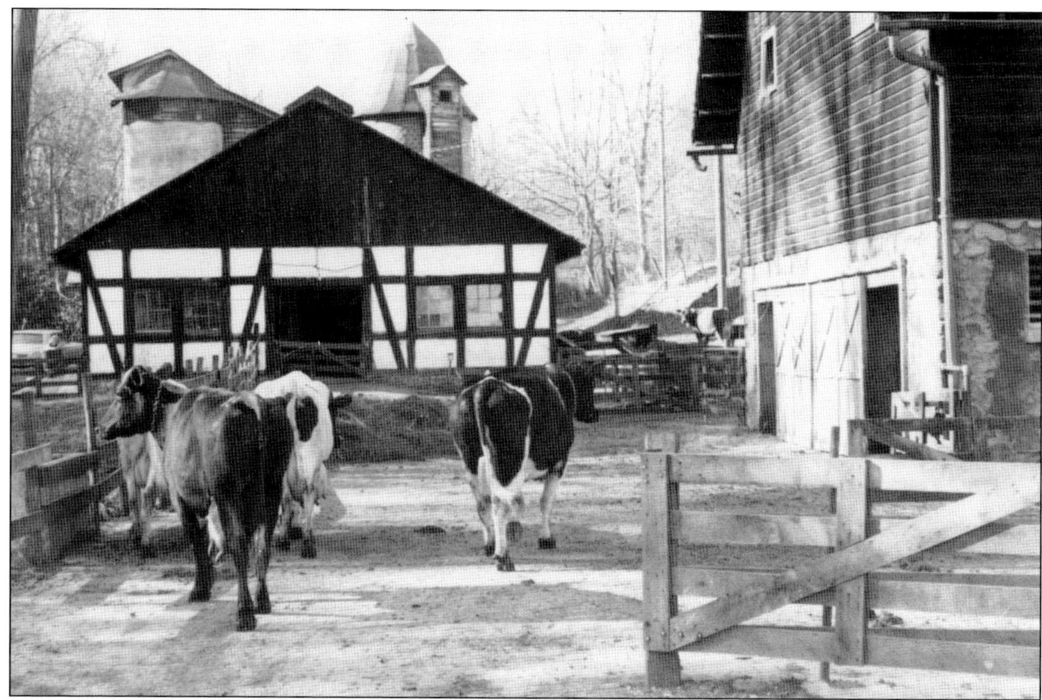

As the school's dairy grew, so did the need for more space to support operations. By this time, the school's farm consisted of dairy production and livestock trades, including these Holsteins that were sold by the Folk School in the late 1960s. The growing and changing herd expanded beyond the designated space of the original milking barn (left), built in the 1930s.

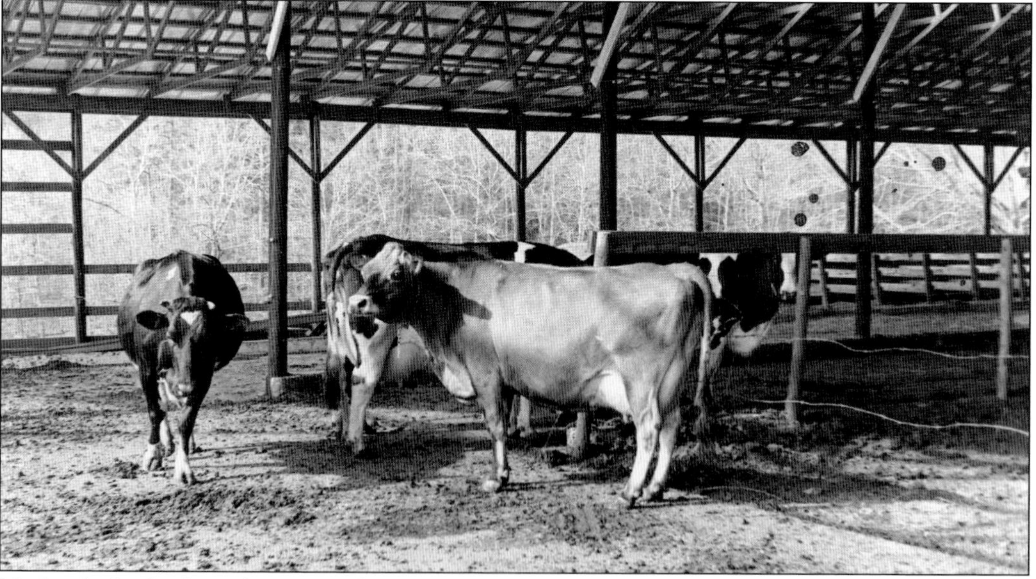

Under the leadership of executive director John Ramsay, who emphasized agriculture, the structure now known as Festival Barn was completed in 1967. It served as a much-needed location for part of the dairy cattle operation. Like many of the original farm sites and buildings, the space has since been reimagined and serves as a prime location for Fall Festival vendors, a classroom space for Little Middle Folk School, and a venue for concerts.

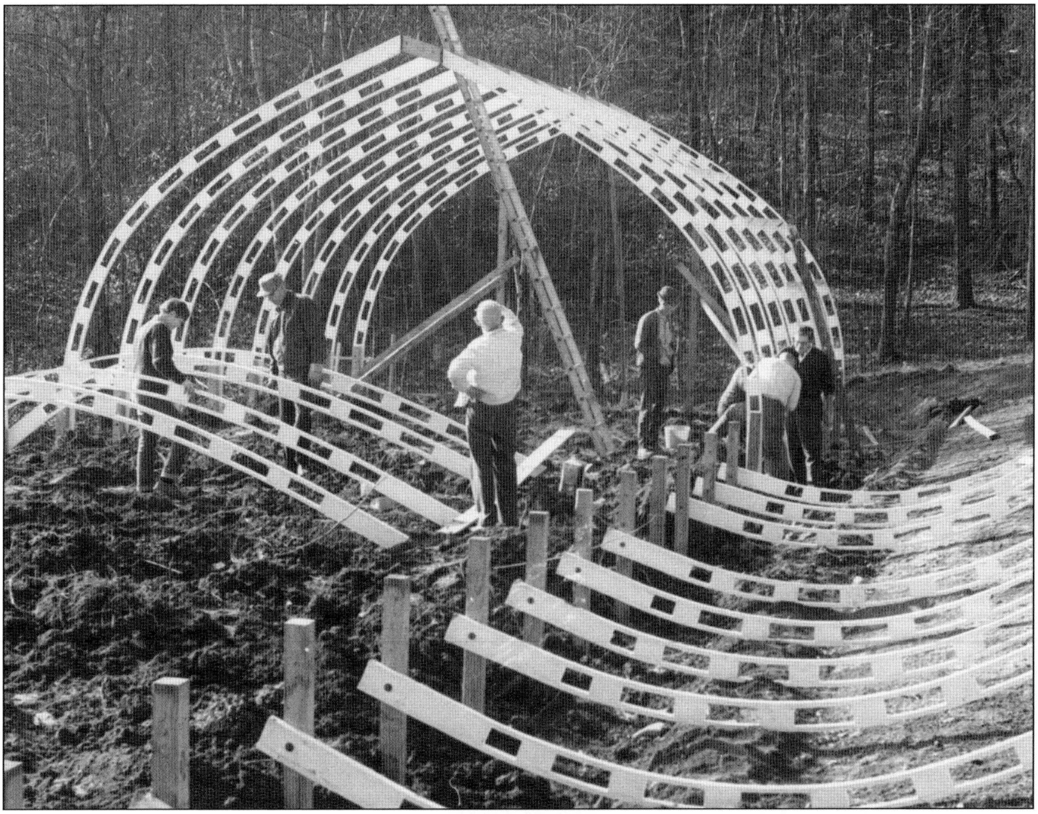

Farming practices on the school's campus also included a variety of growing crops. In 1969, a greenhouse was constructed to support the continuous demand for fresh produce. Potatoes, tomatoes, corn, and more often made their way from the garden to meals served throughout the day. It was also preserved for later use.

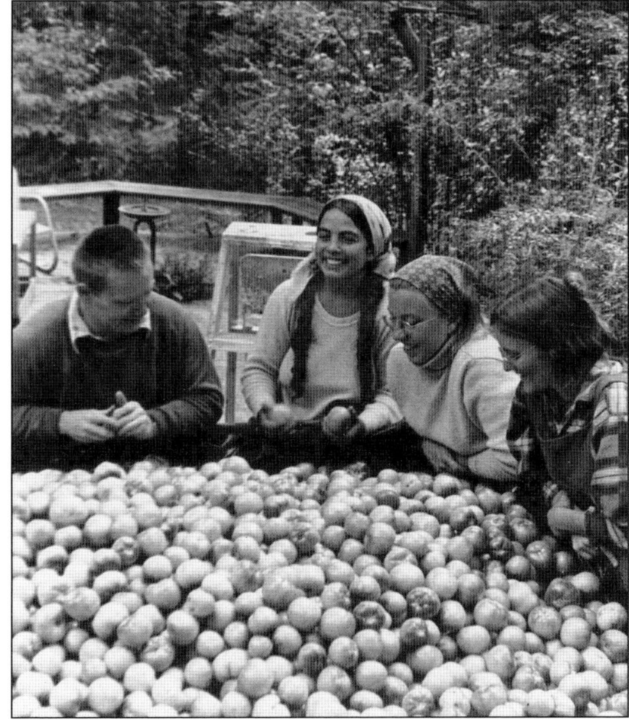

Much of the garden work relied on work-study students who lived on campus and received several tuition-free classes in exchange for labor. Decades later, the work-study program remains the largest source of assistance for all gardening activities, which includes planting, tending, harvesting, and processing freshly picked herbs, vegetables, and craft products.

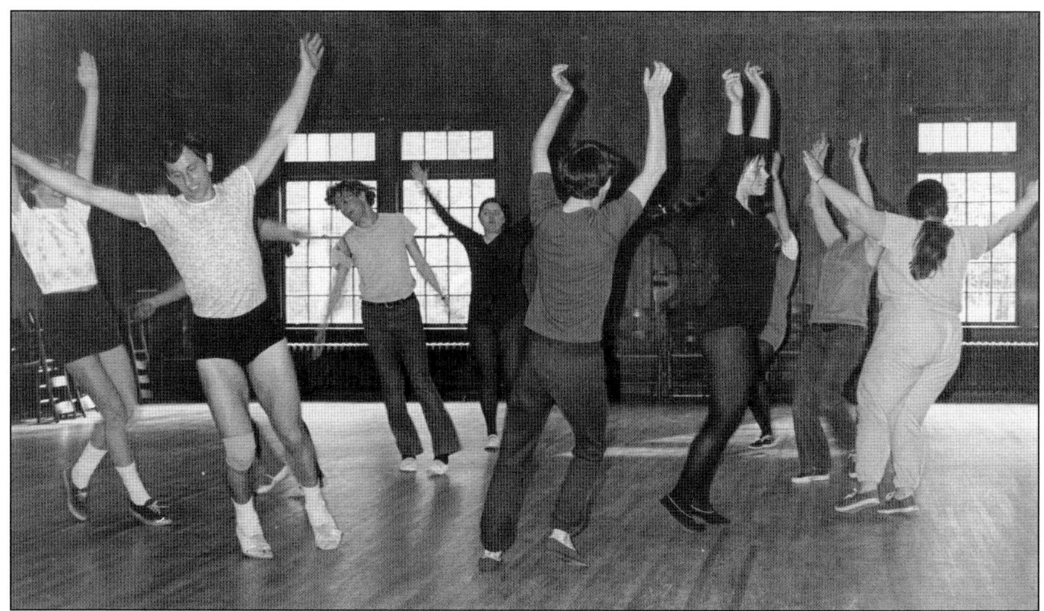

During Georg Bidstrup's tenure as director, he made Danish gymnastics a core activity for students, often as a teacher. Having grown up in Denmark and participated in the Danish Folk School movement, Bidstrup's influence brought the roots of the *folkehøjskole* to Brasstown. When he retired in the late 1960s, the tradition of gymnastics continued under the guidance of instructors, including Daniel Eihler (below), also from Denmark. Much like community dance, gymnastics provided a holistic approach to the Folk School experience by blending social and cultural learning through movement. While it is no longer a core activity, it remains part of the Folk School story. In 2022, a group of senior gymnasts from Denmark, known as GYS87, spent a week in Brasstown sharing a workshop and performance.

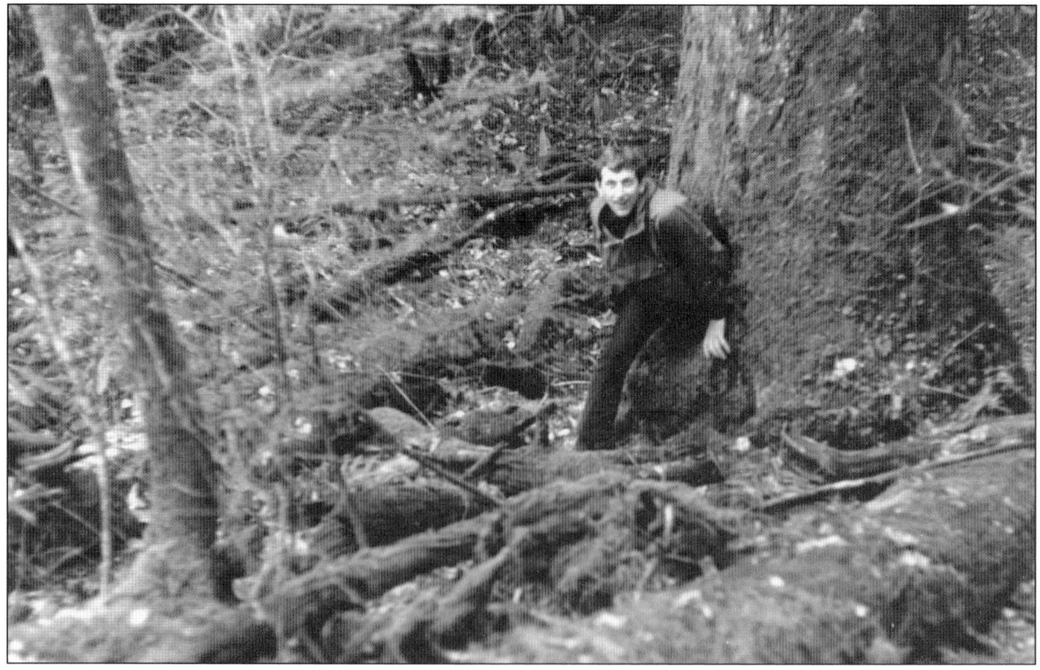

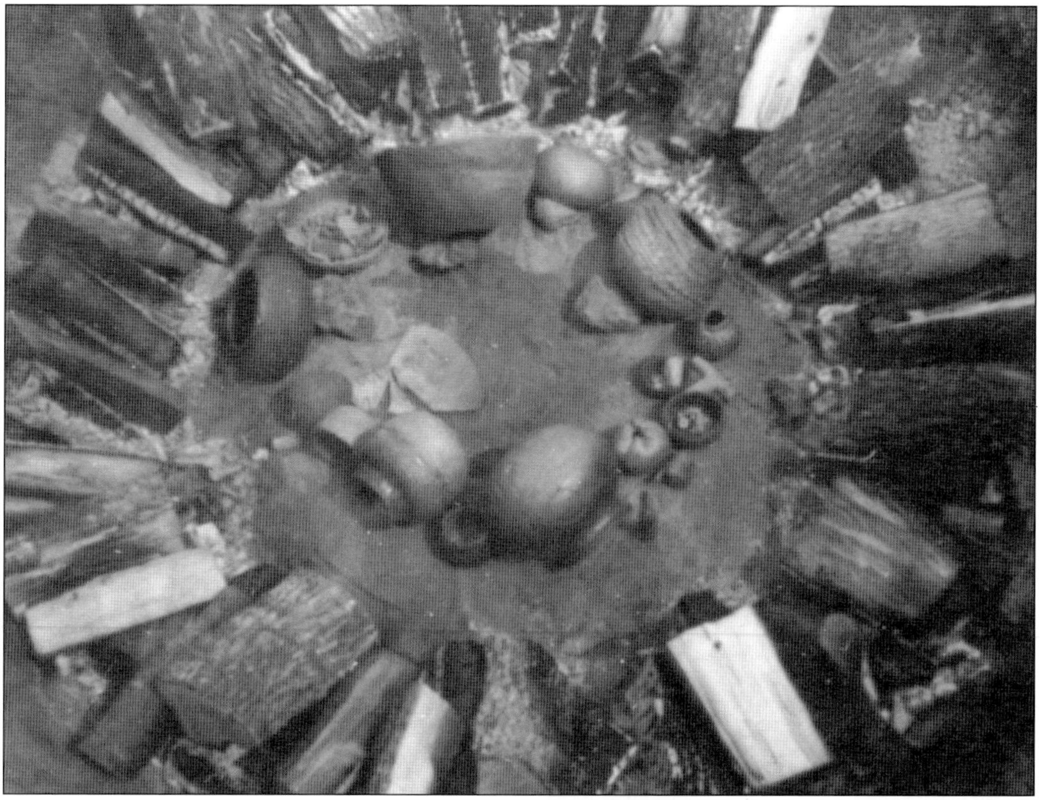

As programs like Little Middle Folk School and operations like the dairy farm moved ahead, the Folk School also received financial support from the North Carolina Arts Council (NCAC). Classes in traditional Appalachian crafts like pottery and woodworking benefited from the organization's emphasis on arts awareness. Pottery was especially popular during the early 1970s, requiring a new space with more room for students and supplies. Fortunately, a cannery that had been built on the property in 1952 and operated by Cherokee County as a communal service facility for decades was donated to the school in 1969. Clay classes moved to the building in 1970.

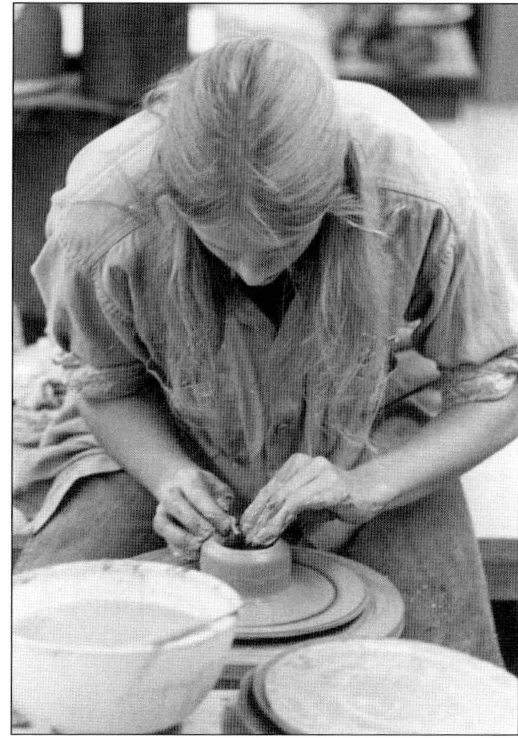

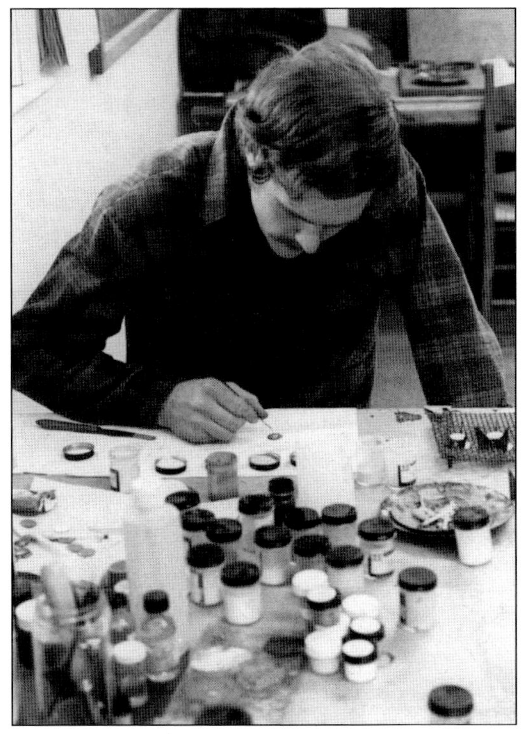

Classes in the craft of enameling were also expanded due to NCAC financial support. Despite this growth, student enrollment decreased, and the school faced the possibility of closure. Enamel artists Gus and Maggie Masters (below), pictured here at a celebration held to honor their contributions to the Folk School, were appointed as codirectors in 1974. To save the school, they transitioned it toward an arts and culture-focused curriculum. Part of this transition included the first annual Fall Festival. The weekend celebration of craft, music, and dance created a new and beloved tradition for the Folk School, for artists, and for community members and regional visitors.

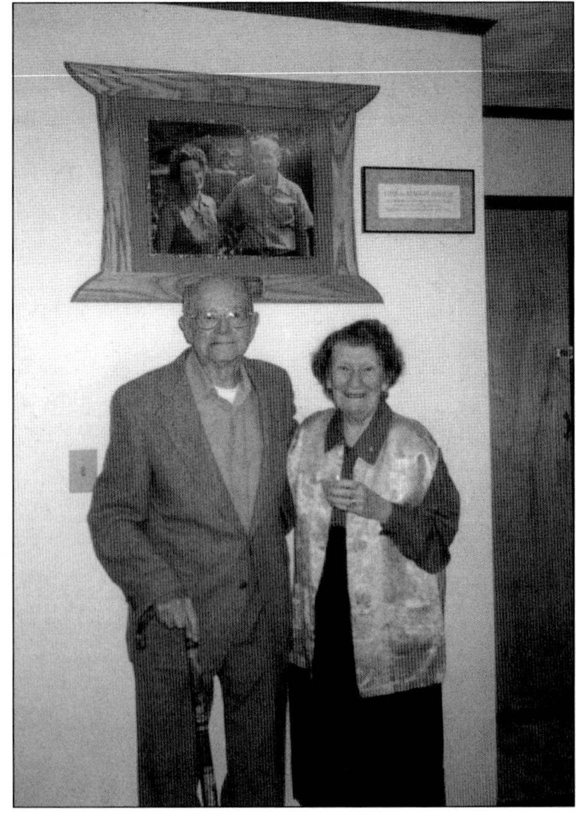

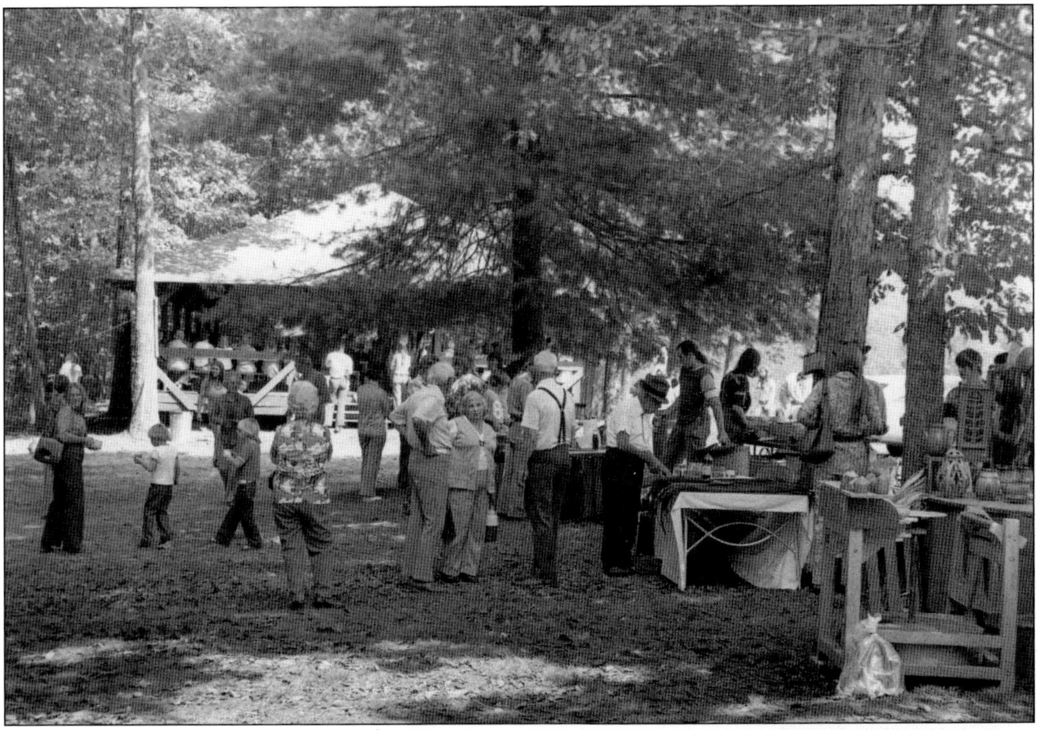

The inaugural Fall Festival was held October 5–6, 1974, with Open House and the surrounding grounds as the main site. The event invited artists to display and sell their work, musicians to entertain the crowd, and dancers to showcase steps and turns in tune. Visitors, including those who had not yet experienced the Folk School, watched demonstrations that highlighted old-time traditions like making hominy and sorghum, while also soaking up the energy of autumn weather in the mountains. It was a positive turning point for the school, and one that established the annual gathering that now welcomes thousands of people to Brasstown every October.

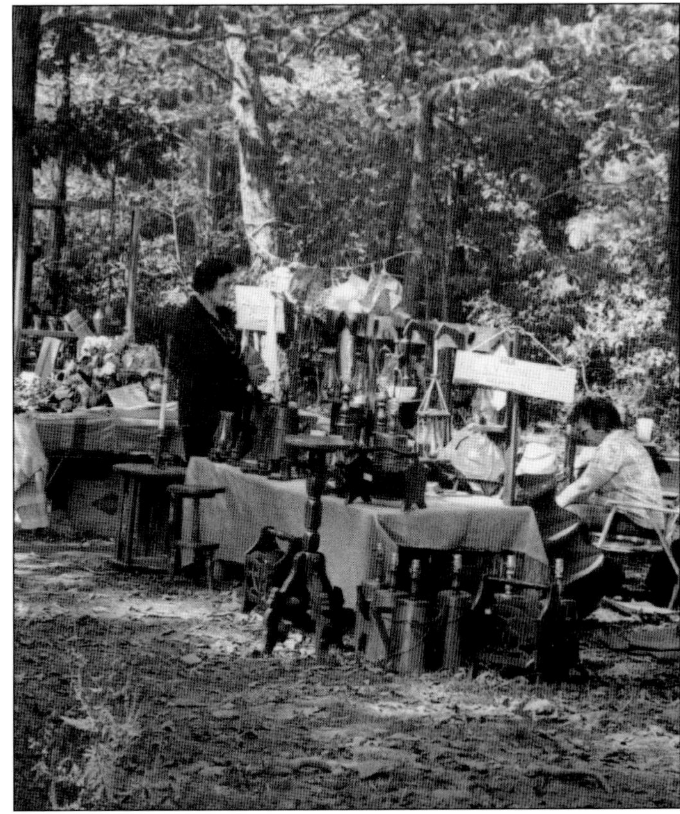

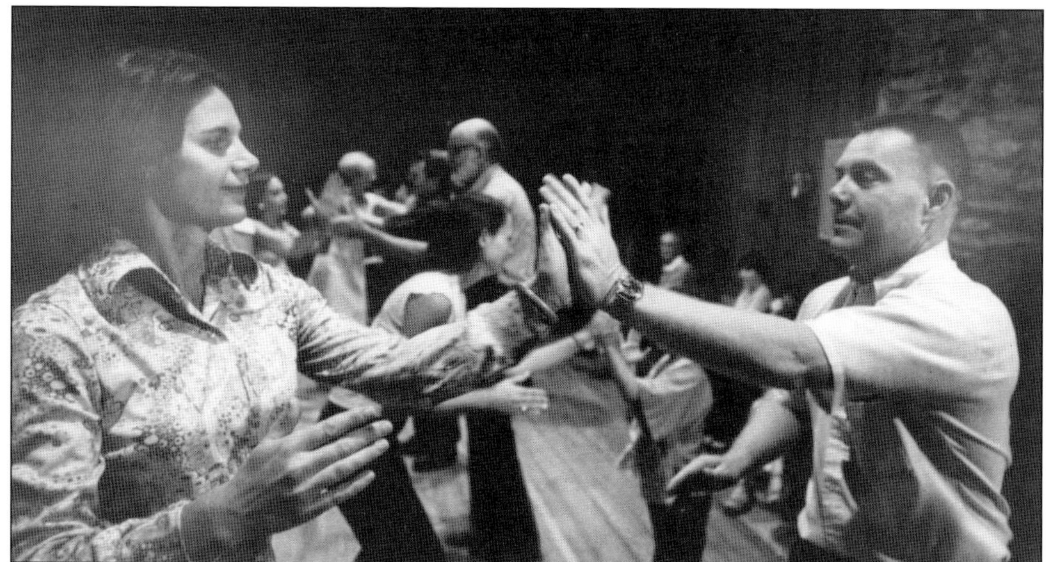

Following the success of the first Fall Festival, the Folk School broadened its class offerings in both session length and subject matter to attract a larger audience. A growing interest in the school's rural setting was highlighted when the first mountain-born director, Esther Hyatt (above, left), was appointed in 1976. Under Hyatt's guidance, the school continued its growing emphasis on folk dancing and music classes. Her familial roots, artistic vision, and business acumen helped the revitalization of these traditional program areas. In 1979, the Folk School held its first Winter Dance Week, an annual event scheduled between Christmas and New Year's Day. The following year, Hyatt recruited well-known dancer and dance caller Bob Dalsemer to organize the second Winter Dance Week. Her decision led to a significant influence on the future of the school's music and dance scene.

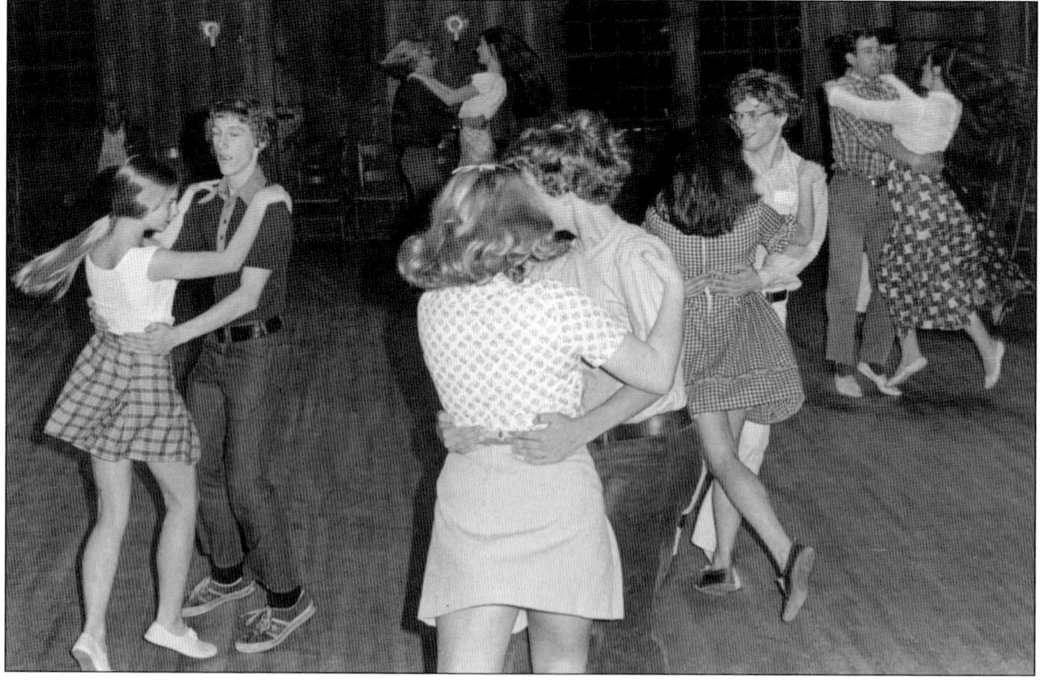

Six

Fall Festival

Going to the Fair

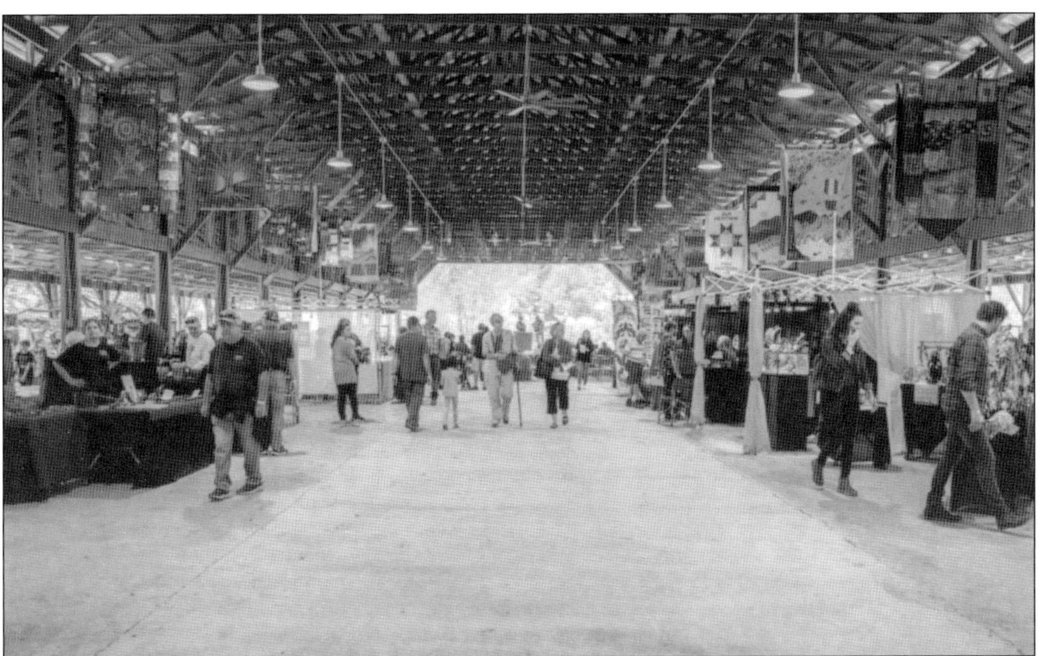

The first weekend of October has been drawing residents and visitors to the scenic setting of the Folk School's campus since 1974. Hundreds of regional craftspeople present works for sale, studios host traditional and contemporary craft demonstrations, and music and dance performances provide continuous entertainment across stages throughout the two-day event. It is a much-anticipated celebration of Appalachian craft, culture, and heritage.

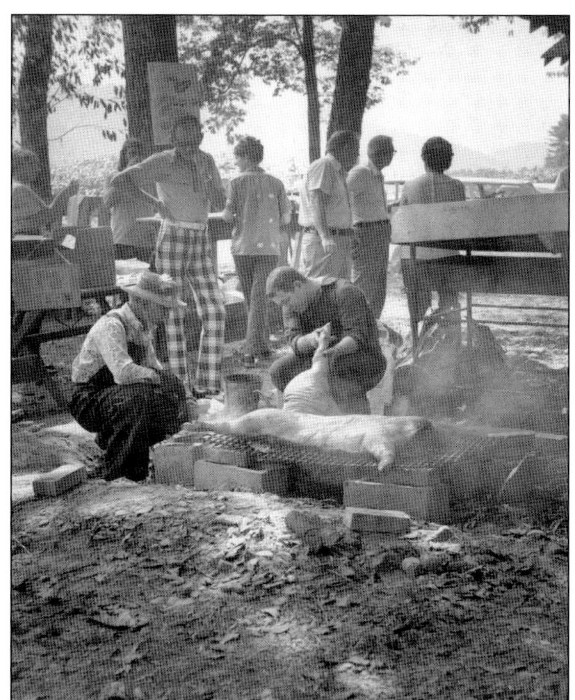

Regular Fall Festival attendees know that the Folk School's famous barbecue is a long-standing favorite. David Hyatt (right, holding leg) started the tradition at the first event in 1974 with a slow-smoked pig. David Hyatt was married to Esther Hyatt, who later served as executive director for the Folk School and initiated the homesteading program.

One notable guest at the first Fall Festival was Marguerite Butler Bidstrup (in chair). Following her retirement from the Folk School, she remained a resident of Brasstown. Having shared in the school's founding and witnessing both the challenges and opportunities that came with an ever-evolving curriculum and student population, Bidstrup's presence was significant to the school's origin and ongoing stories.

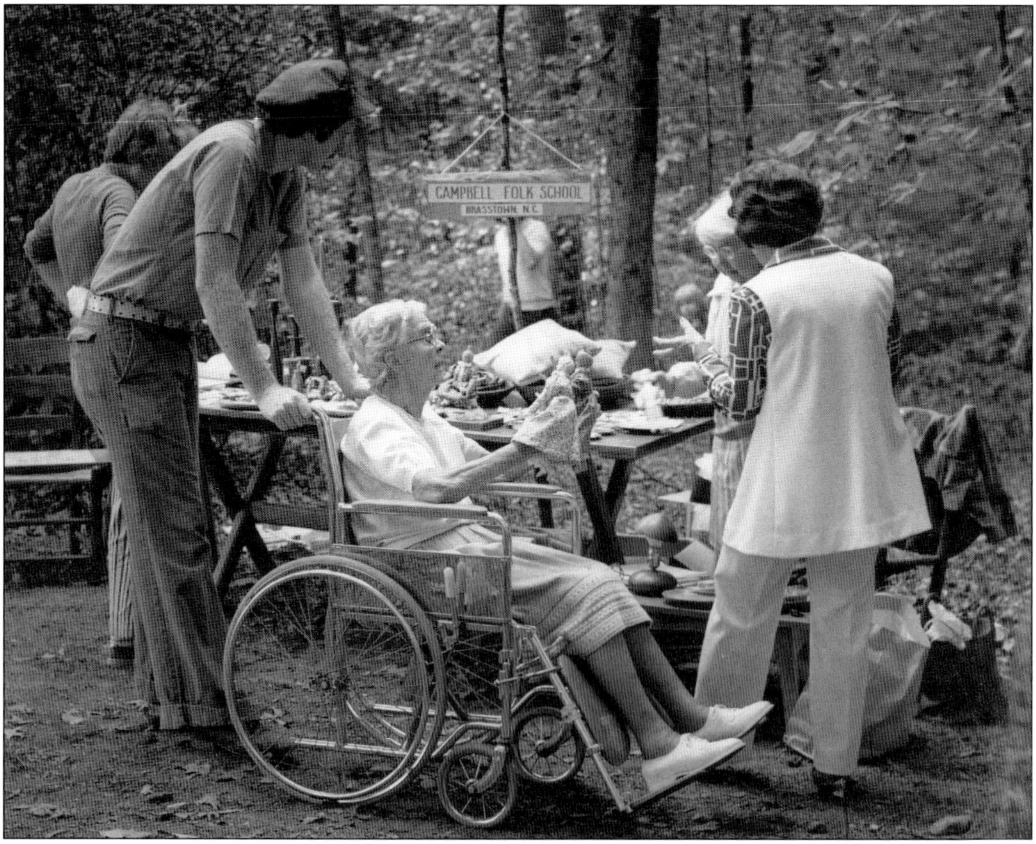

Musical performances over the years have included several well-known folk singers. Clark Jones, a North Carolina banjo (as well as guitar, ukulele, autoharp, and the mountain and hammered dulcimers) player, visited the 1976 festival to share his love of traditional songs. The image of Jones with one of his many instruments served as the cover art on his 1982 album, *Early American Folk Music and Songs.*

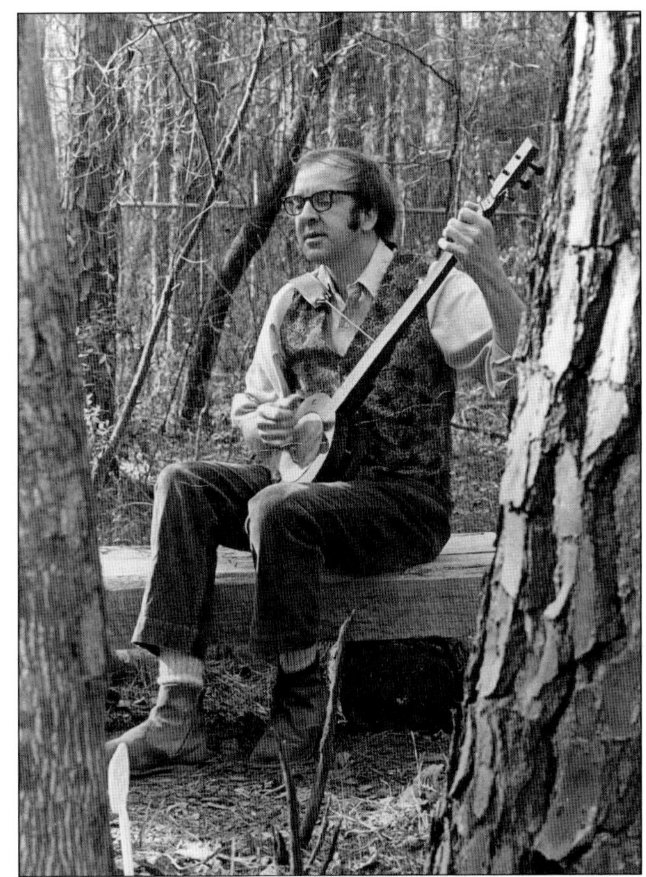

Another icon of Appalachian folk music, Jean Ritchie, shared her talents at the 1979 Fall Festival. Ritchie's original connection to the school came through her sister May Ritchie Deschamps, who was married to Leon Deschamps. He was well-known for the design and construction of many stone structures on the school's campus. Ritchie often spent summers in Brasstown, taking classes while visiting her sister and brother-in-law.

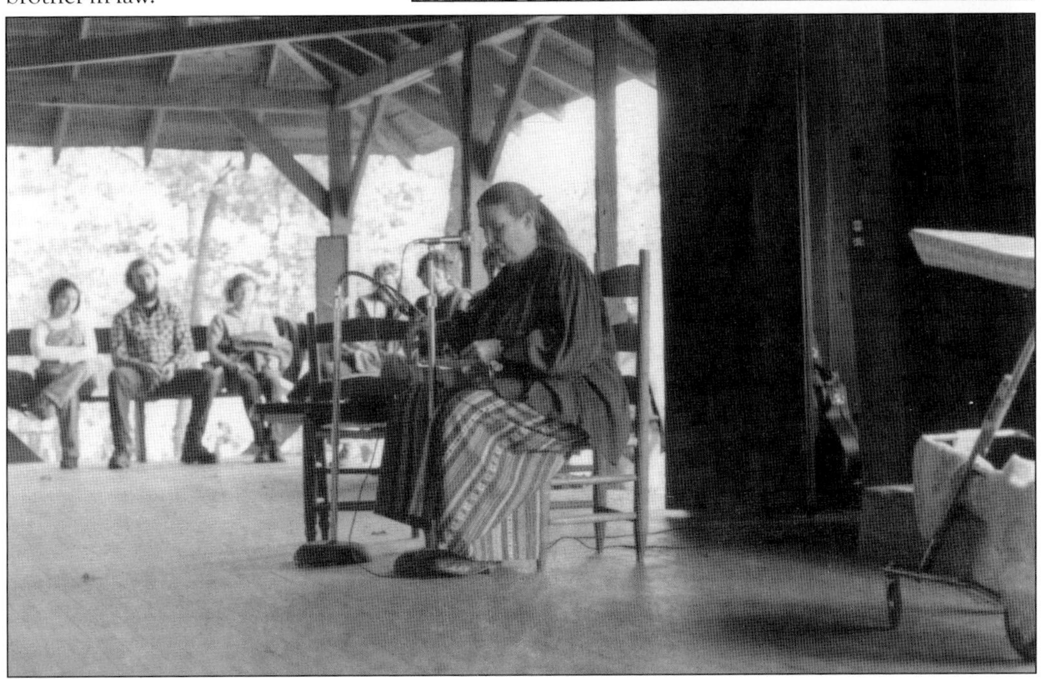

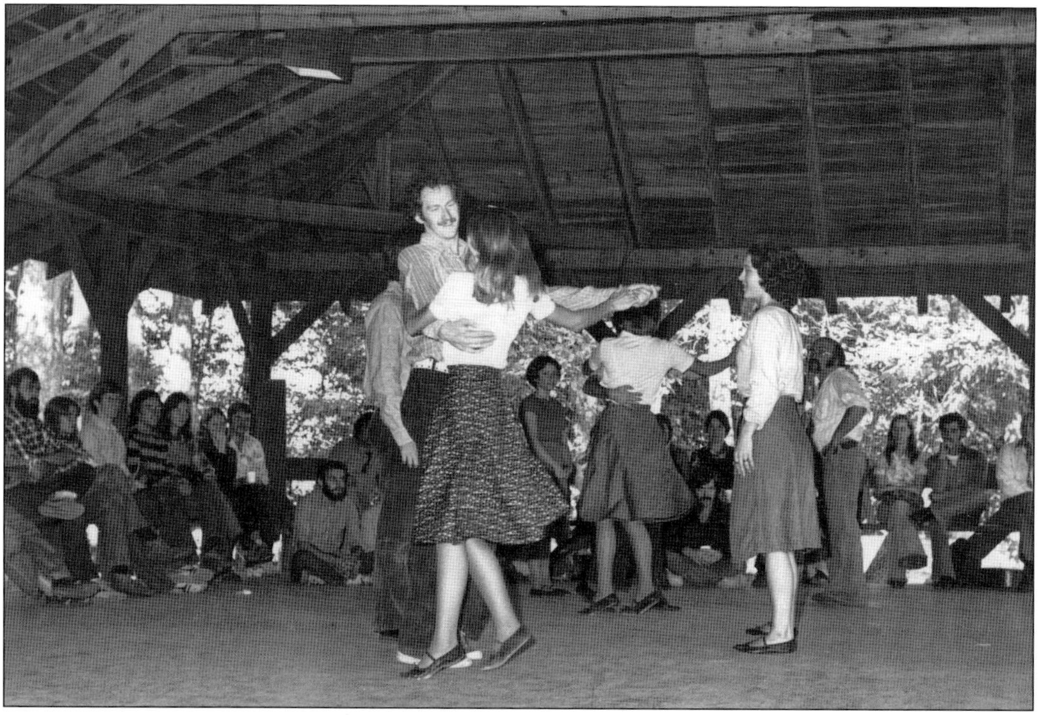

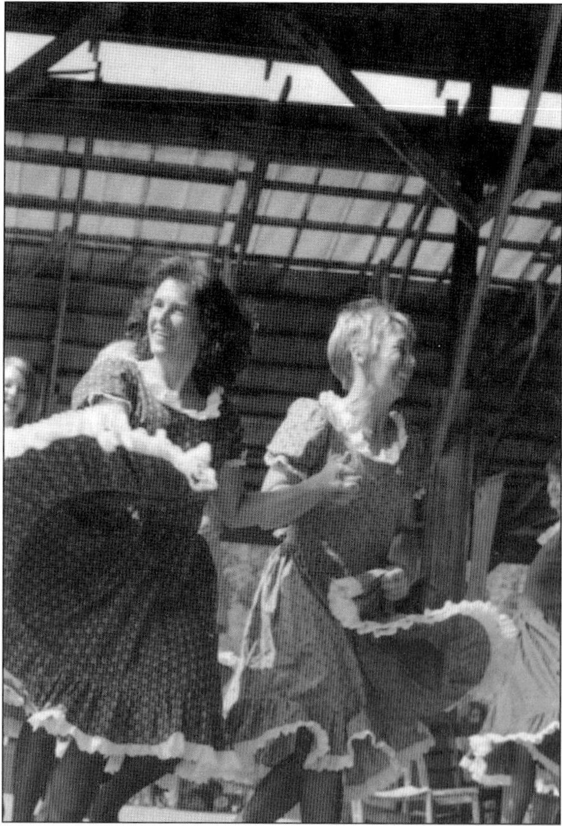

Dance performances have played an important role in the weekend celebration since the early days of Fall Festival. In formative years, including the 1976 demonstration above, Open House served as a dance floor and stage for performers. During the growth of nearly five decades of hosting this weekend celebration, dance teams now grace multiple stages. The Folk School Cloggers, featured in Festival Barn at left, have continued the percussive dance form in Appalachian style, often to bluegrass or old-time music and accented by the distinctive sounds of taps on their leather-soled shoes. From partner dances to communal choreography, fancy feet have been entertaining visitors for almost 50 years.

The parade of Morris Dance musicians and teams is a highlight of Fall Festival music and dance performances. Members of the multiple dance teams make their way to the Festival Barn stage, led by musicians on drums, accordions, and more. Leaders of this parade include Rosemarie Kelischek (first row), Jan Davidson (second row, left), David Liden, Bob Dalsemer (third row, left), and Carl Dreher.

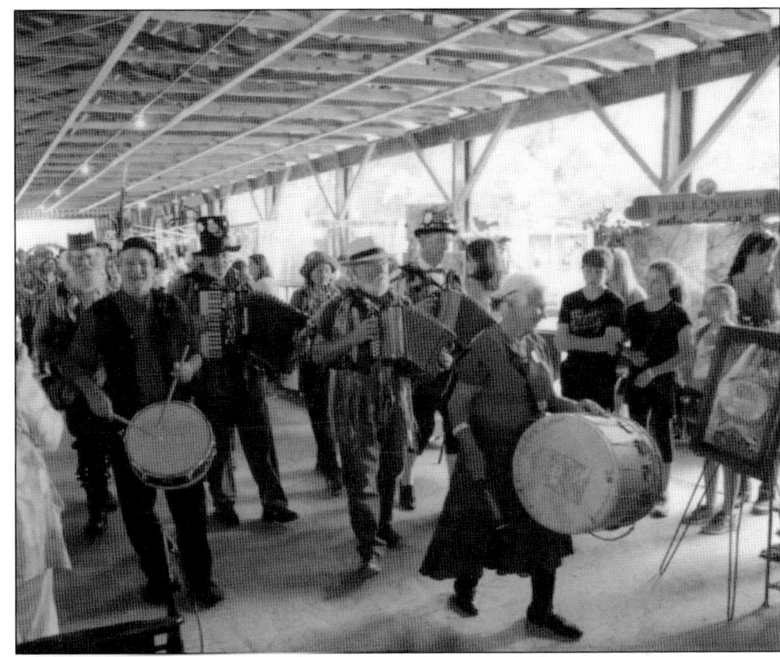

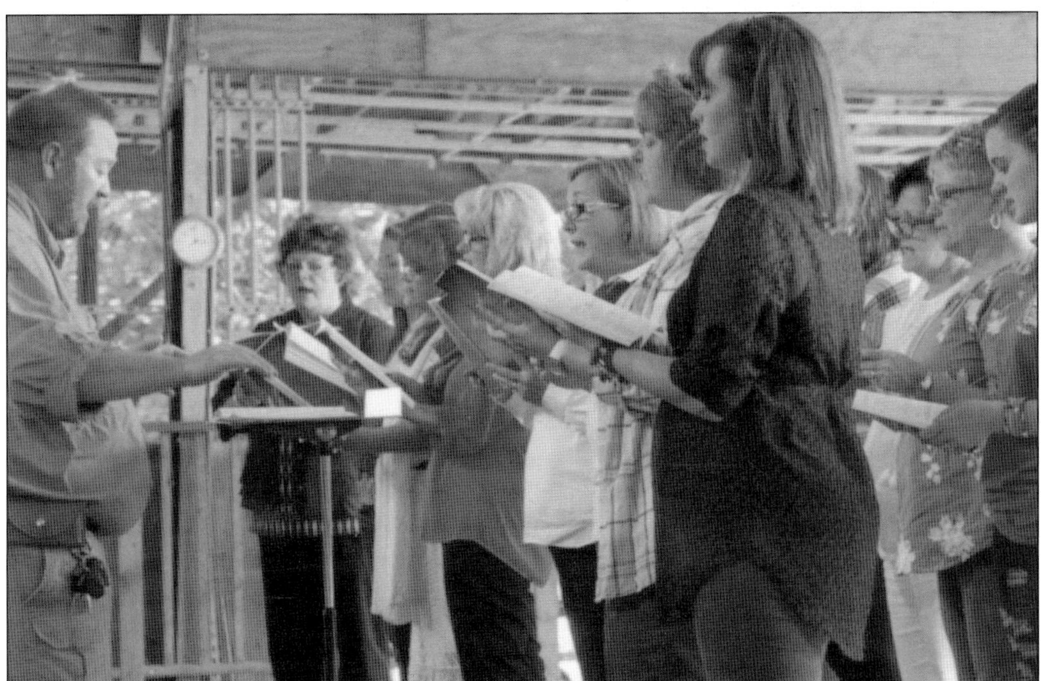

Fall Festival regularly welcomes church choirs to share their music. These gospel hymns are sometimes sung without the accompaniment of instruments. Under the direction of Rick Carter (left), the Little Brasstown Baptist Church Choir, which has long shared a connection with the Folk School, has often made a joyful noise.

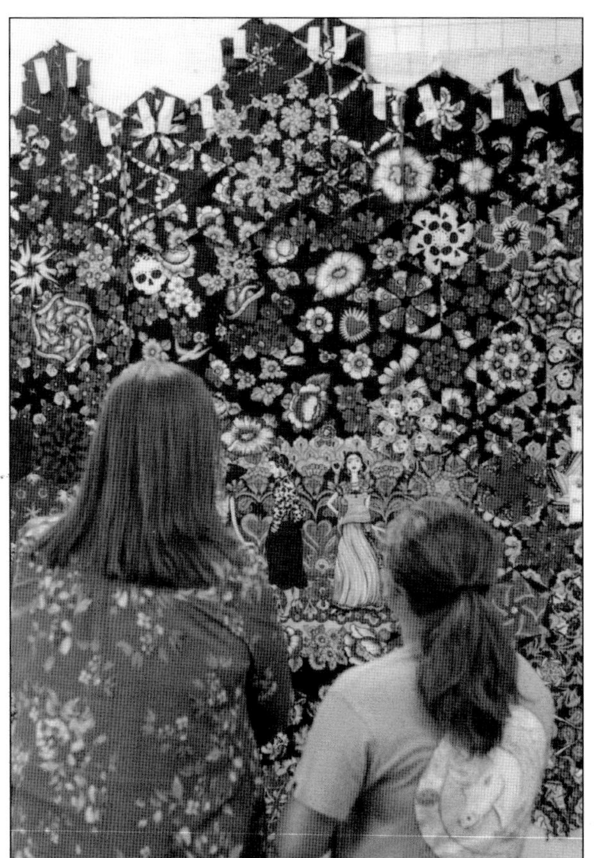

Inside the studios, works-in-progress take center stage. The Louise Pitman Fiber Arts Studio, which houses spaces used for weaving, lace, sewing, and quilting, welcomes visitors to view wall boards with masterpieces made from colorful fabrics and interesting patterns. Seeing the progress of designs helps those unfamiliar with the details of craft to understand the extensive work involved in creating something by hand.

Along with music and dance performances, craft demonstrations can be found throughout the sprawling grounds of the festival. As enthusiastic attendees peruse booths filled with handmade items, they also stop along the way to watch makers in their element. Here, former clay resident artist Marcia Bugg showcases her work on the potter's wheel.

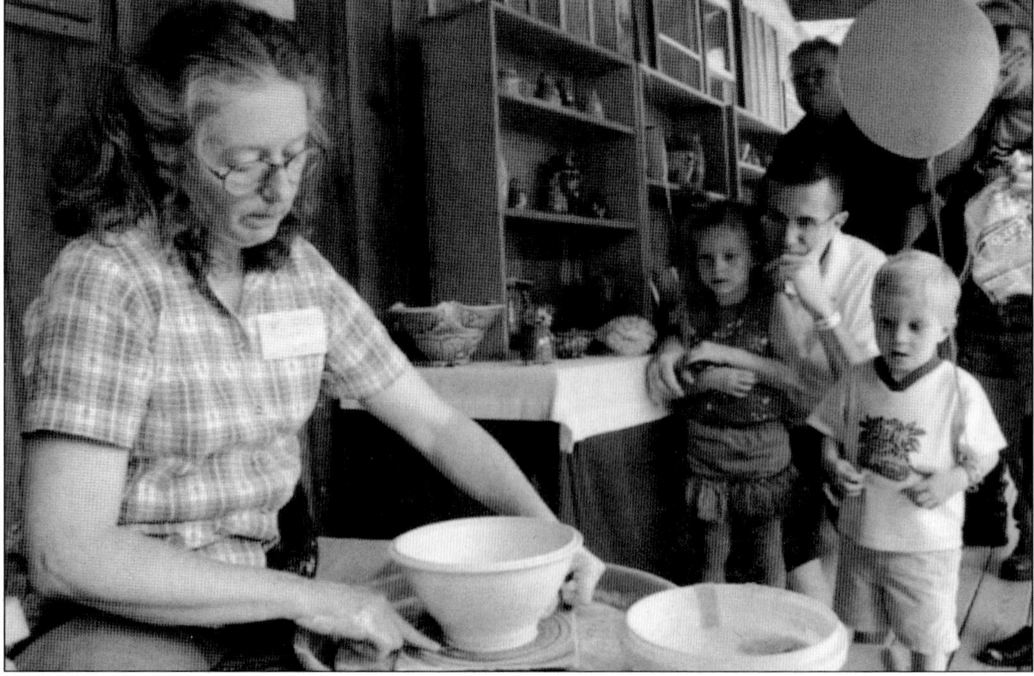

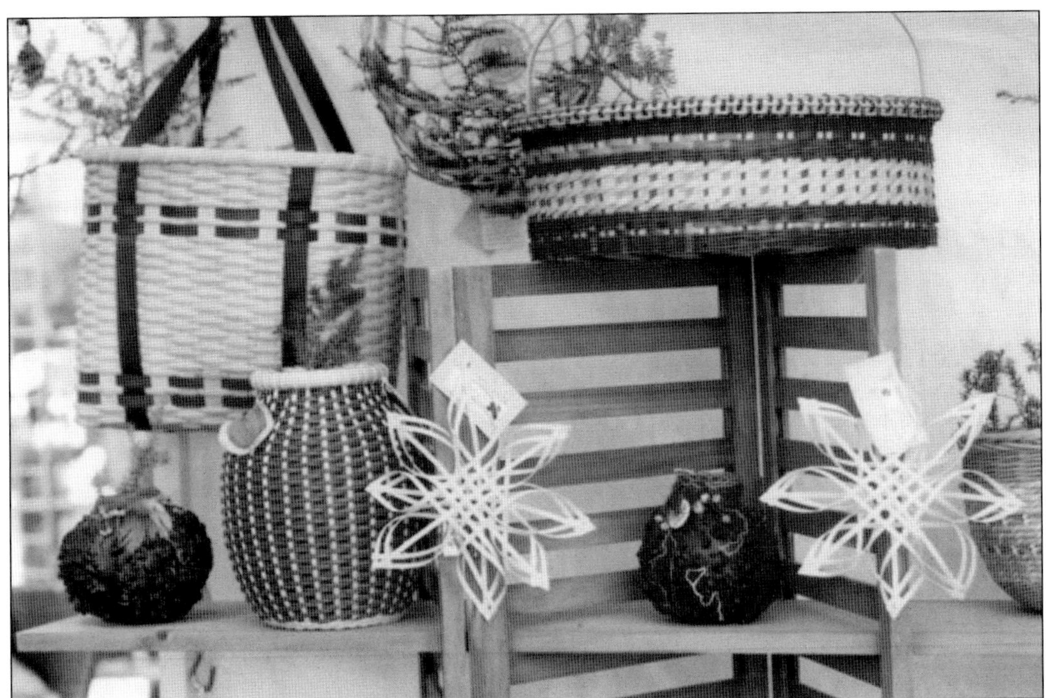

Baskets are one of many ways natural fibers, including reeds, willow, vines, bamboo, and honeysuckle, are woven into decorative and functional forms. These fibers can also be used to create ornaments, totes, straw art, and even backpacks. Many of these items can be found among the crafters whose experience brings a keen eye for design and a deep familiarity with materials to the final products.

While some demonstrations are held inside or on the front porch of a studio, others offer an inside look to passersby as they stroll through rows of craft booths or make their way to a music or dance performance. Former resident blacksmith Paul Garrett always draws a crowd as he takes a hammer to hot iron.

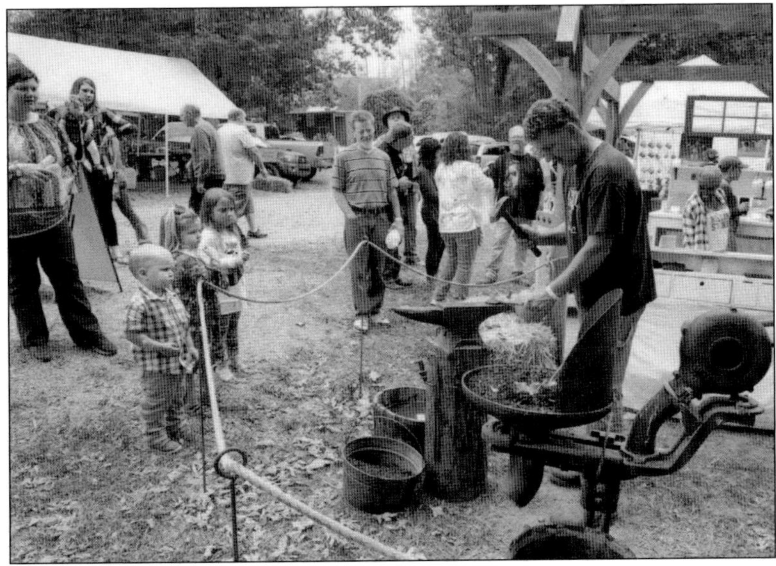

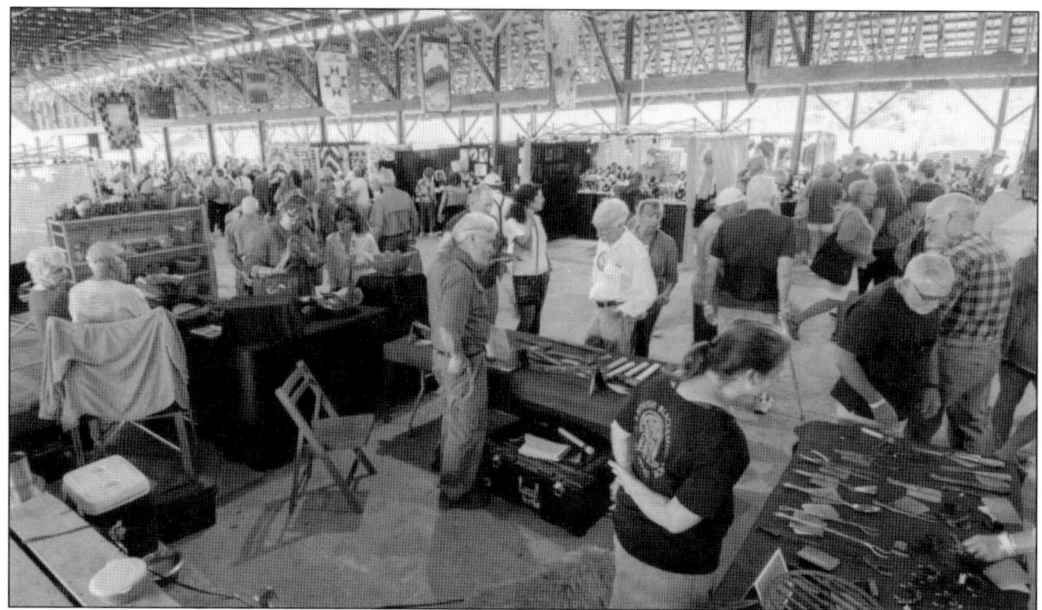

Fall Festival welcomes more than 200 vendors annually, selling items such as enameled jewelry, patchwork quilts, paintings and prints, felted hats, wood turned bowls, and so much more. The range of crafts, along with music and dance performances, now attracts an average of around 10,000 attendees. It honors the origin story of the Folk School while also providing a positive economic impact for Cherokee and Clay Counties.

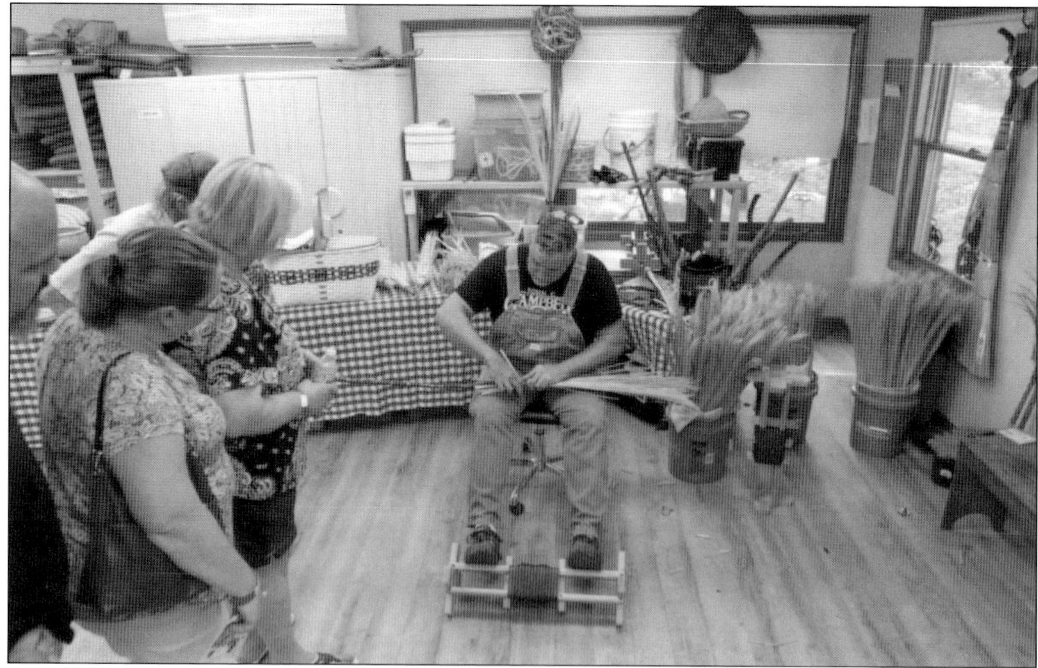

Demonstrations invite festival attendees to witness the preservation of traditional and nontraditional craft. It also offers artists the opportunity to talk about the history of a craft, discuss materials, and answer questions. In this demonstration, broom and basket maker Max Hendry uses a foot winder as he attaches broomcorn to a handle.

The array of Fall Festival craft vendors ranges from jewelers and painters to rug makers and metal workers. While many crafts include pieces made from scratch, like wood-carved spoons or woven scarves, others include upcycled materials that turn often discarded remnants into practical designs and unique pieces. What was once simple Kraft paper can be transformed into a one-of-a-kind book cover. Soup pots, aluminum lunch boxes, and cookie tins can also take on new life as wall art or front porch decor. By incorporating sustainable practices into their craft, these makers create fun and functional pieces that offer eco-friendly options for interested buyers.

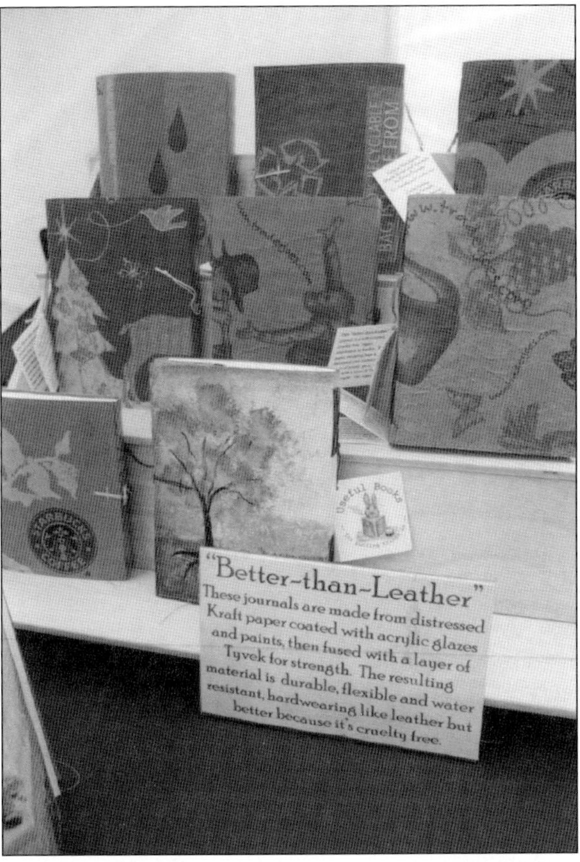

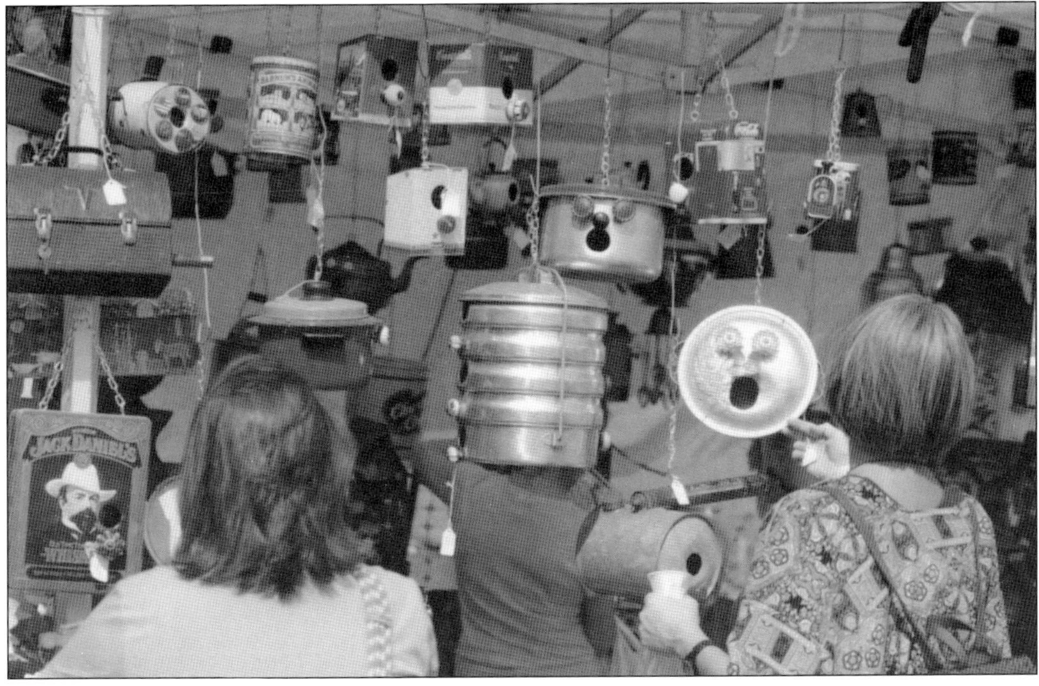

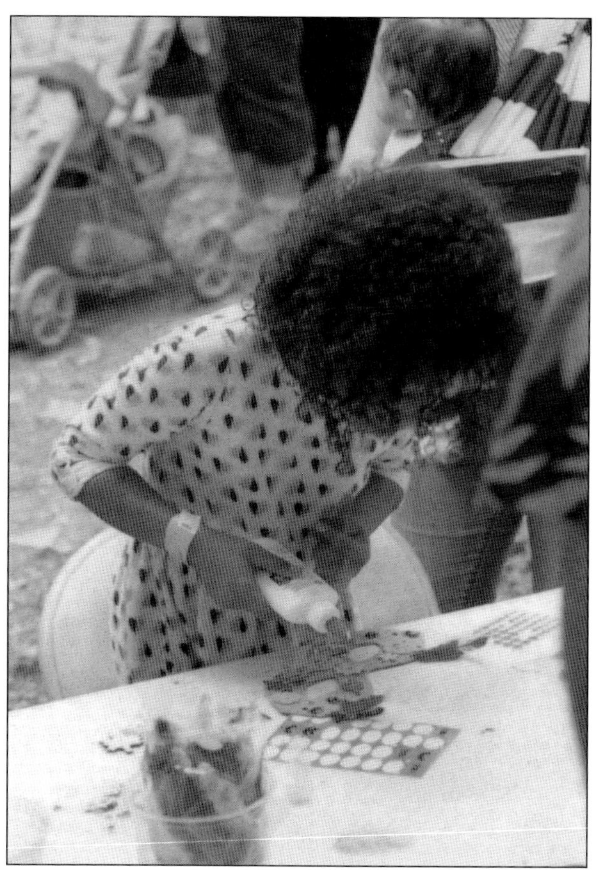

Fall Festival is a family-friendly event that provides special activities for children and youth. These artistic opportunities often include face painting, dancing, and crafts, such as face masks decorated with feathers, rhinestones, and a variety of foam shapes. Young people take home something they have put together with their own hands, encouraging creativity and individuality.

Animals are always a big hit with children and adults. Alpacas are especially beloved for their fluffy appearance. When fiber from an alpaca is spun into wool, the yarn can then be turned into hats, socks, mittens, blankets, and more. Bringing these animals to the festival allows farmers and fiber artists to share information about renewable resources used in making various products.

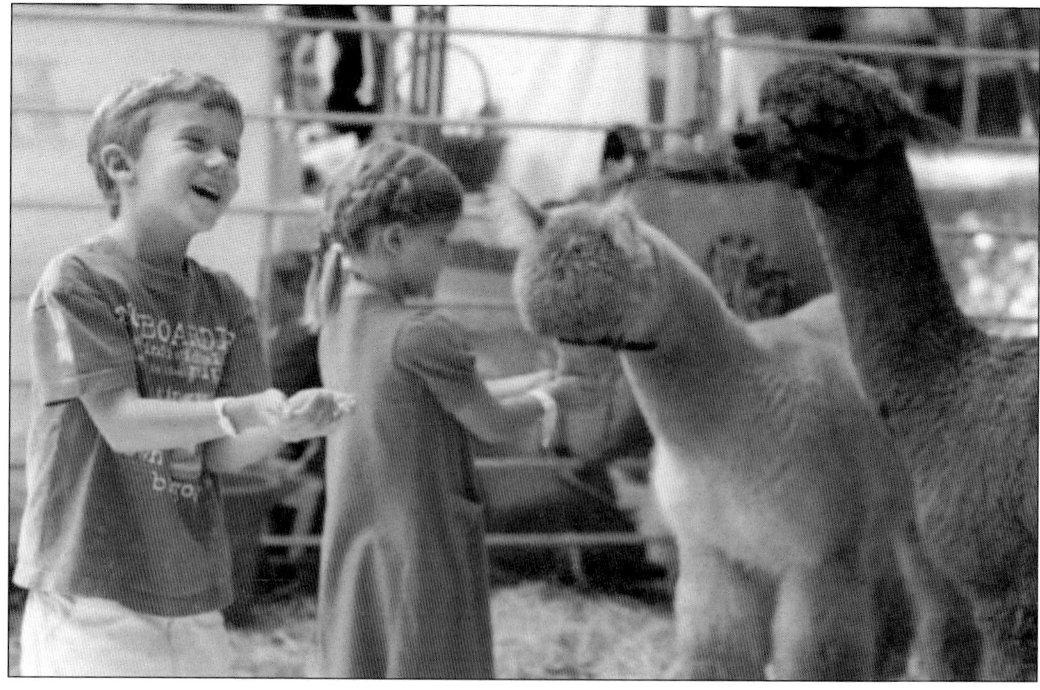

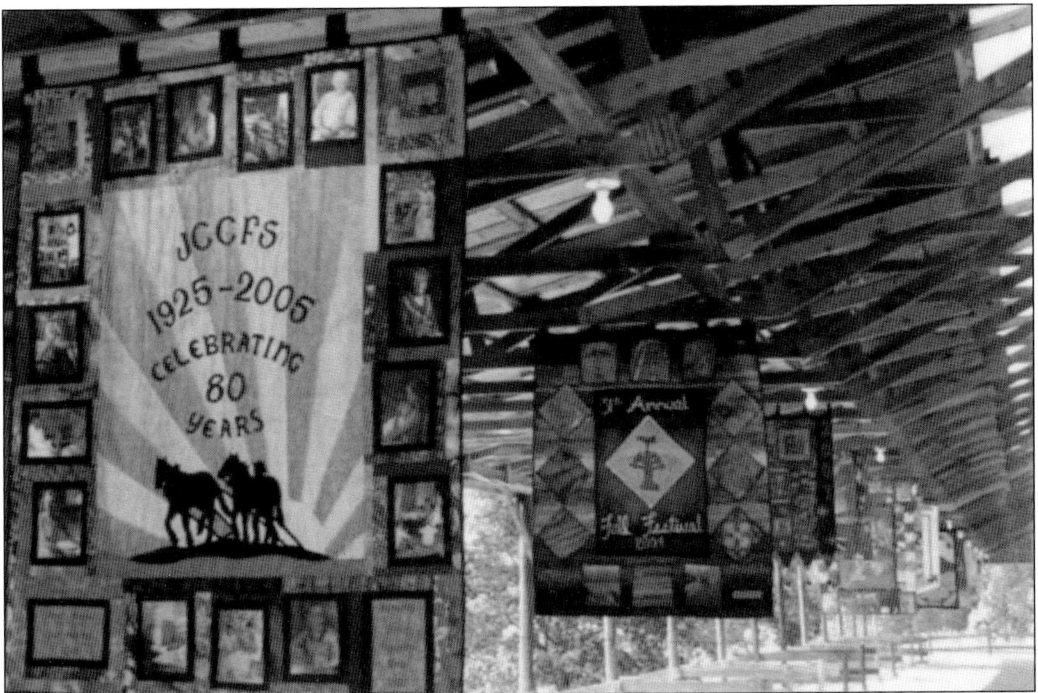

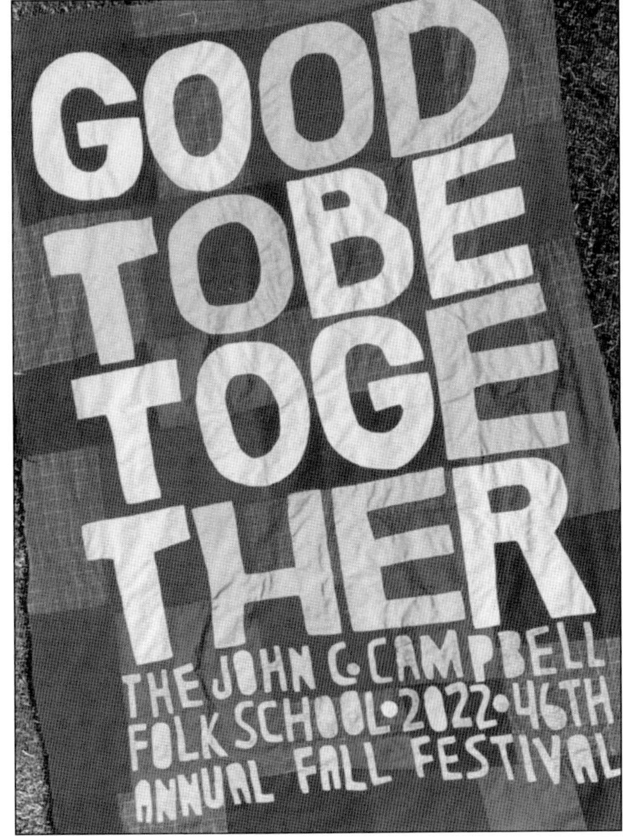

The Fall Festival quilt banner is a significant part of the weekend celebration. A new banner is crafted annually to represent that year's festival. Multiple techniques, images, and patterns incorporate classic and modern quilting practices, including piecing and appliqué, batiks, photograph prints, and hand stitching, among others. These banners are hung throughout the Festival Barn, representing decades of quilting expertise. The 2022 banner, created by former artist-in-residence Zak Foster, marked the return of Fall Festival after a two-year absence during the COVID-19 pandemic. The back of the quilt invited festival attendees to sign their names, bringing home the reminder that it is always good to be together.

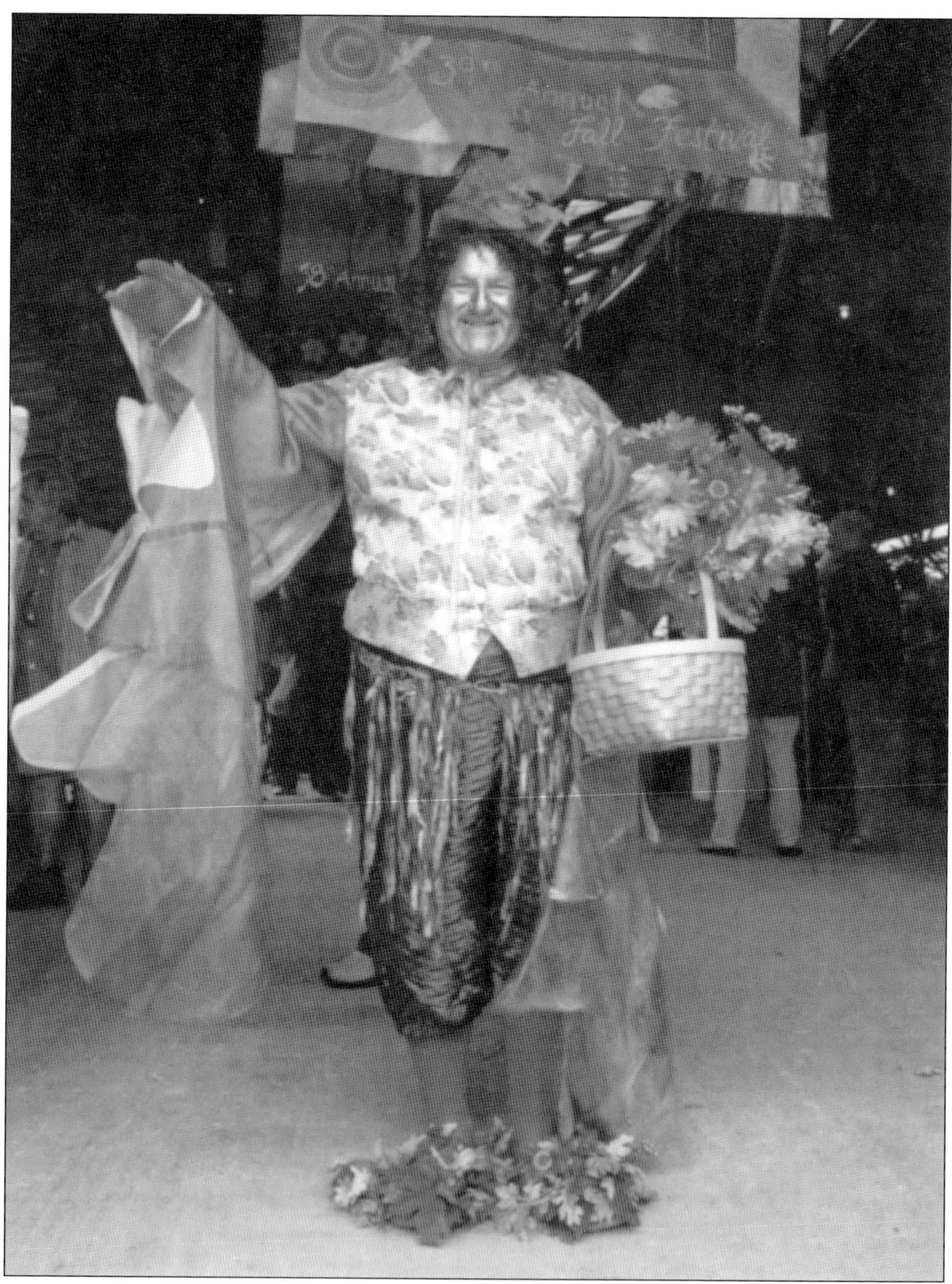

For many years, stained-glass and kaleidoscope artist, the late David Baker, captured the spirit of seasonal celebrations. His "Mr. Autumn" or "Fall Festival Fairy" attire and accessories delivered joy to visitors, vendors, and volunteers. Baker embodied the spirit of Fall Festival, relishing in the beauty of the season, the connection to community, and the cycle of life. He was known for saying, "Love wins," and his words, alongside the genuine happiness he brought to every class, every costume, and every celebration, echo those found in Olive Dame's Campbell Danish folk song translation: "Love life. Hate no one. With joy and sorrow, hope and faith, you shall build here on earth a bridge up to the stars."

Seven

1980s–1990s

Wake Up, Wake Up

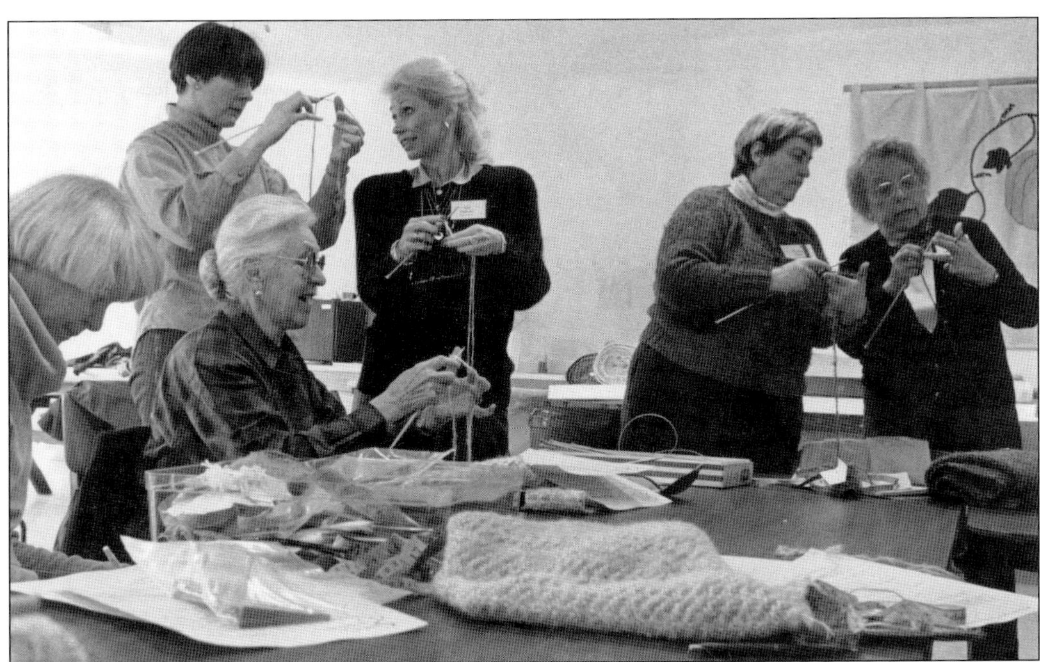

After harnessing its focus on arts and crafts programming, the Folk School entered a new period of growth. The Francis Whitaker Blacksmith Shop became the largest teaching blacksmith shop in the country, and the campus became a Historic District on the National Register of Historic Places. Student enrollment increased, new construction provided much-needed studio and dining space, and the music and dance programs took on new life.

Marguerite Bidstrup

april 19th 1982

It is unlikely that anyone could fashion a finer legacy than the one Marguerite Bidstrup, who died last week, gave to Western North Carolina. She spent most of her 90 years seeking to educate the human family and instill into it the vision that comes in knowing that each individual has worth and dignity.

She and the late Mrs. John C. Campbell founded what became the John C. Campbell Folk School at Brasstown. That institution during its more than 50 years of existence has served as a vehicle for creative adult education, which has contributed greatly to the social, cultural and economic condition of the Southern Highlands.

Mrs. Bidstrup surely recognized that her Vassar education and other gifts were meant for a purpose. And she immediately put them to work in the Pine Mountain Settlement School in Kentucky, from which she rode horseback into isolated areas to serve mountain people.

Her later work at Brasstown brought the Folk School worldwide attention and attracted visitors from around the globe to the North Carolina mountains.

Through it all, she maintained the dignity and joy of a rich life, made the richer by her teaching folk dances to literally thousands of people.

Marguerite Bidstrup helped the mountain people to preserve a heritage and to build on it for a richer legacy to be passed on to future generations.

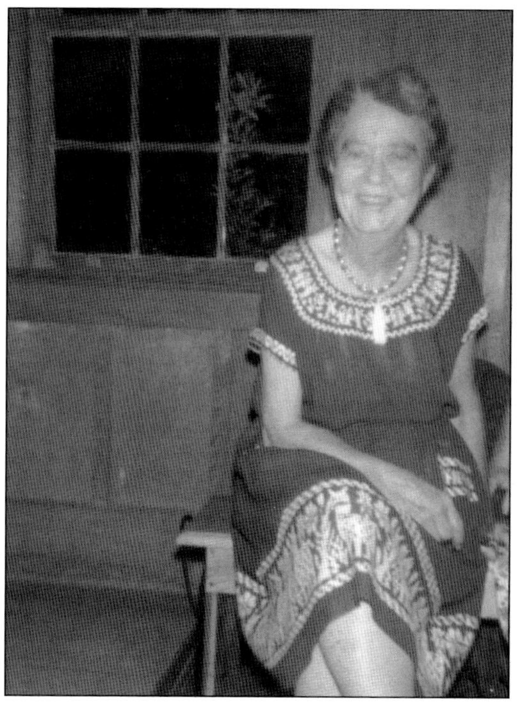

Marguerite Butler Bidstrup died in 1982 and was remembered as a woman who "spent most of her 90 years seeking to educate the human family and instill into it the vision that comes in knowing that each individual has worth and dignity." From her first trip to Brasstown, which forever changed the story of a small community, to the nearly six decades she spent as one of its residents, Bidstrup helped preserve a way of life that emphasized creativity, service, and dance. During her Folk School tenure, she served as the assistant director and treasurer, and she often joined students and community members in dance. This image of Bidstrup was taken by six-year-old Marianne Varley in 1963.

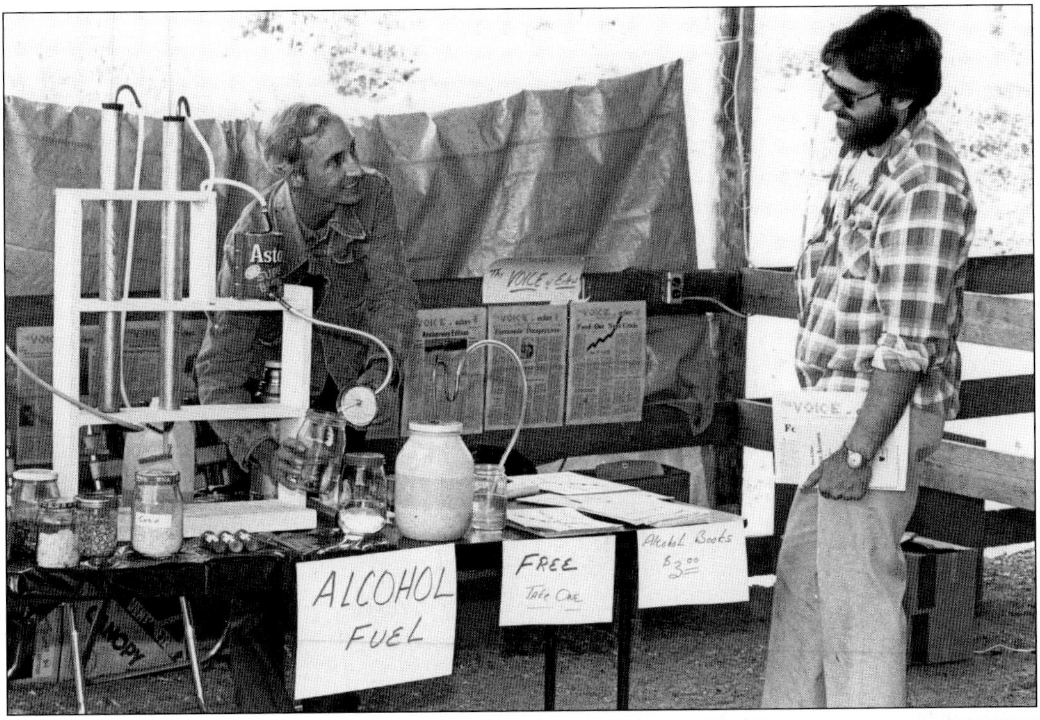

In the 1980s, the Folk School offered a homesteading program, a six-month course for teaching back-to-the-land skills and food production. Students studied shelter design and construction, organic gardening, and homestead planning. In 1981, the school held a homesteading festival with demonstrations and information booths, including alcohol fuel, which can be used to provide light and heat in an off-grid setting. The event was intended to teach people about their options and decide what might work best for their individual situation. Interdependence, rather than independence, was the goal. Carla Owen (right) was involved in the homesteading program and is pictured here re-digging a raised bed. Owen was an integral part of the Folk School community who also managed the dining hall, served as the resident artist in weaving, and later served as coresident artist in cooking.

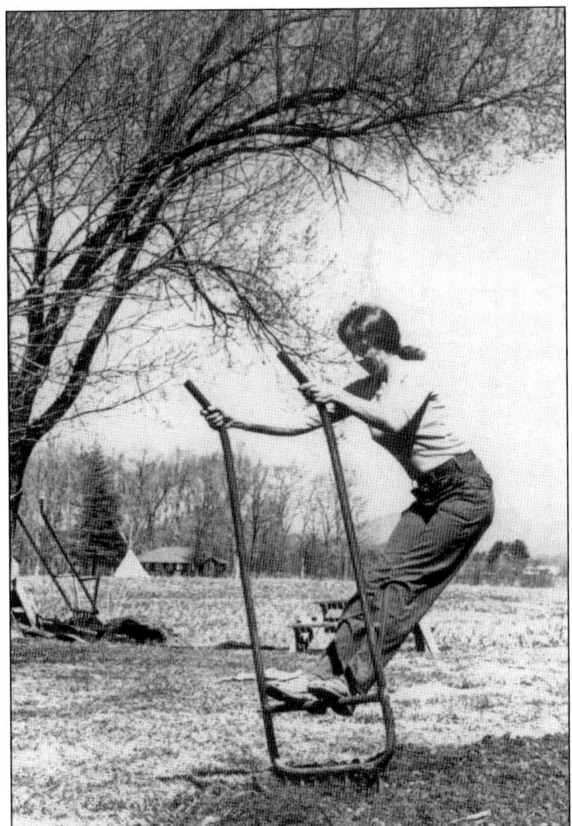

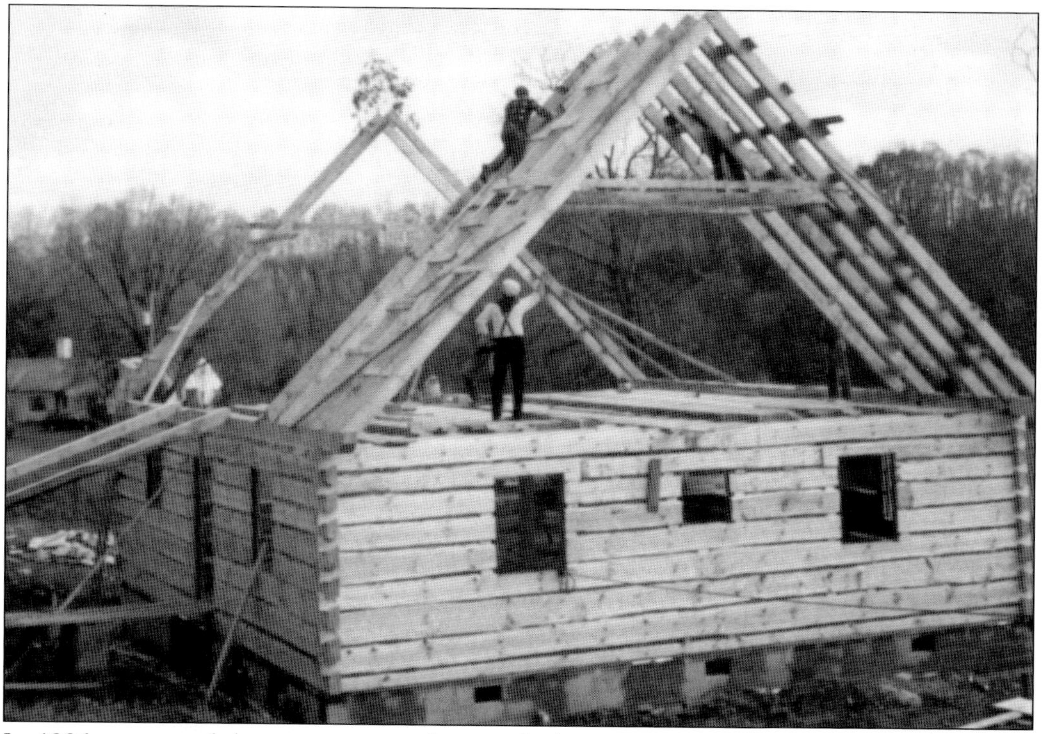

In 1986, a two-week log construction class taught by Peter Gott resulted in the frame for Log House. Built for student housing, which was a growing need, the final details of the structure were completed in 1988. Gott initially mastered log construction for his own dreams of living off the land and eventually started teaching classes to other interested builders.

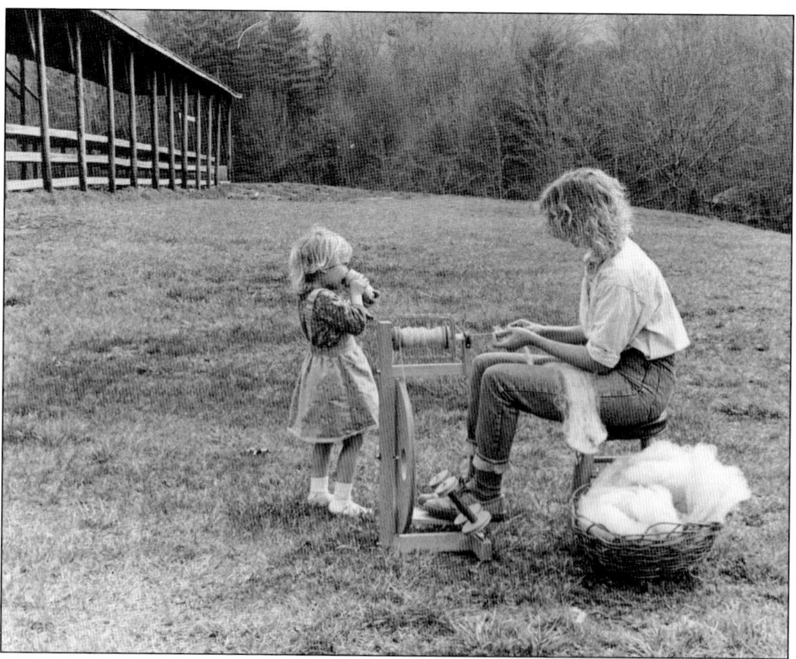

Martha Owen (right) first came to the Folk School as one of a few kids in Little Folk School (later Little Middle). She took her first spinning class in 1978 and has stayed with the craft ever since. In this 1988 photograph, she is spinning wool into yarn outside Festival Barn while her youngest daughter, Emolyn Liden, was "drinking a grape coke and trying to be good."

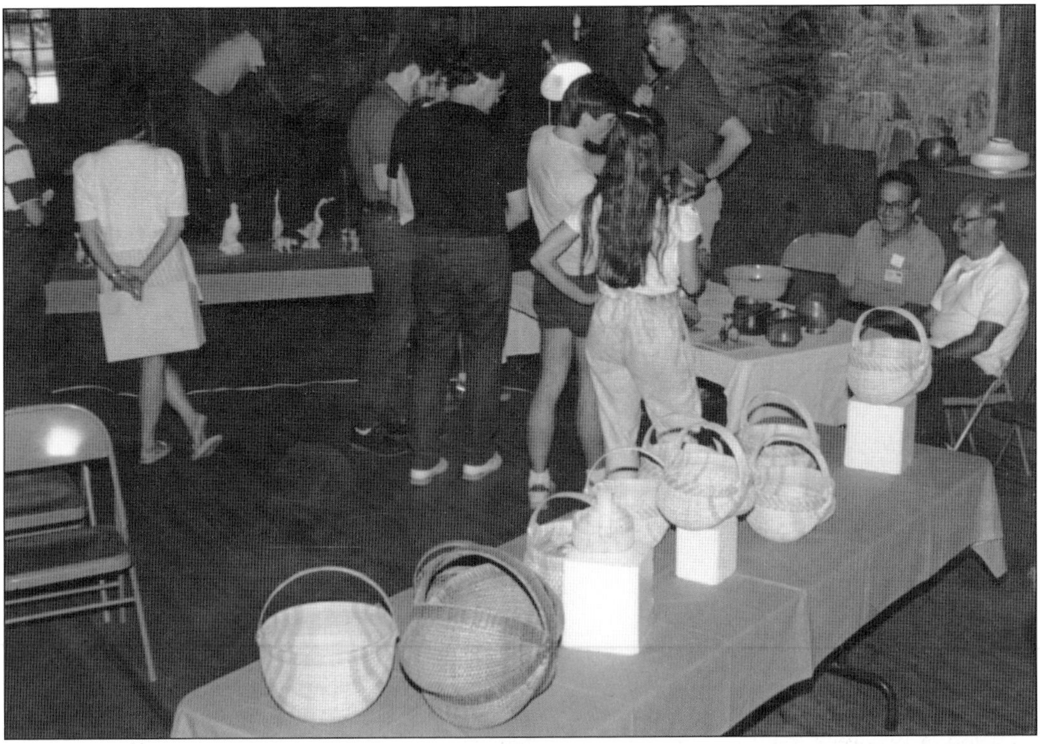

As enrollment continued to grow in the 1980s–1990s, so, too, did the student showcase. Held as a final celebration of weeklong classes, the display of crafts from different studios and program areas brings students, instructors, staff, and guests to Community Room in Keith House. In this image, tables are filled with finished pieces from basket makers, wood-carvers, and potters.

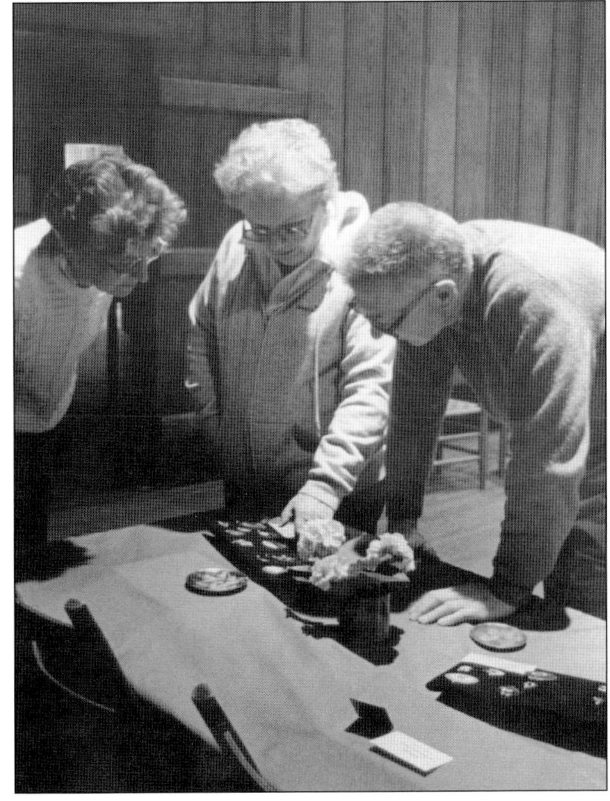

Enameling classes at the Folk School were given new life under the direction of Gus and Maggie Masters, who started the official program in the 1970s. Thanks to their dedication, these pieces shared at a student showcase in the 1980s were produced in an enameling studio now recognized as one of the best and most respected in the United States.

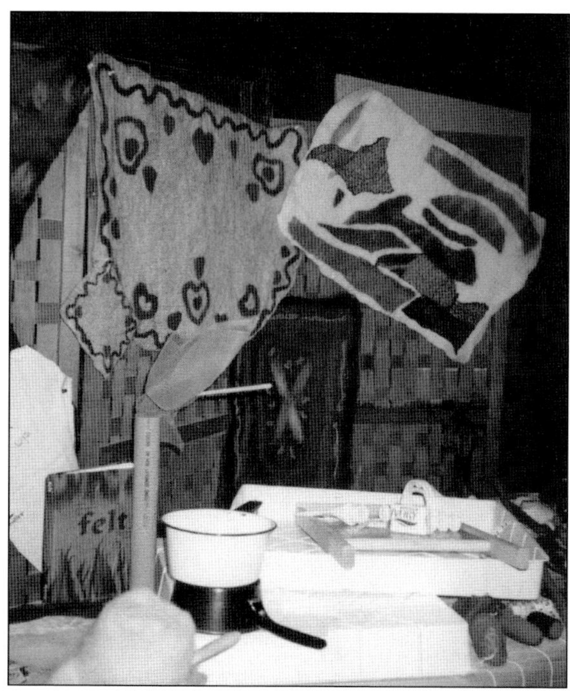

A felting display at the student showcase demonstrates the versatility of the craft. By pressing layers of wool together, students make rugs, wall hangings, and other decorative pieces. Felting classes now include backpacks, embellishments, hats, and more. When combined with silk dyeing, nuno felt results in pieces, patches, or yardage that can add color and texture to works ranging from quilts to books.

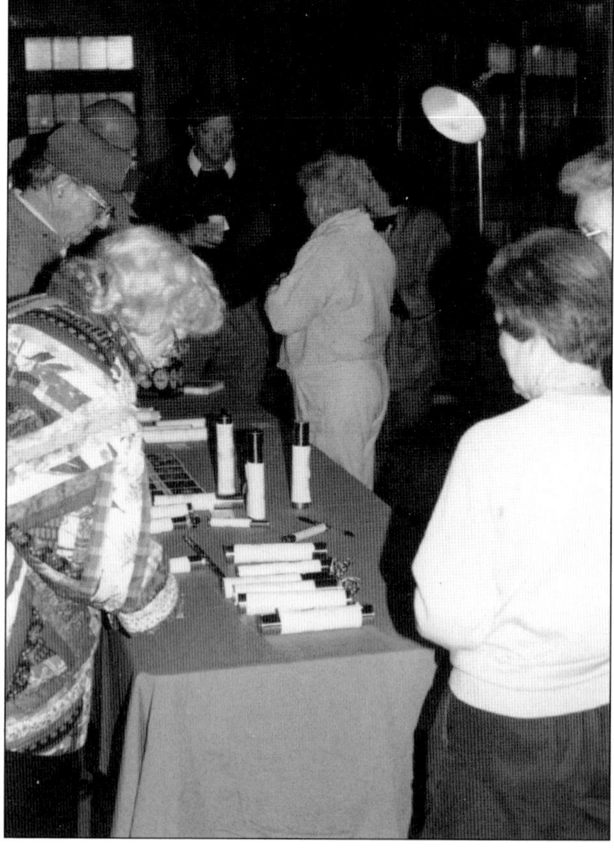

The sense of discovery and wonder that comes with looking through a kaleidoscope is something Folk School students have been creating for decades. Using the components of a tube or soldered glass along with colorful objects, including beads, the magic of symmetrical patterns provides an experience that requires precision and playfulness.

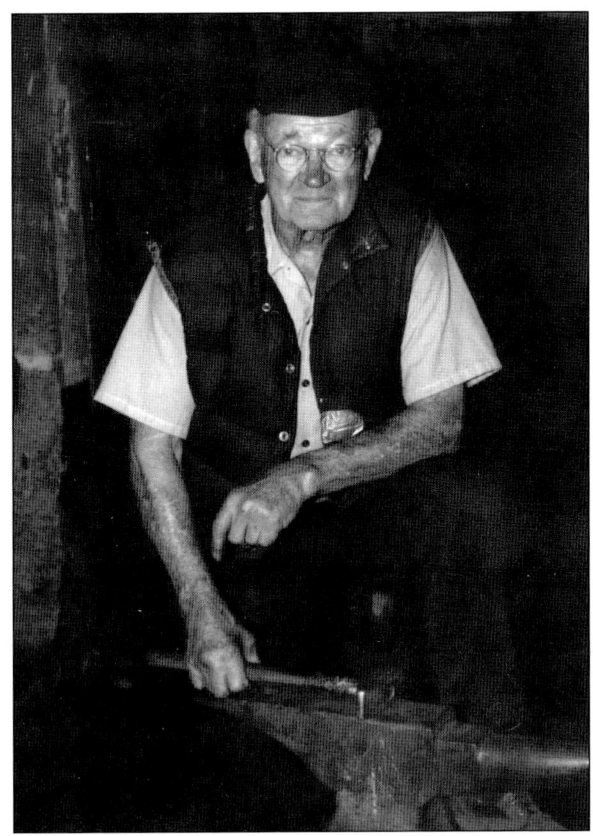

Francis Whitaker was known as the "Dean of American Blacksmiths" and devoted his life to keeping the art of blacksmithing alive. Whitaker first visited the Folk School in the mid-1970s and taught his first class in the Oscar Cantrell Shop. He served as a Folk School blacksmithing instructor for 18 years and was instrumental in building the program from a one-forge shop to a 13-forge shop. From 1991 to 1993, he led three workshops that resulted in the chandeliers that hang in the Olive Dame Campbell Dining Hall. Whitaker taught his last two-week advanced class at the Folk School in 1997. The Francis Whitaker Blacksmith Shop, which once served as the primary location for blacksmithing classes, now provides additional space for tools and serves as a finishing room.

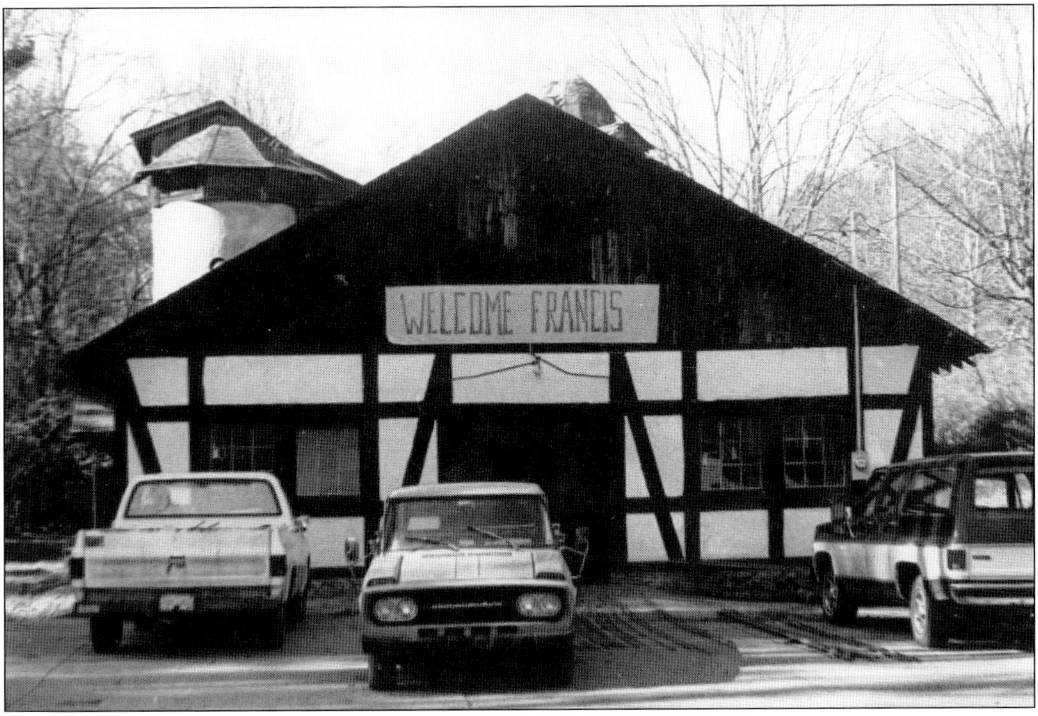

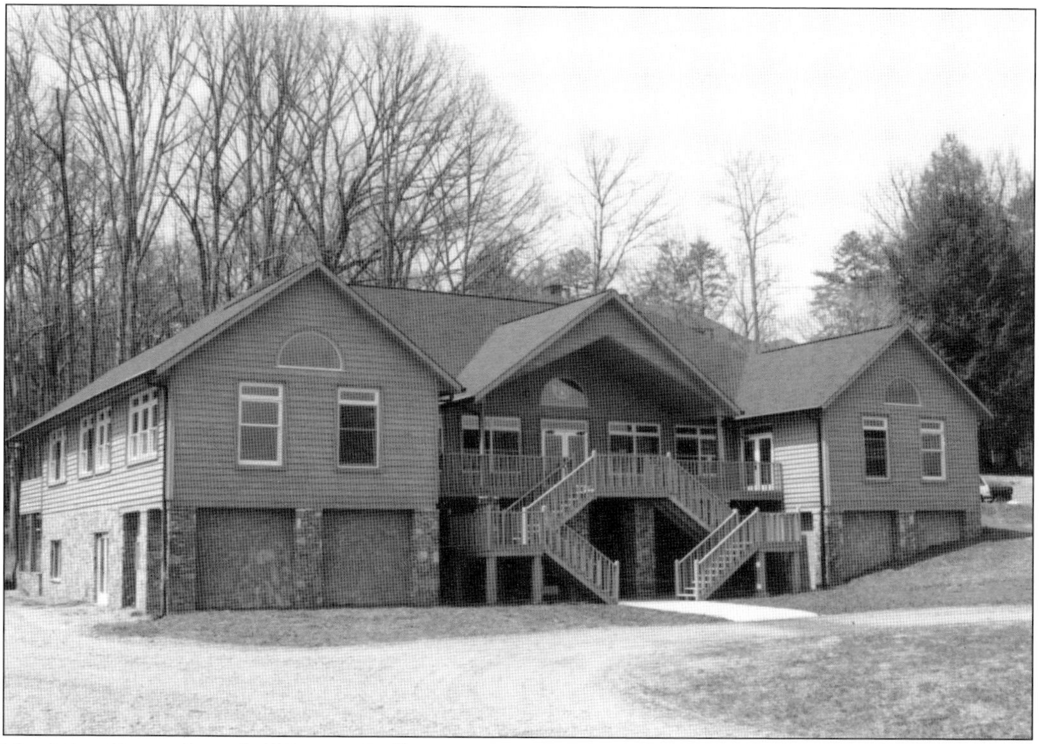

The Olive Dame Campbell Dining Hall was constructed in 1992 and serves as a campus centerpiece. Students, instructors, and staff visit daily for delicious meals. The dining room has also provided space for community events, including Empty Bowls, which raises funds for food pantries in both Cherokee and Clay Counties.

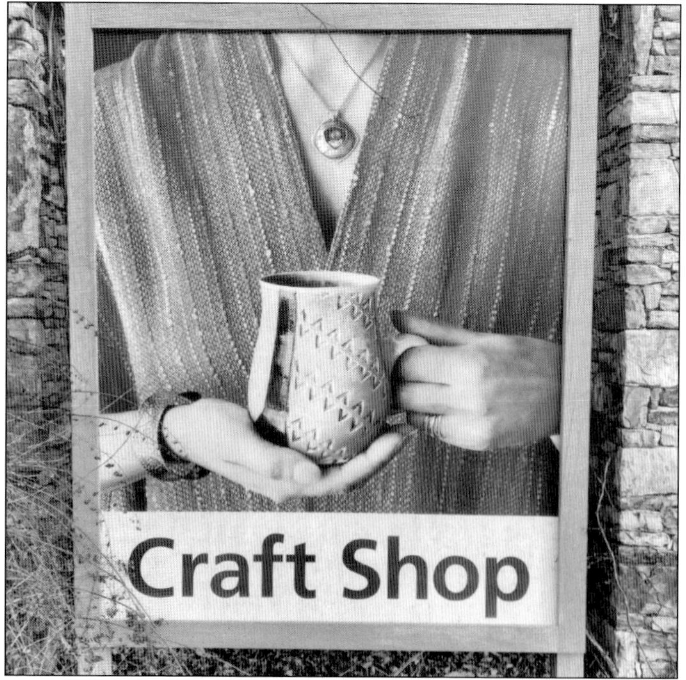

The school's Craft Shop is located on the bottom floor of the building and represents a number of juried craftspeople. Traditional and contemporary pieces are available for sale, showcasing the diverse media offered through year-round classes and workshops. The Craft Shop also serves as the home of the world-renowned Brasstown Carvers.

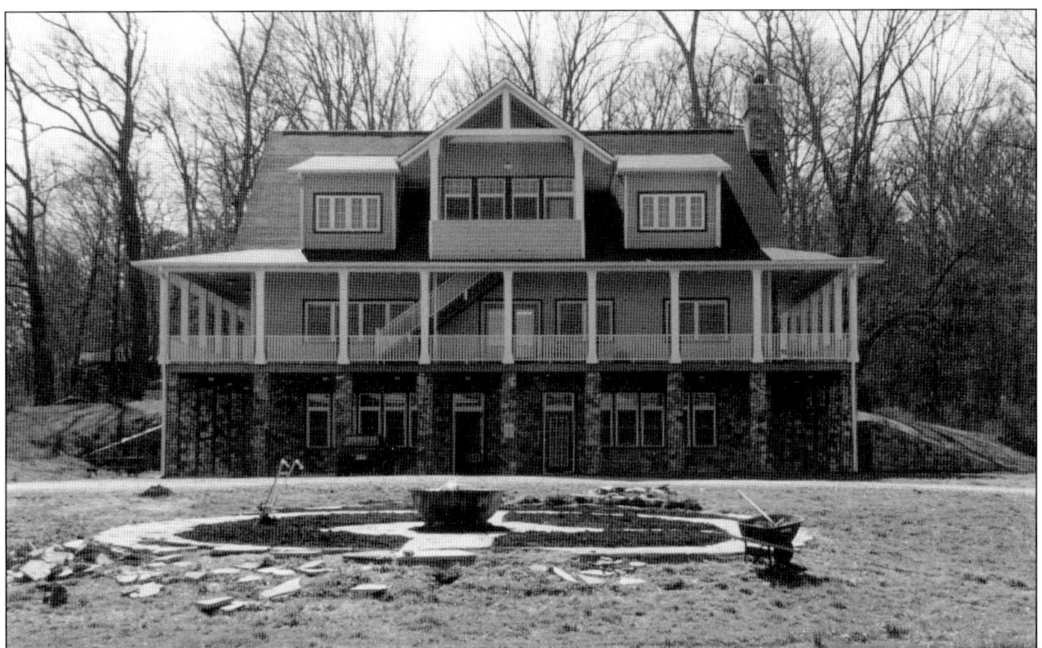

Davidson Hall was constructed in 1999 and serves as a multipurpose building. The ground floor houses the Wet Room, used for spinning, knitting, crochet, felting, dyeing, and surface design classes, and the Cooking Studio. The school's Music Studio can be found on the second floor, and student housing is available on the third.

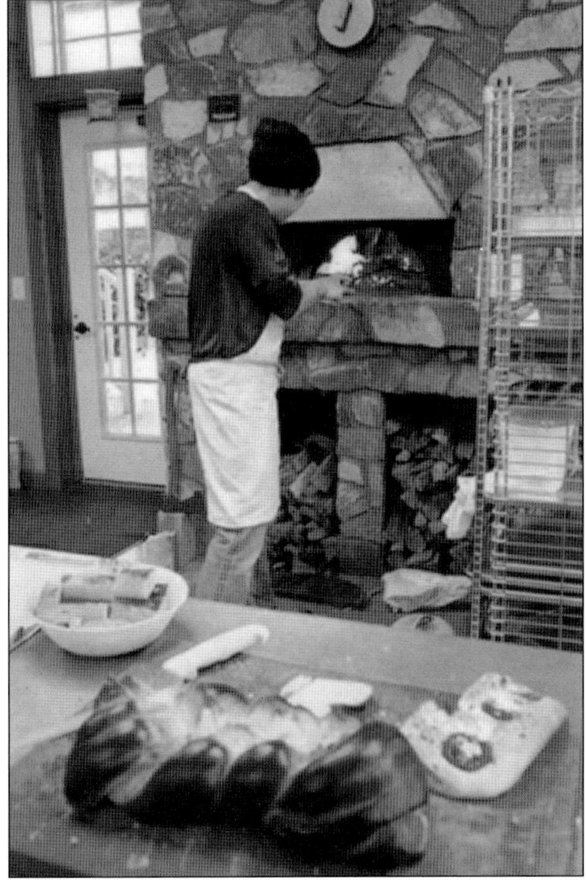

The Cooking Studio was built with a wood-fired oven, a method that requires practice building fires, cooking in rotation, and studying heat. It was one of the first cooking programs to invest in brick ovens. The popularity of the in-studio oven inspired a second, outdoor, student-built oven, housed under a student-built, timber-framed pavilion. Pizzas, flatbreads, and endless loaves yield perfectly crunchy crusts.

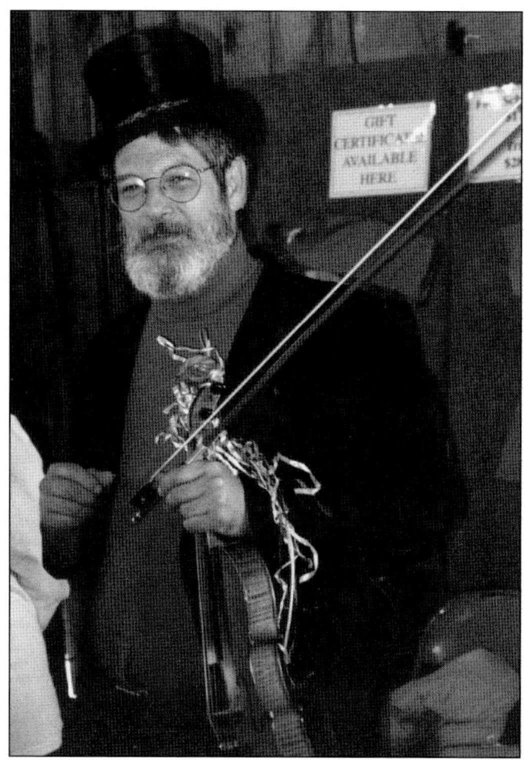

Jan Davidson was appointed as executive director in 1992. Under his guidance, the Folk School flourished. He focused on programming, facilities, fundraising, historic preservation, and conservation. Throughout his 25-year tenure, enrollment more than doubled, from an annual average of 2,500 to 6,000 students. Davidson's Murphy, North Carolina, roots and his deep love of the Folk School created a lasting legacy in Brasstown.

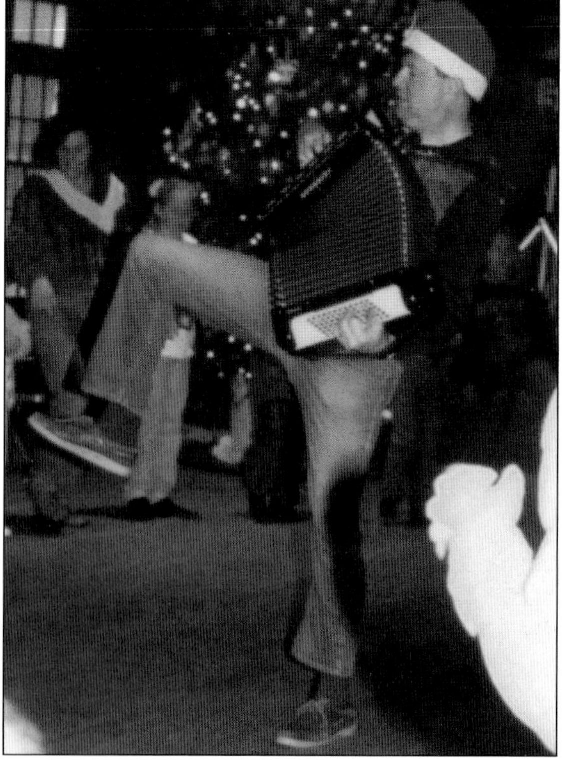

Bob Dalsemer joined the staff in 1991 as music and dance coordinator. He started free Friday night concerts and created Dance Musicians' and Dance Callers' Week. He also developed a robust offering of music and dance classes throughout the year. Dalsemer often served as a dance caller, and he played with a house band for community dances. His dedication forever changed the music and dance scene at the Folk School.

Eight

Music and Dance
Old Play Song

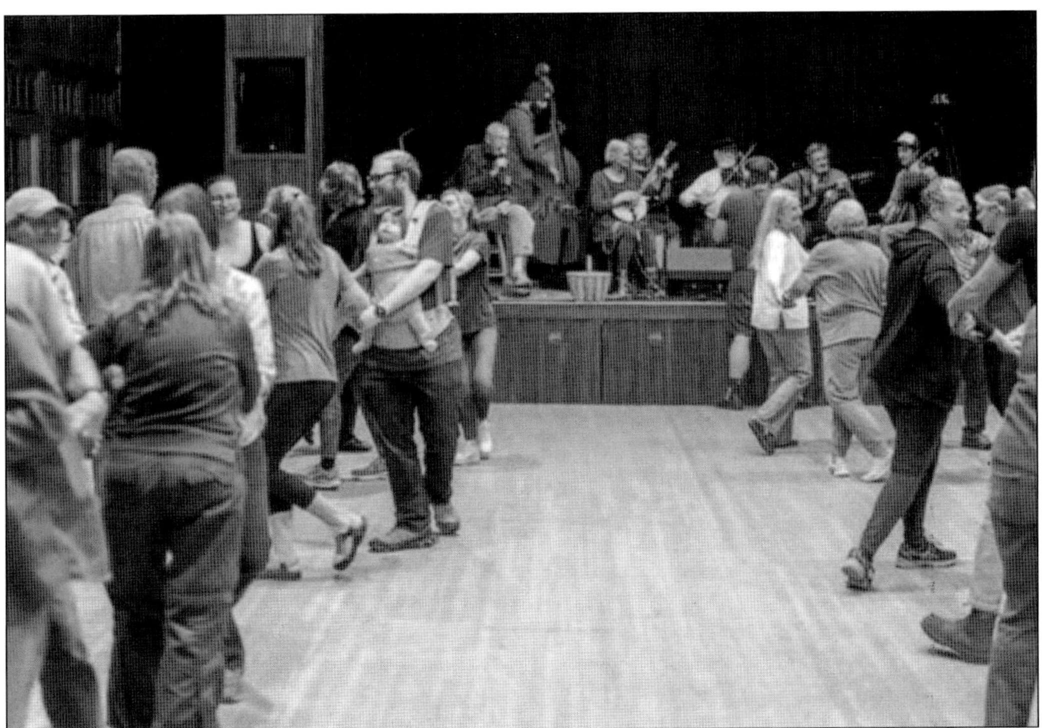

Music and dance offerings have been a core part of John C. Campbell Folk School's identity since its founding in 1925. Contra dances, evening concerts, May Day celebrations, the Junior Appalachian Musicians program, and traditional and contemporary classes teach new and old friends how to strum along or swing their partner round right. Brasstown is also the home to several dance teams that further the English Border Morris dancing tradition.

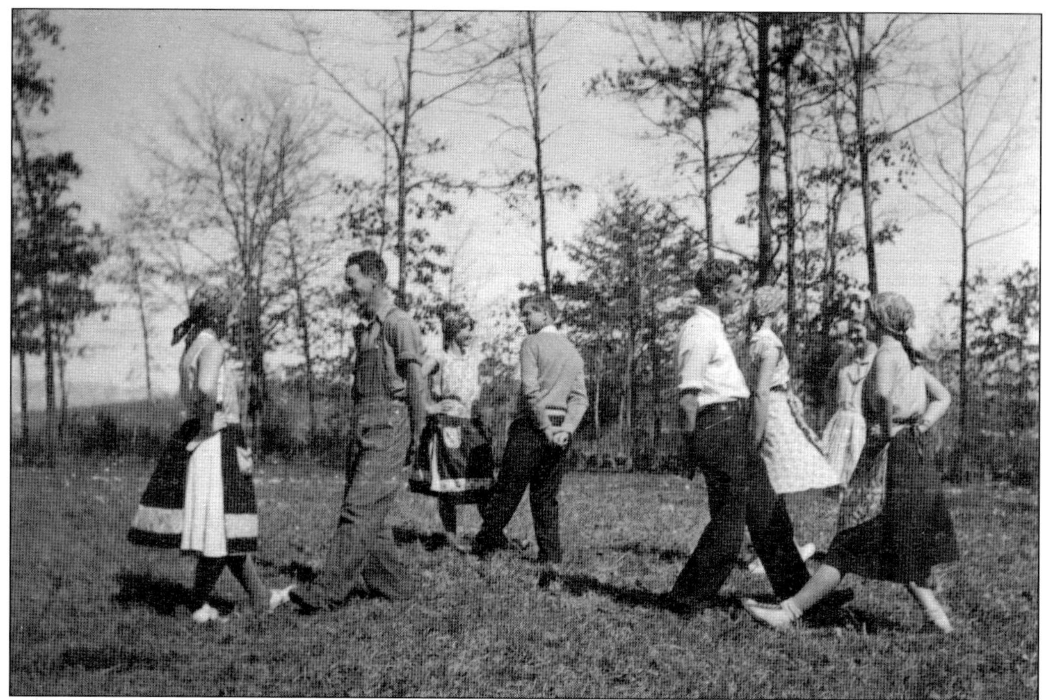

When Marguerite Butler Bidstrup and Olive Dame Campbell visited the south of England in 1923, they attended English folk dances and decided to incorporate folk dancing at the school they were then planning. Friday Night Games, as they were originally called, included Scandinavian folk dances and English country dances. Between the 1940s and 1970s, as the school worked to accommodate the growing and changing needs of the student and community populations, Friday Night Games became Saturday Night Dances. These iconic images from the late 1930s and early 1940s have been repeated thousands of times in the Community Room and Open House as people continue to gather for dance.

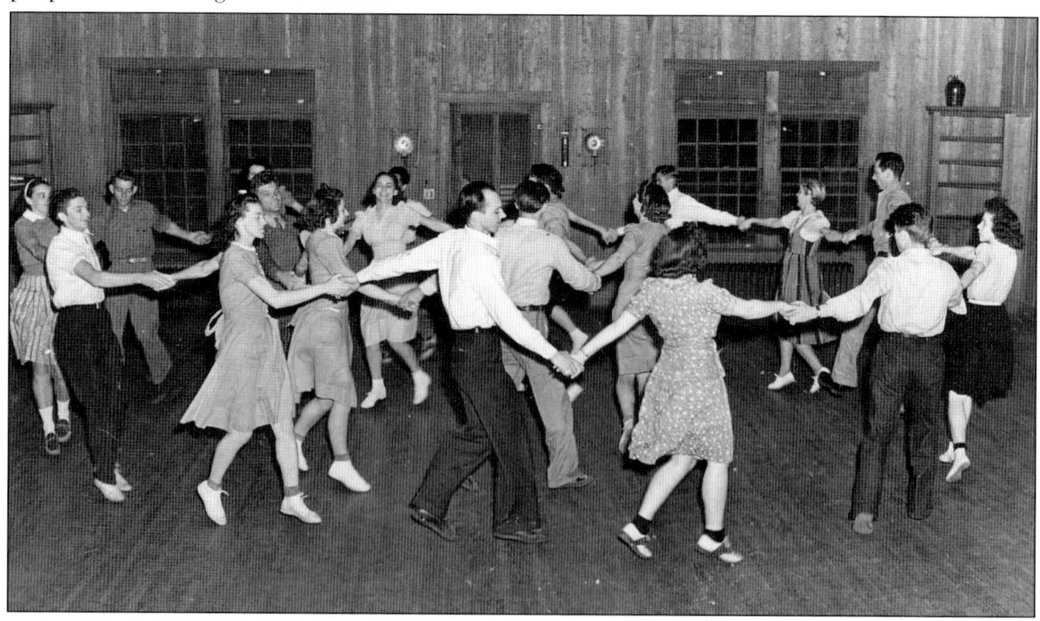

Much like dance, music has played a significant role in the communal atmosphere of the Folk School since its beginning. Weeklong short courses, originally established in 1932, were geared toward country dancers and recreation leaders, including musicians. Creation of the short course has been attributed to Marguerite Butler Bidstrup, who regularly participated in both music and dance classes and events. In the image at right, students in a 1945 short course played the recorder, a traditional folk music instrument. In the photograph below, Bidstrup (first row, center) shared the joy of the recorder in a larger music class with various woodwind instruments.

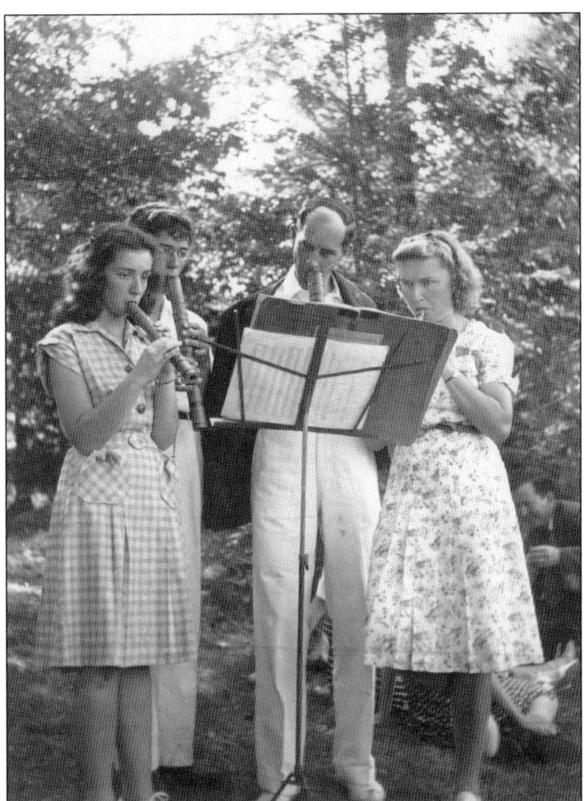

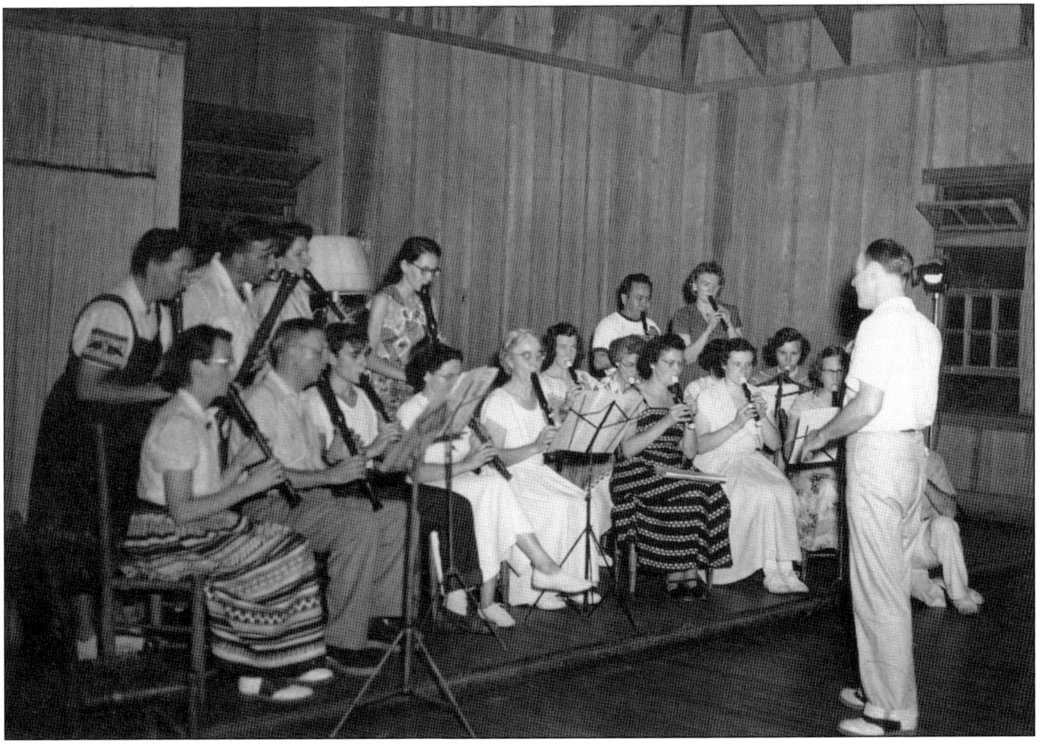

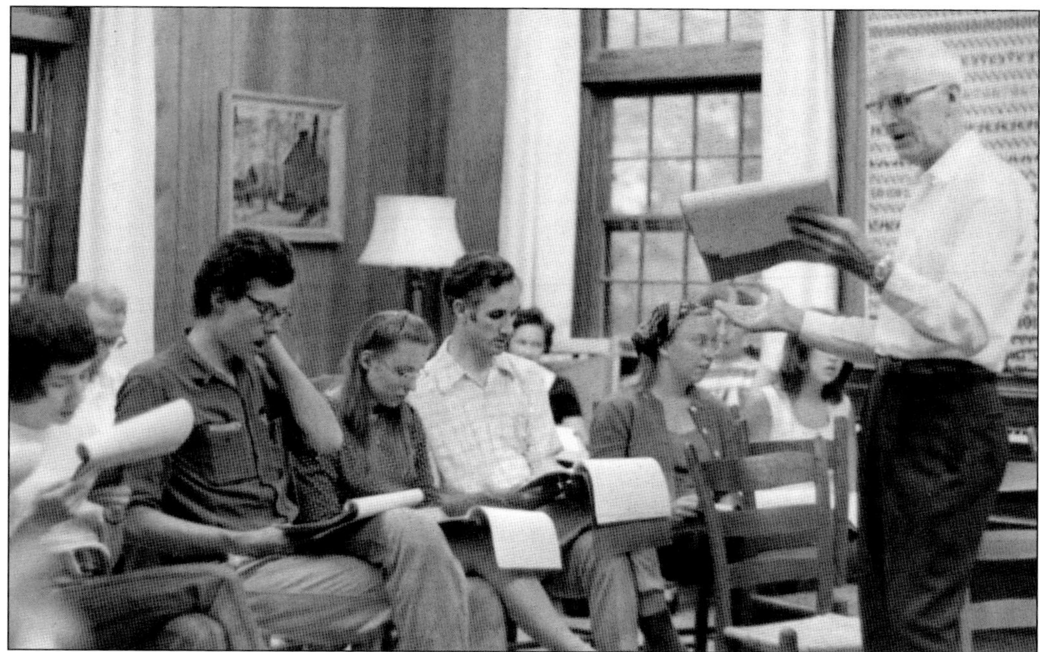

The annual Shape Note Singing invites voices from surrounding states for a day of vocal harmonizing. Beginner and experienced singers use *Sacred Harp* and *Christian Harmony* books, originally published in 1866. It is the oldest seven-shape-note collection to have remained in continuous use, primarily in Western North Carolina and North Georgia. This 1978 Shape Note Singing was led by Richard Moss.

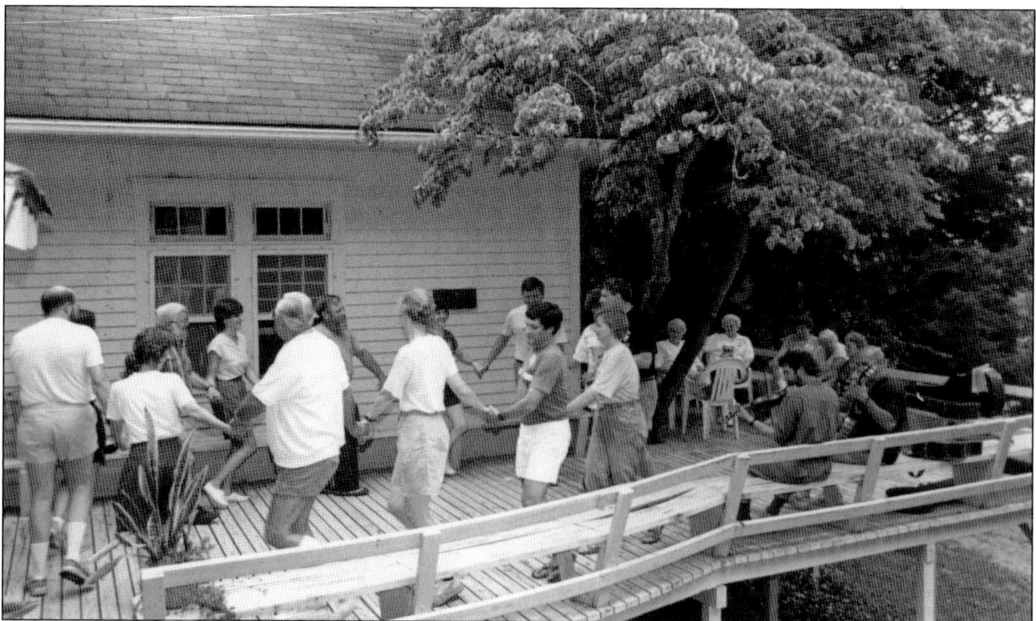

Music jams are a common occurrence around the Folk School campus. On a nice day, musicians bring their instrument of choice to an outdoor gathering place and join in tune. If dancers are present, those jams become a bigger shindig for all involved, including these spectators on the back porch of Keith House.

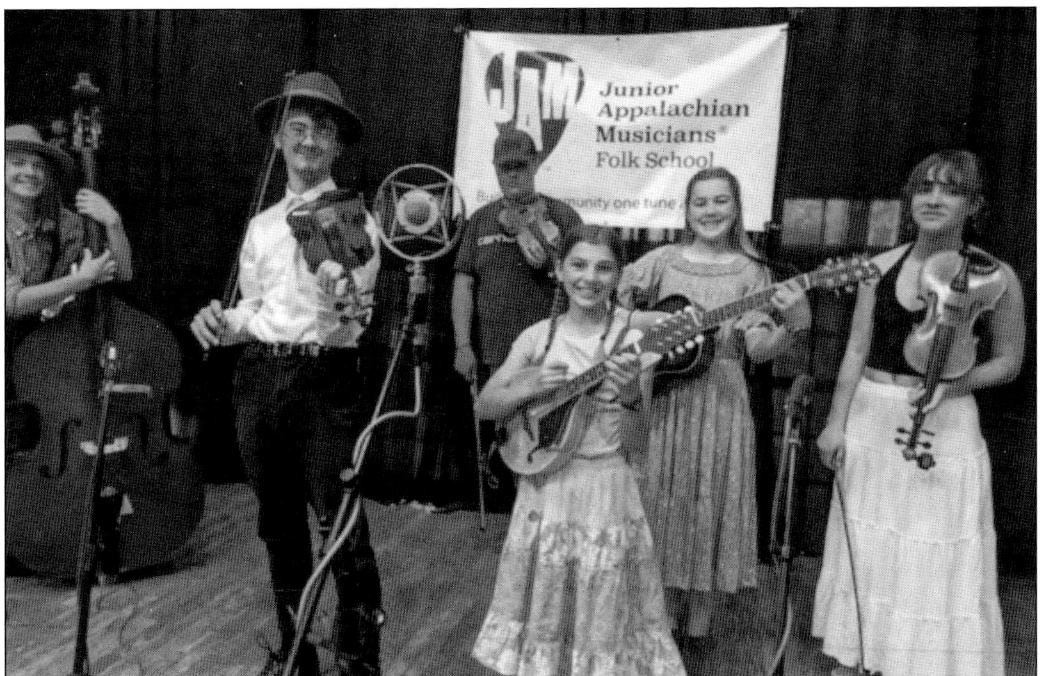

The Junior Appalachian Musicians (JAM) program offers students between the ages of 12 and 18 the opportunity to learn stringed instruments in traditional old-time and bluegrass music, including guitar, banjo, and fiddle. The young musicians practice together in a band, connecting to the heritage of rural Appalachia. JAM students hold concerts at the end of their season and perform at the annual Fall Festival. What began as a small group in Alleghany County, North Carolina, in 2000 has now expanded into a nonprofit that offers programs in Virginia, West Virginia, Kentucky, Tennessee, Georgia, and North Carolina. With its roots in traditional craft, music, and dance, the Folk School is an ideal site for JAM.

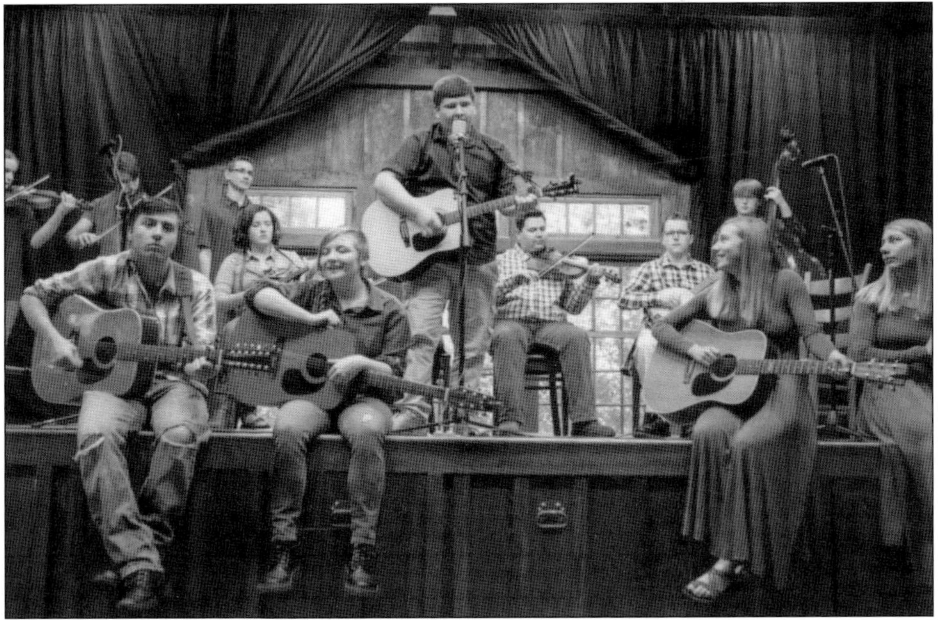

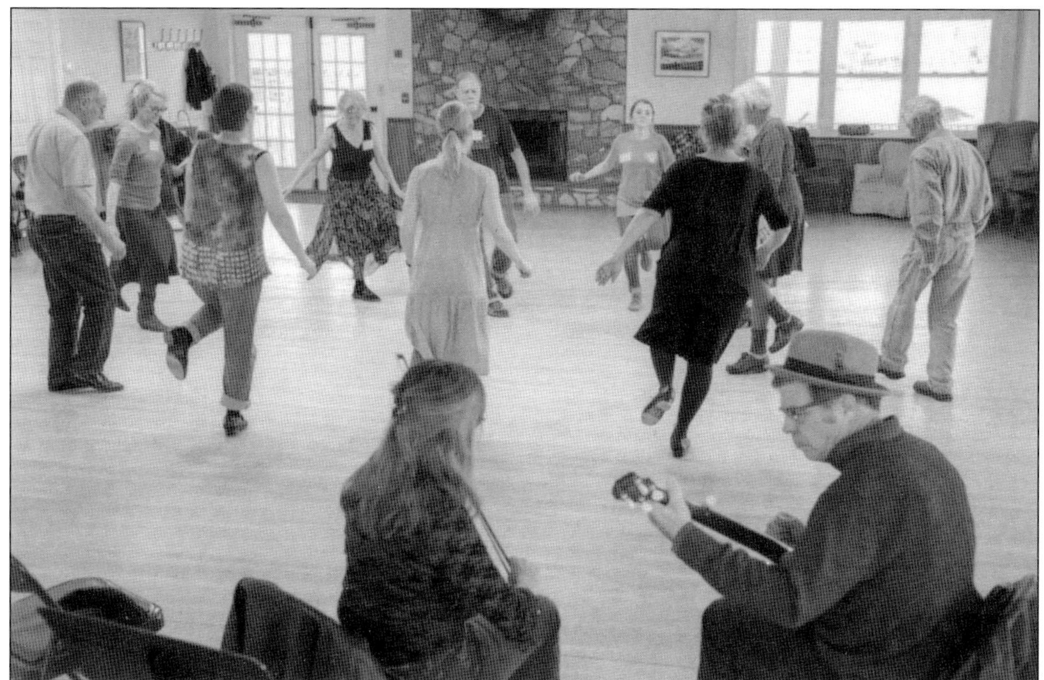

Dance classes include offerings for those who find themselves on the dance floor and for those who stand behind the mic and guide movement on the dance floor. Some are focused on areas like contra, square, or clogging. Special weekends incorporate English country dance, Balfolk, and more. Whether dancing or calling, classes help students of all levels learn how to navigate steps, feel rhythm, and connect with others.

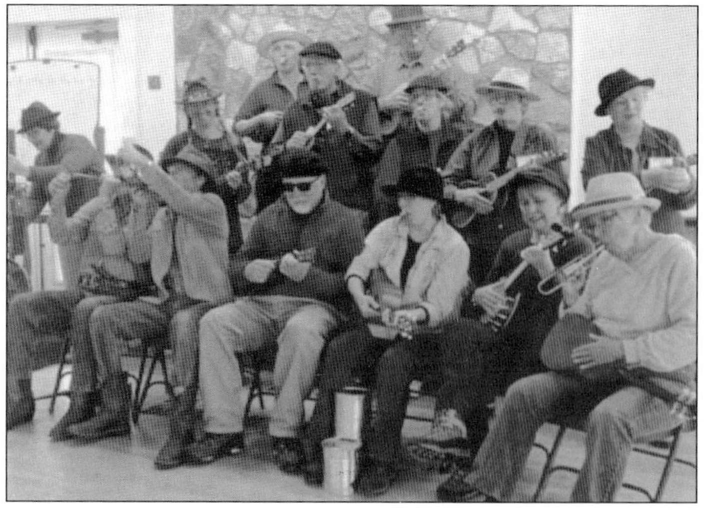

In music classes, students try their hand at guitar, banjo, dulcimer, Native American flute, ukulele, and more. They can also learn the art of playing with other musicians in a jam, explore singing traditional ballads and folk songs, and study African American contributions to Appalachian music. Whether first-timers or experienced musicians or singers, the span of music classes offers something for everyone.

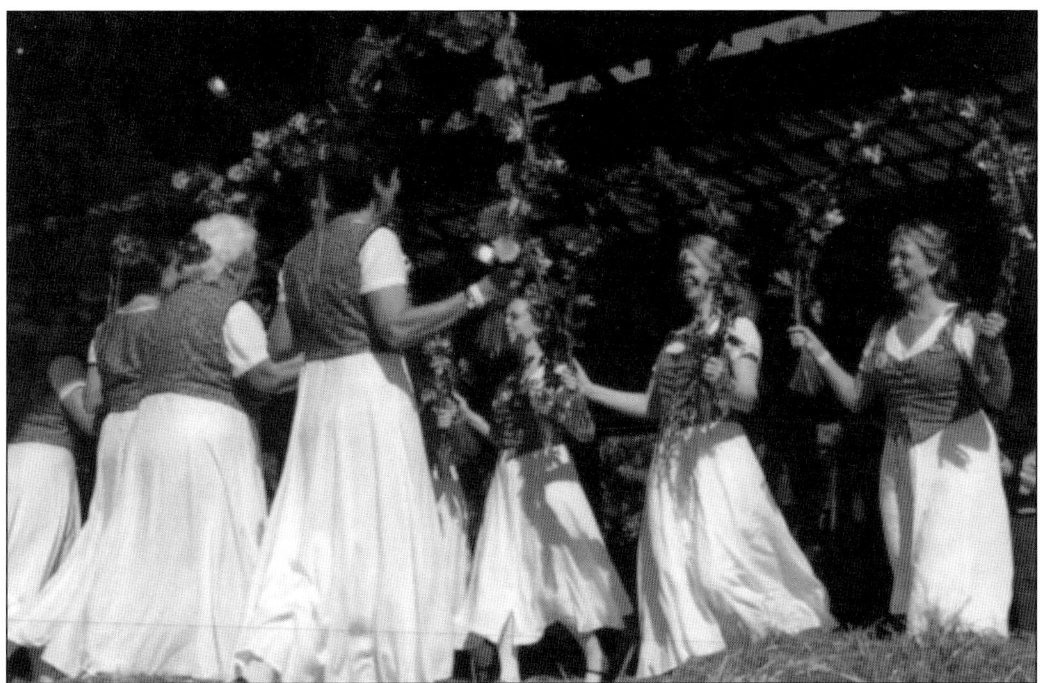

Brasstown Morris includes individual teams, known as "sides," who perform traditional English Morris dances with an American flavor. The teams are accompanied by a large band with accordions, fiddles, drums, and other instruments. All performers are members of the local community. The Rural Felicity Garland Dancers were established in Brasstown in 1983 and spent decades performing at local, national, and international festivals and celebrations.

Morris dancing dates from the aftermath of the Crusades. It was a seasonal, ritual dance done by men in disguise, often at Christmas or May Day. The Stix-in-the-Mud Border Morris Dancers perform with painted blue faces, colorful rag coats, loud leg bells, and a hearty serving of attitude. The Folk School team has been delighting audiences since 1996.

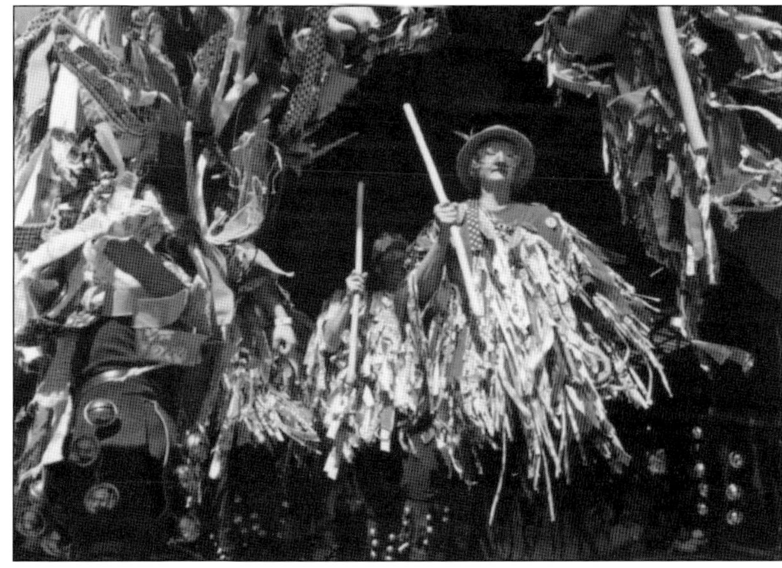

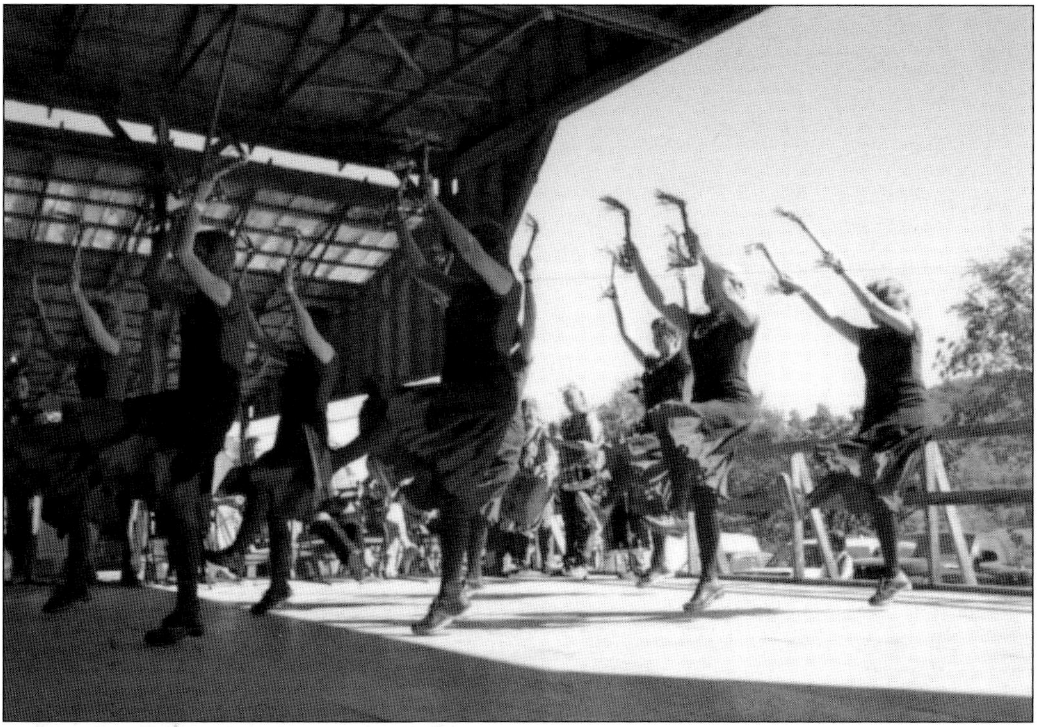

The Dame's Rockets Northwest Clog Morris Dancers, a women's group named after a common flower similar to phlox, was created in 2005. The name also recognizes the school's founder, Olive Dame Campbell. Their celebratory dances are often performed in wooden clog shoes and, for the Folk School team, accentuated with striped tights.

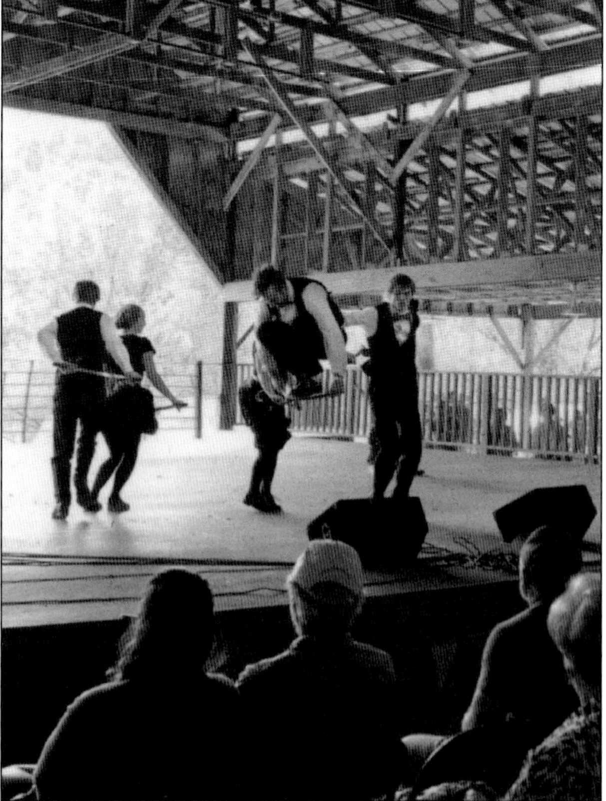

Rapper Magic Sword Dancers use flexible, metal curry combs, called "swords," to create quick, intricate, and seemingly impossible configurations, all while maintaining their swords in hand. In group formations, patterns are created above the dancers' heads with interlinked swords. Footwork also plays an important role in the dance, including impressive jumps.

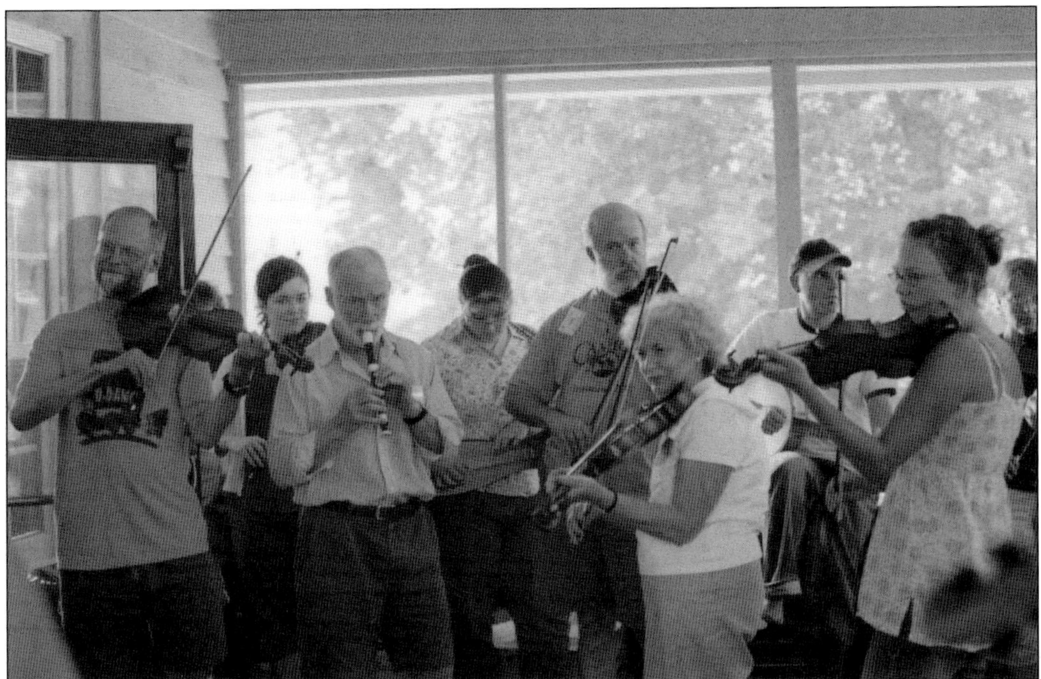

Since 1994, Dance Musicians' Week has honored the ways endless instruments bring folks to the dance floor. Those instruments include piano, guitar, fiddle, recorder, accordion, flute, banjo, tambourine, and more in celebration of all things dance music. On the way to lunch, students, instructors, and staff members walk through a concert. David Kaynor (left) was one of the original organizers behind the special week, helping it run for 25 years.

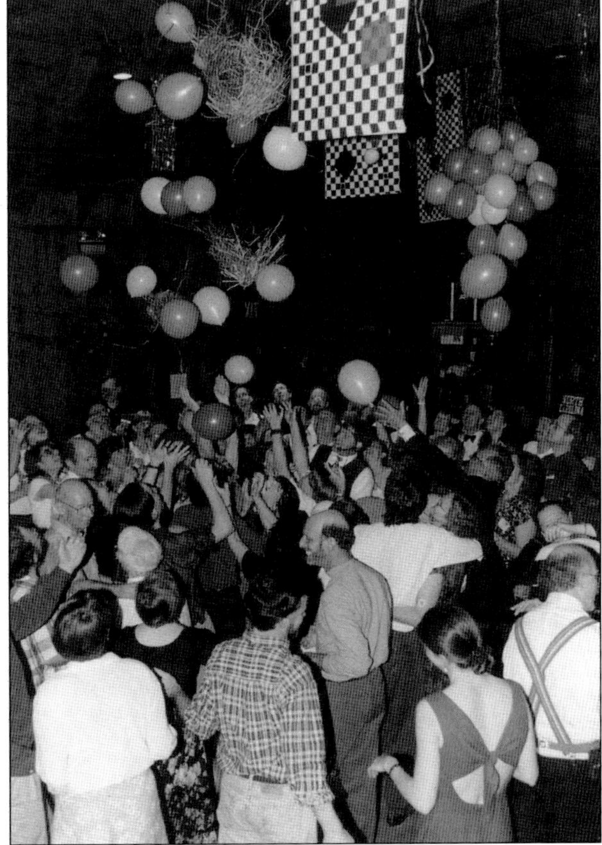

Winter Dance Week was established in 1979 as a year-end celebration of music and dance. It wraps up with a New Year's Eve party, complete with English country dance, contra, and squares, all set to live music. This event draws in students and community members for a meaningful and memorable tradition. A midnight balloon drop rings in the coming year, surrounded by friends old and new.

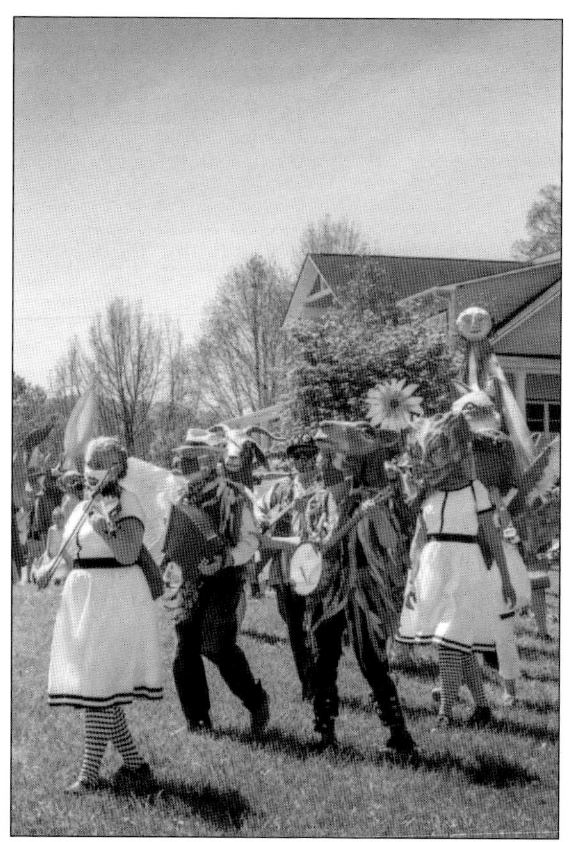

Another annual event, the May Day Parade and Maypole Dance, was founded by Nanette Davidson and is a festive celebration of spring. The parade is led by the Brasstown Morris Dancers and Band and stretches from the Festival Barn to the Maypole, located near Davidson Hall. Dancers then circle around the Maypole and share several traditional dances. Puppets, costumes, and revelry abound. For this very special occasion in 2021, a small puppetry class was held the week prior. Led by the Paperhand Puppet Project, students created unique masks and colorful puppets out of papier-mâché, cardboard, cloth, paints, and upcycled treasures that were on full display during the festivities.

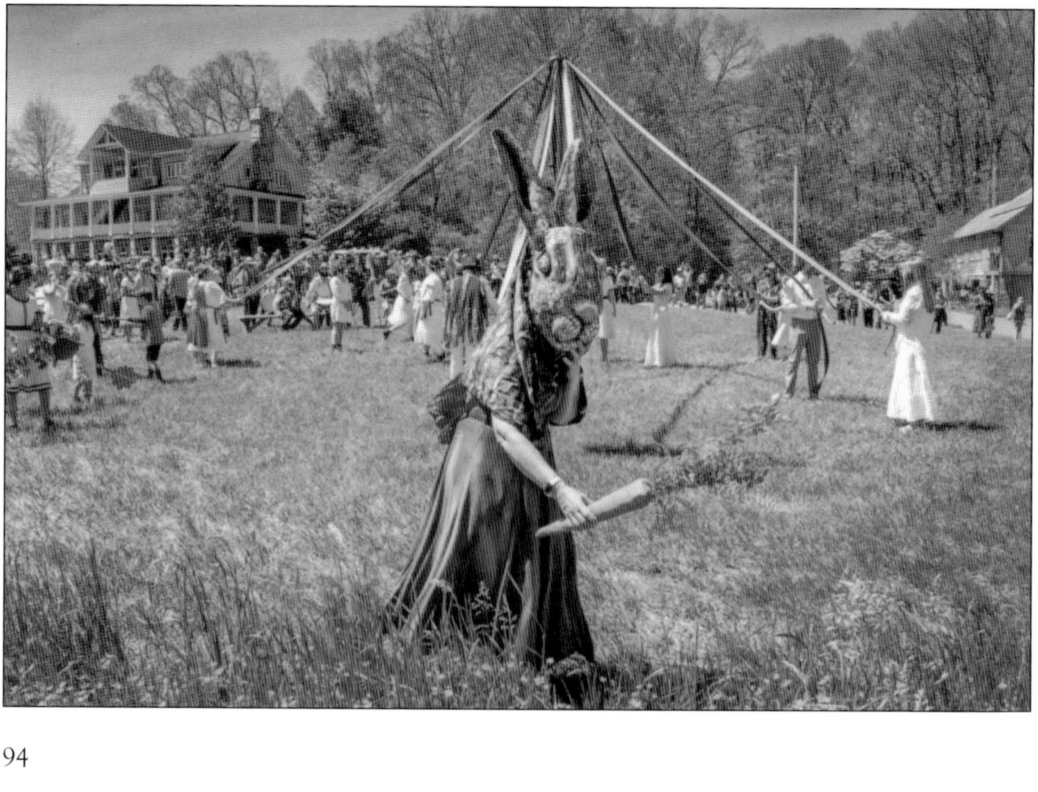

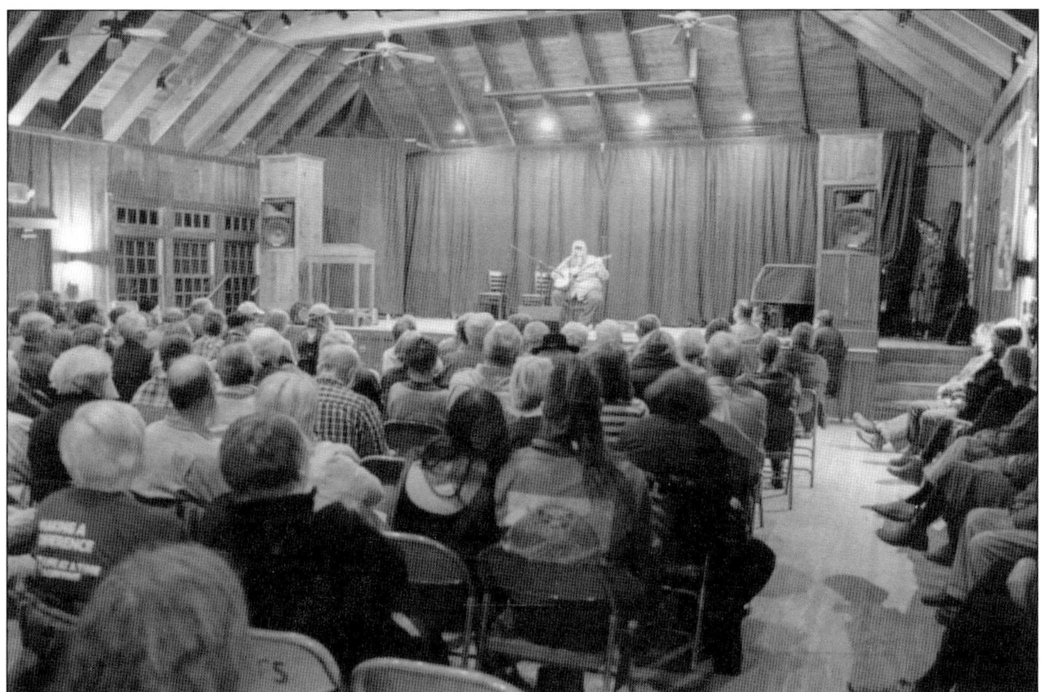

Folk School concerts offer instructors, local artists, and traveling bands a stage to share their music. They often pack the house with students and community members for old-time, bluegrass, country, and eclectic roots music and more. Renowned artist Riley Baugus is a sought-after banjo player, maker, and instructor, whose voice was featured on the *Cold Mountain* soundtrack. Baugus also built the banjos that were used in the film.

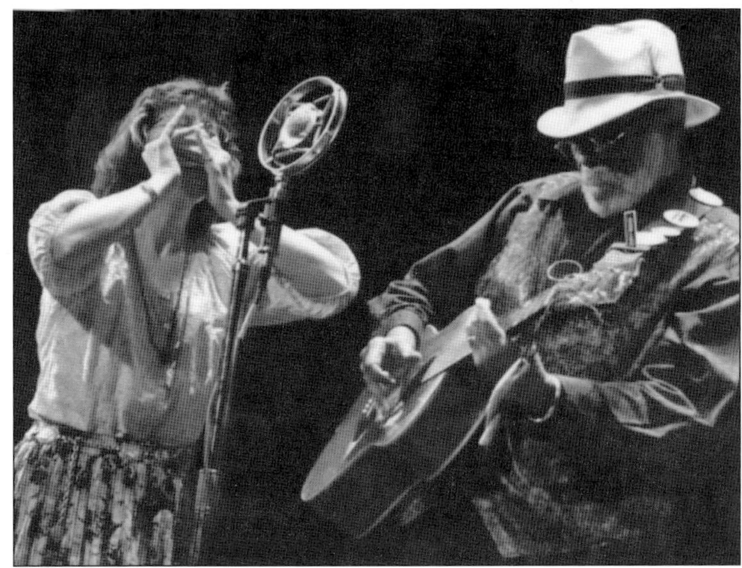

Sparky and Rhonda Rucker have taken the Folk School stage to share songs and tell stories from the American folk tradition. Their performances include old-time blues, Appalachian music, slave songs, Civil War music, spirituals, work songs, ballads, civil rights music, and their own original compositions. They are internationally recognized as musicians, authors, and storytellers. (Courtesy of Sparky and Rhonda Rucker.)

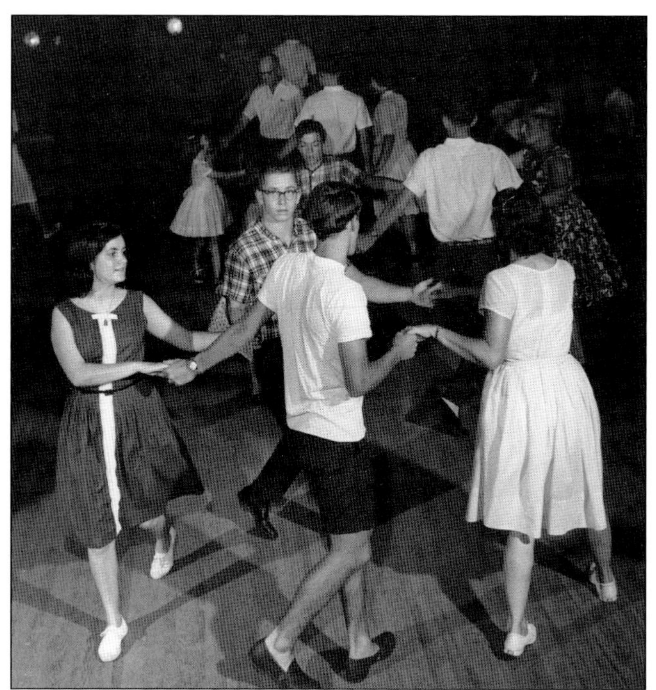

Music and dance events have long been and remain places where brand new connections are made and established friendships are enriched. While decades span these nearly mirror dance scenes in Keith House (left) and Open House (below), the sentiment remains. Strangers and companions are brought together through music. Whether joining a spontaneous jam, taking the stage as a band, reviving traditional English dancing in Brasstown, or guiding each other through steps and turns, rhythm does not exist apart from relationships. Both musicians and dancers themselves, Olive Dame Campbell and Marguerite Butler Bidstrup knew that truth when they created the Folk School 100 years ago.

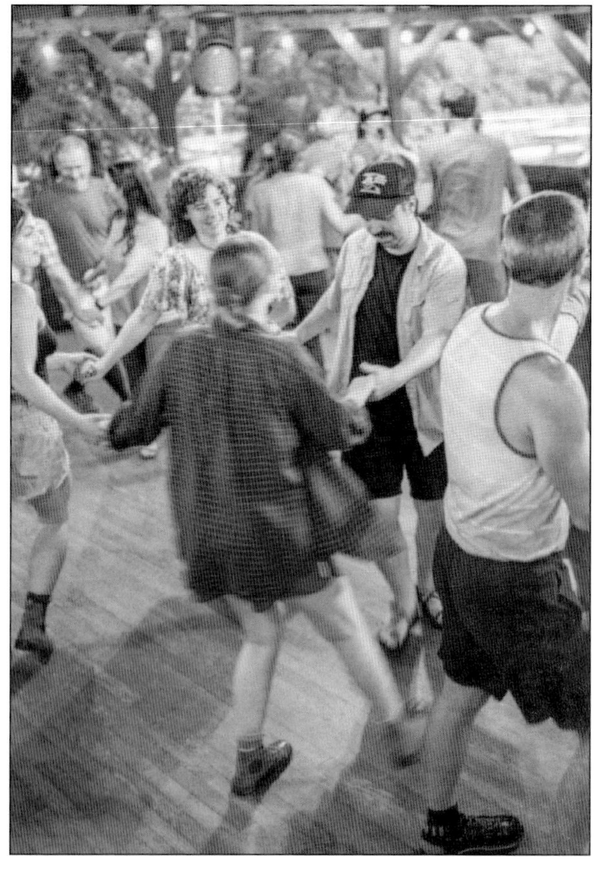

Nine

2000s–Present Day

I Can Feel the Sweet Winds Blowing

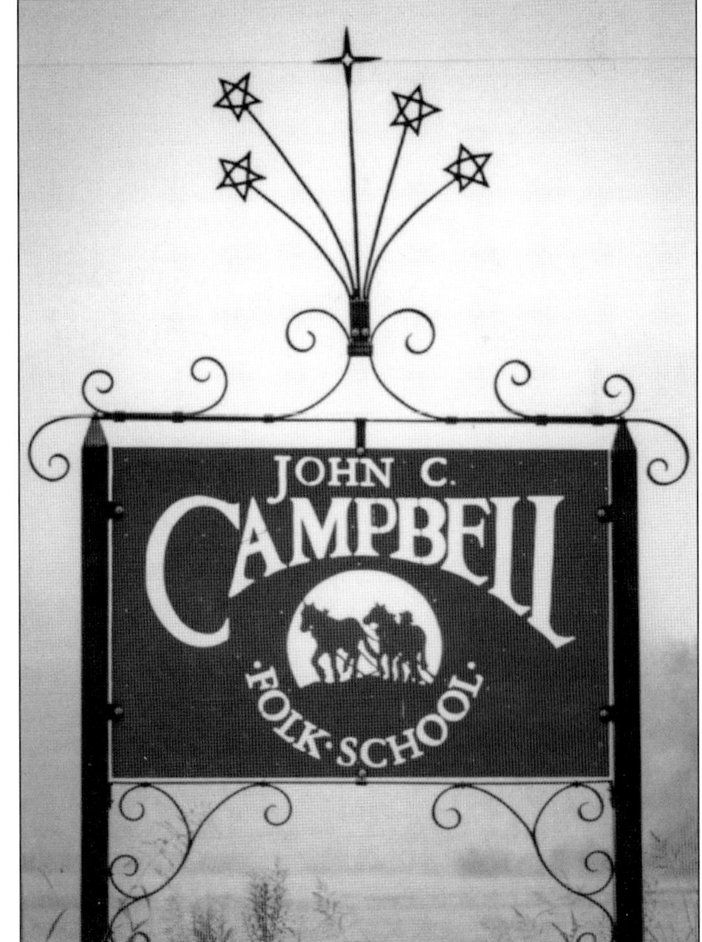

Since 2000, new opportunities have carried forward Olive Dame Campbell's original mission "to awaken, enliven, and enlighten" the world. Innovative programming has included artist mentorships and residencies, and Olive's Porch, located in downtown Murphy, North Carolina, has focused on connecting with locals and visitors. Classes draw in thousands of students and instructors every year, and the school continues to provide joy, kindness, stewardship, and a noncompetitive experience for all.

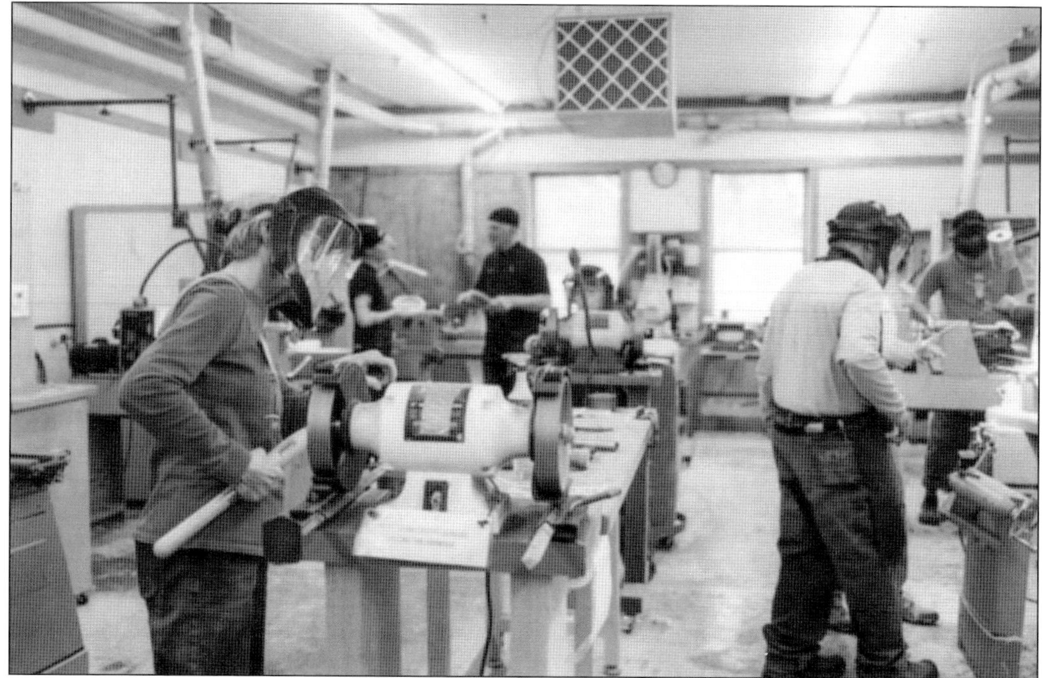

In the 25 years leading up to the school's centennial celebration, the need for upgraded or dedicated space for programming has risen. In 2006, the Willard Baxter Woodturning Studio was constructed. It features a tiered-seating demonstration area and separate spaces for wood preparation, turning, and finishing. Wood turning classes are in high demand, and students always make the shavings fly.

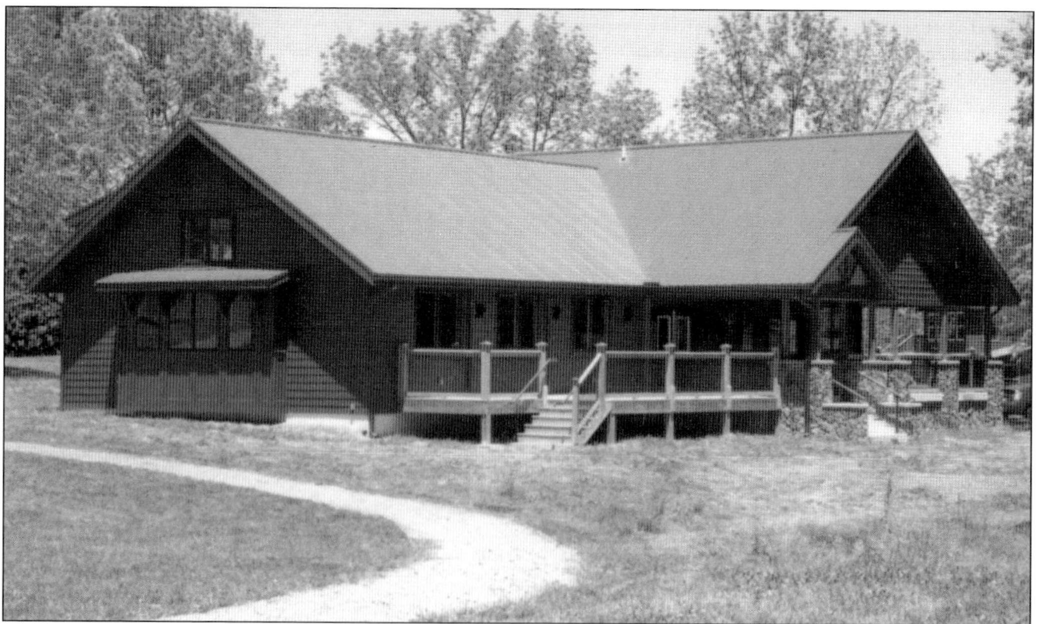

The Book and Paper Arts Studio was completed in 2019 and features three studio spaces on the lower level. With indoor and outdoor work space, the state-of-the-art facility hosts all books and paper arts, calligraphy, marbling, and printmaking classes.

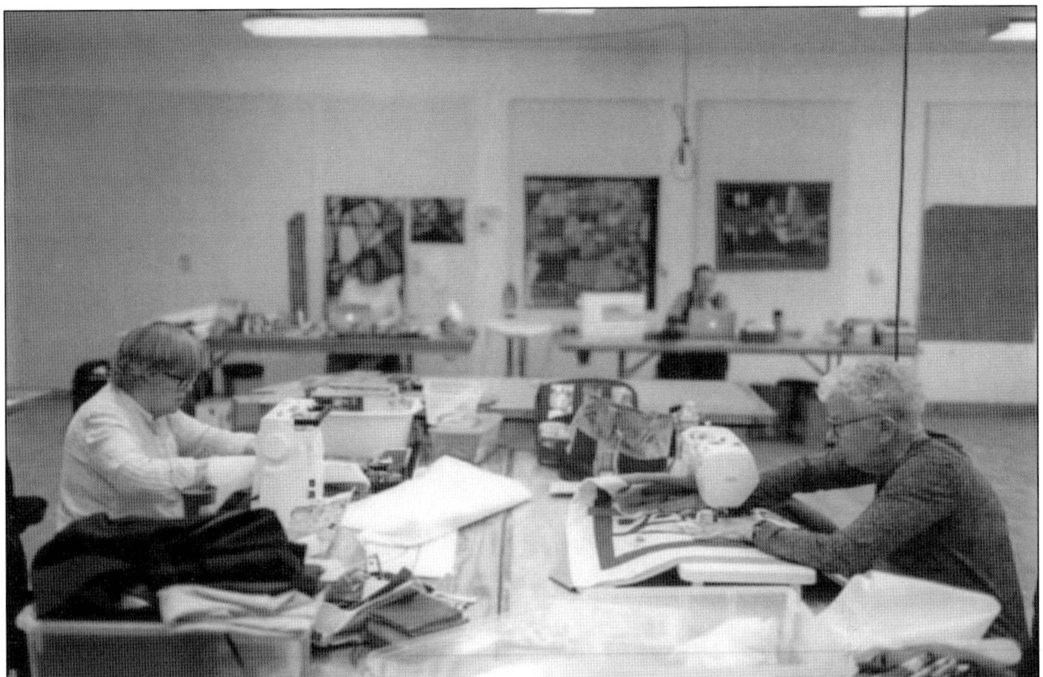

To make one's own clothing, whether a Scottish kilt, a patchwork skirt, or a Scandinavian work shirt, is one reason to learn sewing. Memory bears and unique accessories are others. Through machine and hand sewing, students can master both basic and advanced techniques that turn fabric and yarn into wearable and decorative works of art.

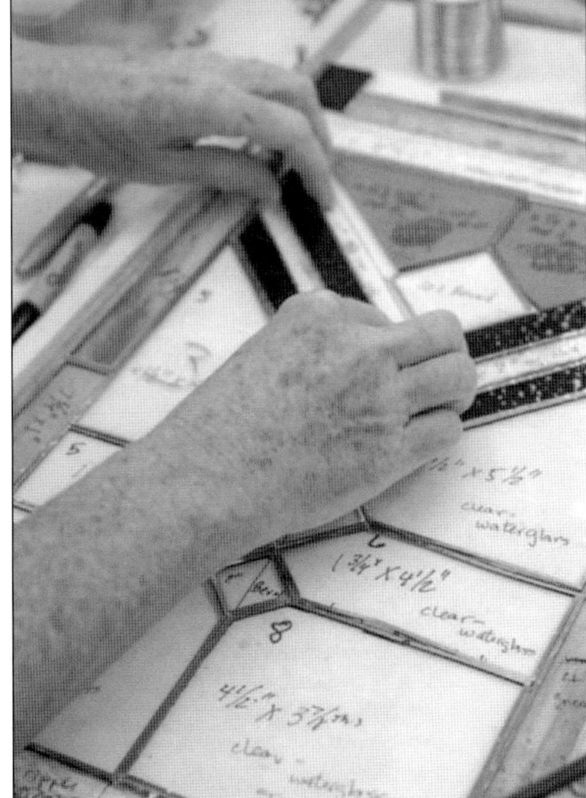

Stained glass can be appreciated in decorative panels, lamps, kaleidoscopes, jewelry boxes, ornaments, and more. Students learn to design a project, cut glass, apply foil, and solder pieces together to create the final product. The craft invites beginners and established artists to continue an art that can be traced back to the 7th century.

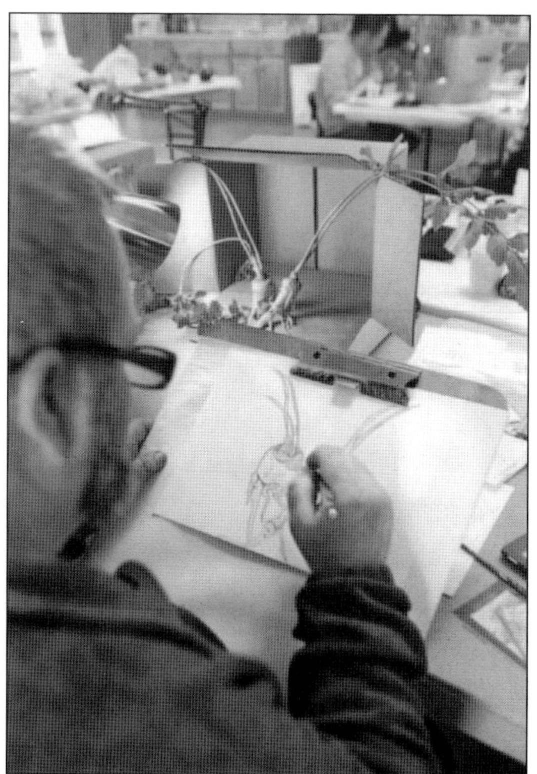

Learning to draw means learning about lines, shading, proportion, and perspective. It can also mean exploring the surroundings to study plants and people. Drawing is a medium that pairs well with watercolor and mixed media. Whether quickly capturing a sketch or focusing on the particulars of root vegetables, drawing teaches the importance of both observation and detail.

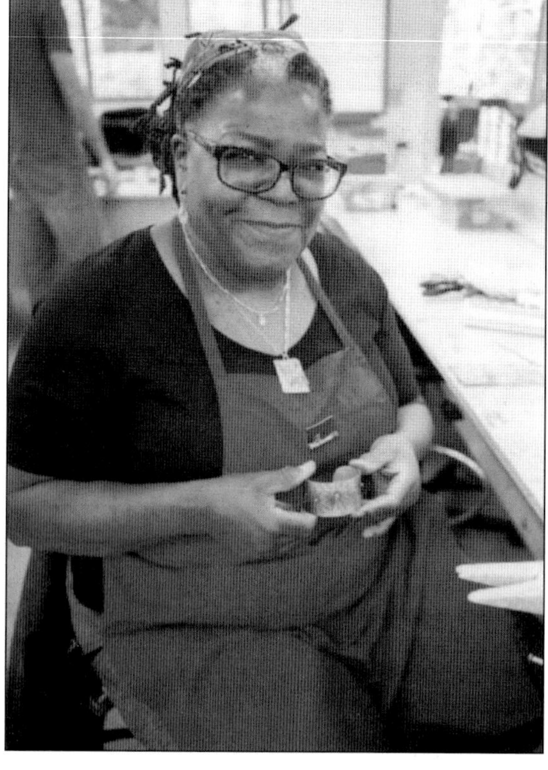

Jewelry classes offer students the opportunity to work with a variety of materials to create a variety of pieces. Stones, enamels, and fabrics are cut, hammered, and shaped into pendants, earrings, bracelets, and rings that are set in sterling silver, silver metal clay, copper, or brass. Metal surfaces can also be enhanced with drawings, paintings, and even photograph transfers.

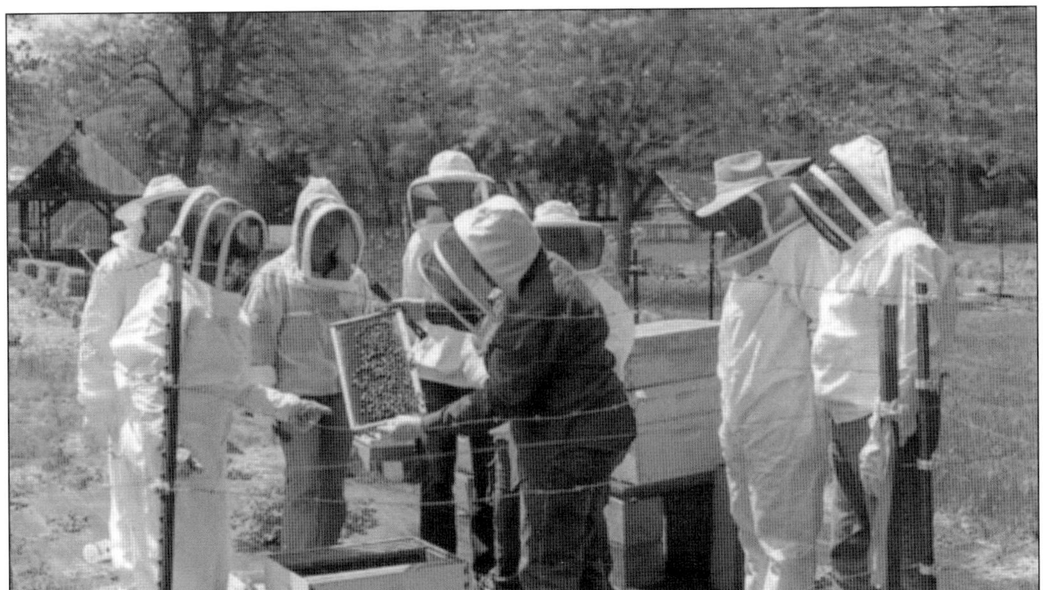

Gardening, homesteading, and nature studies classes find students digging in the dirt, hiking through forests, foraging for mushrooms, exploring bird life, crafting tea blends, studying herbal medicines, and harvesting honey. Surrounded by mountains and lush gardens, the Folk School grounds offer natural treasures for these hands-on areas of programming that take the classroom experience outside.

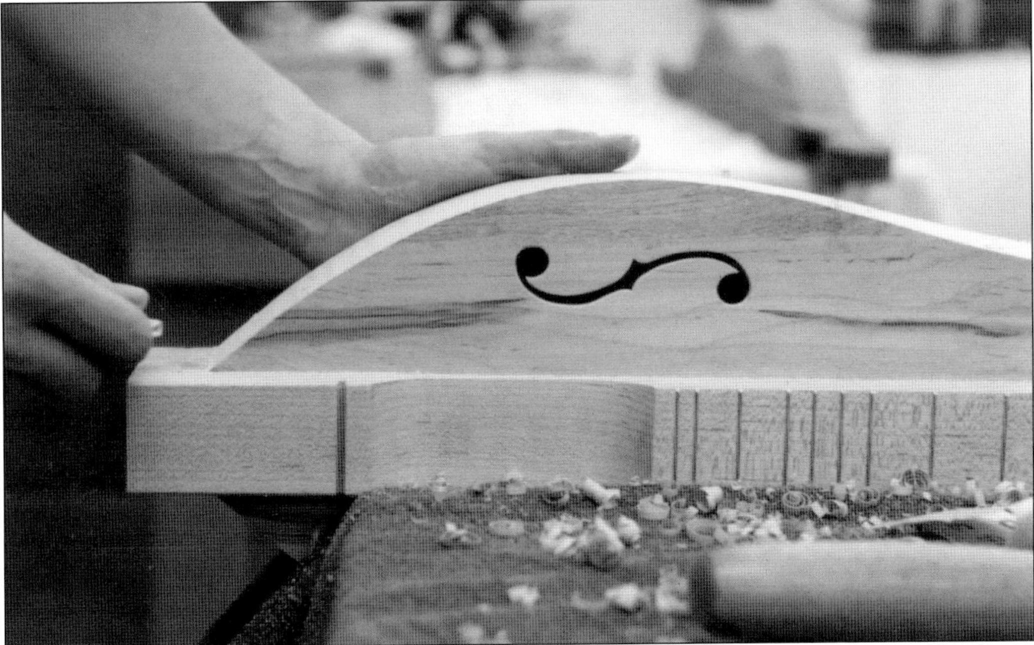

Shaker tables and boxes, Windsor chairs, furniture, marquetry, toys, and musical instruments can all be found in woodworking classes. Students learn how to safely use tools and equipment, how to prepare and assemble individual components, how to measure and correctly cut a dovetail joint, how to secure pieces together, and much more. From side tables and bookshelves to cigar box guitars and mountain dulcimers, woodworking offers a wealth of creative opportunities.

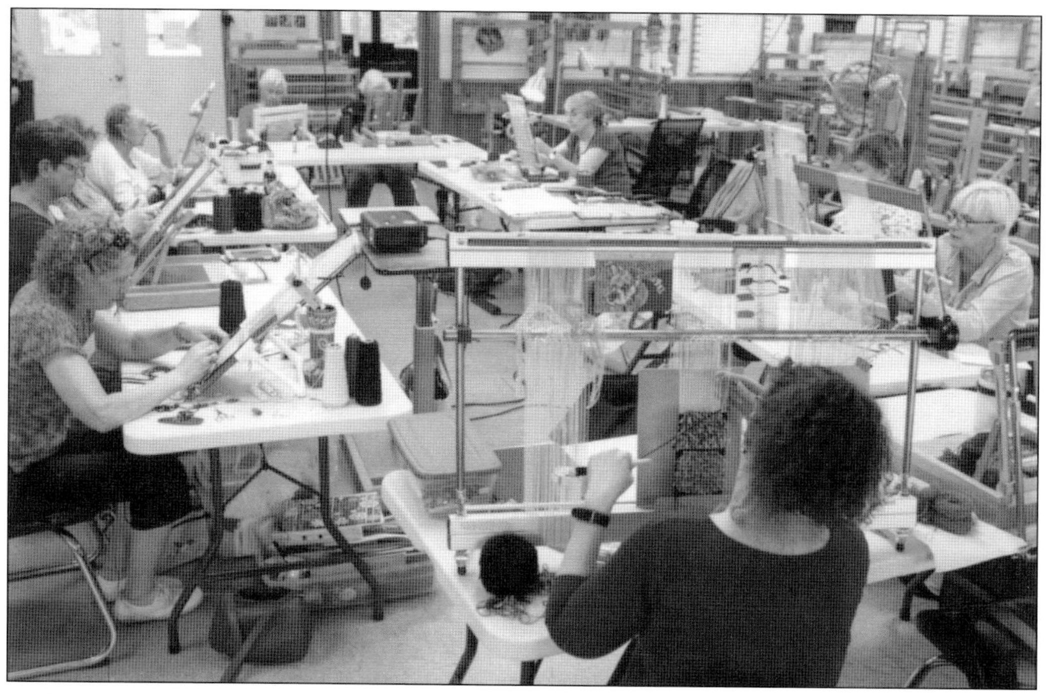

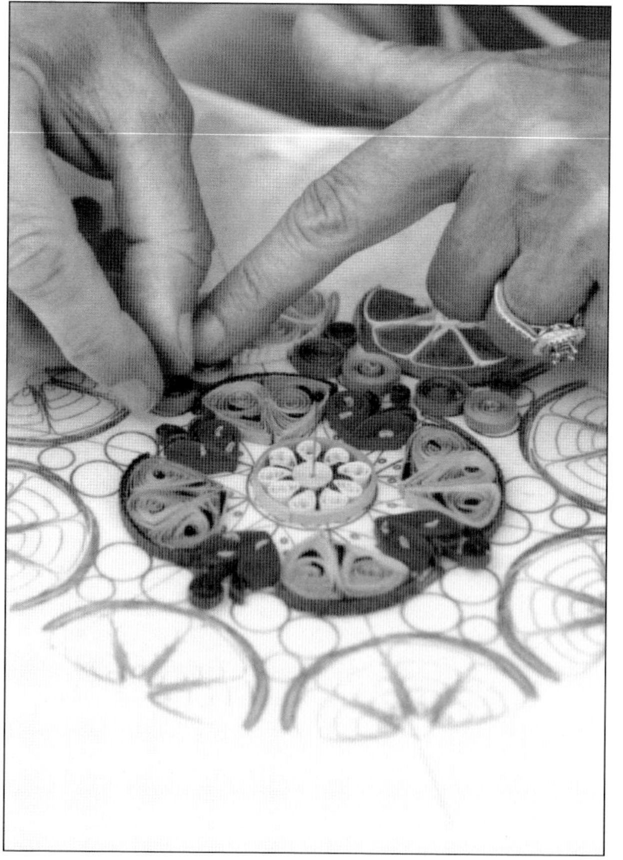

Weaving classes range from creating scarves and rugs to purses and yardage for garments. Tapestries, another woven creation, are constructed by weaving threads together on a loom to form a piece that is both fabric and image. Weaving is an Appalachian tradition that blends labor and art. It also holds deep roots in the history of the Folk School.

Paper quilling is the art of shaping paper strips into various designs. Curled, rolled, and twisted paper is transformed using quilling needles, tweezers, pins, and other tools. The distinctive craft can be used to decorate greeting cards and boxes, create elaborate scenes, or make unique jewelry. Quilling can also help develop fine motor skills while completing a design.

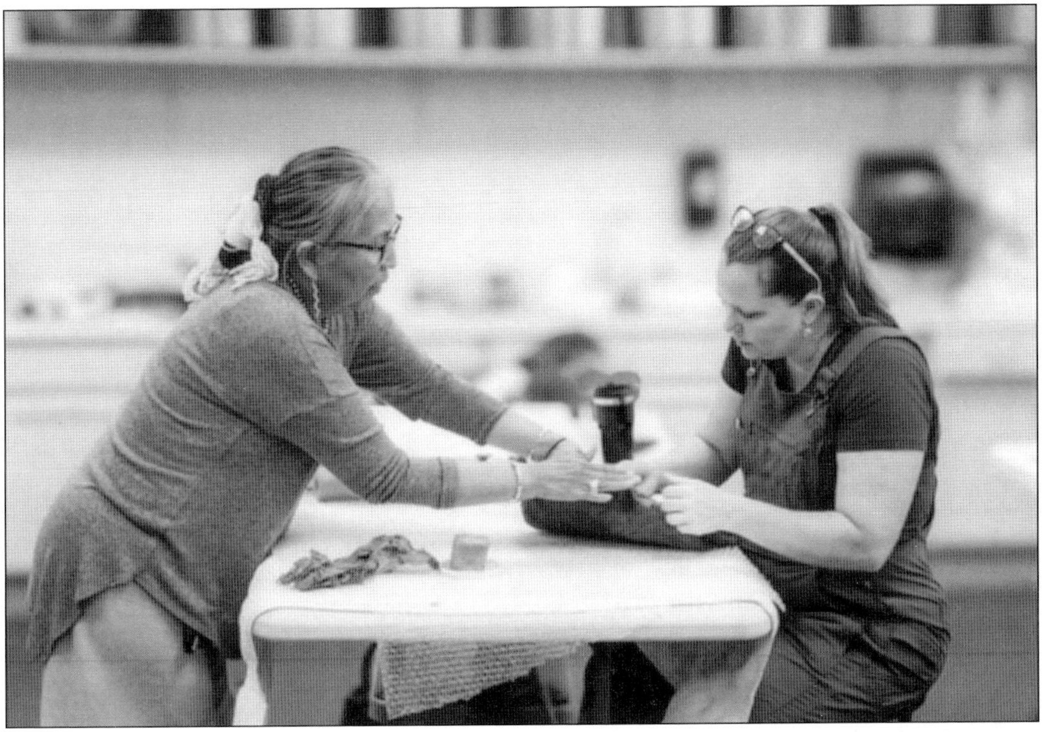

In 2024, the Folk School welcomed Navajo fiber artist TahNibaa Naataanii to teach two classes focused on wool. TahNibaa raises a heritage breed, the Navajo-Churro, and shared the unique wool with her felting students. While the Folk School has long emphasized traditional Appalachian craft, the opportunity to introduce students to techniques and materials from other traditions has expanded creative connections.

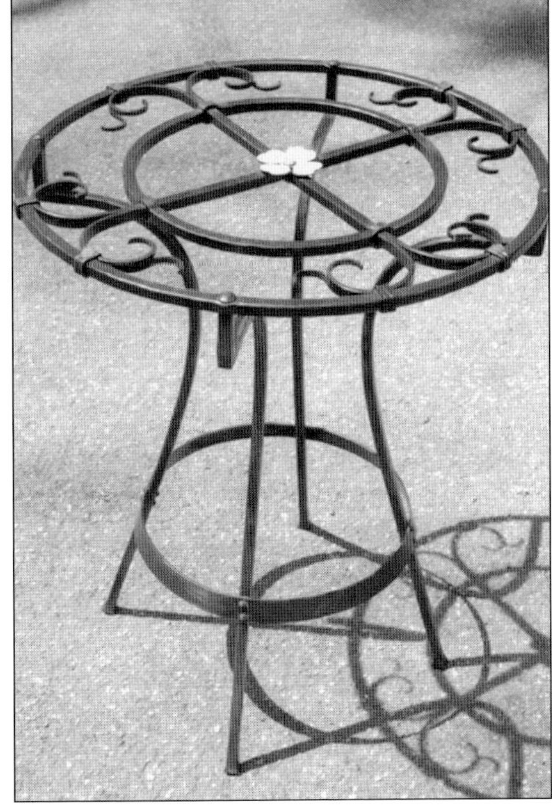

The Folk School's blacksmithing program is known as one of the best in the country. It is also one that dates to the earliest days of the school. Beginners learn the basics of coal fire, forging skills, and hammer control, creating coat racks and hooks. Experienced smiths learn how to make their own tools or craft a classic occasional table using techniques taught by Francis Whitaker.

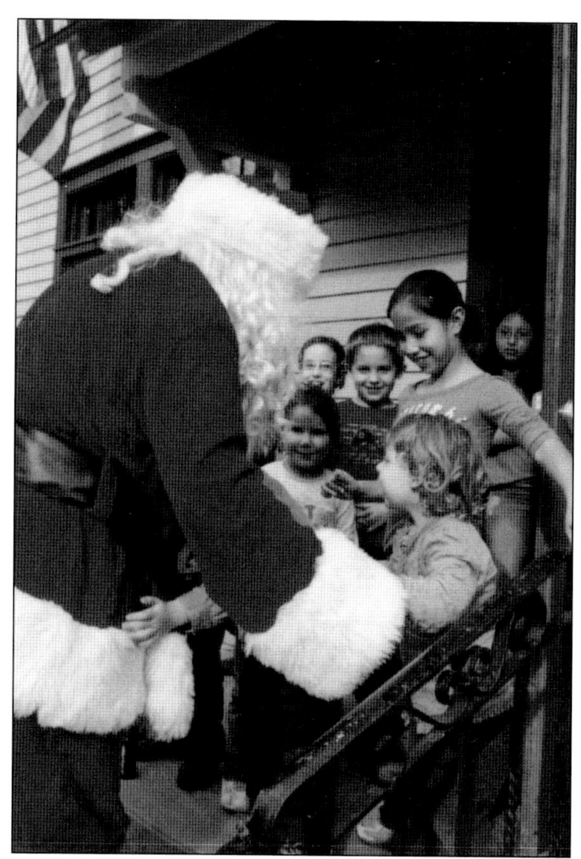

The Kids' Christmas Party is a highlight of holiday activities. Children share in games, crafts, music, dancing, storytelling, and tasty treats. Santa Claus also stops by—these days by fire truck—for an afternoon filled with joy and cheer. The heartwarming event celebrates the magic of the season and is enjoyed by all ages, from little ones to grandparents. It is one of many annual holiday traditions, including the Fireside Sale, a live reading of *A Christmas Carol*, wreath making, and the Olde Folks' Party. Hosting these special events is a distinctive way the Folk School stays connected to the local community.

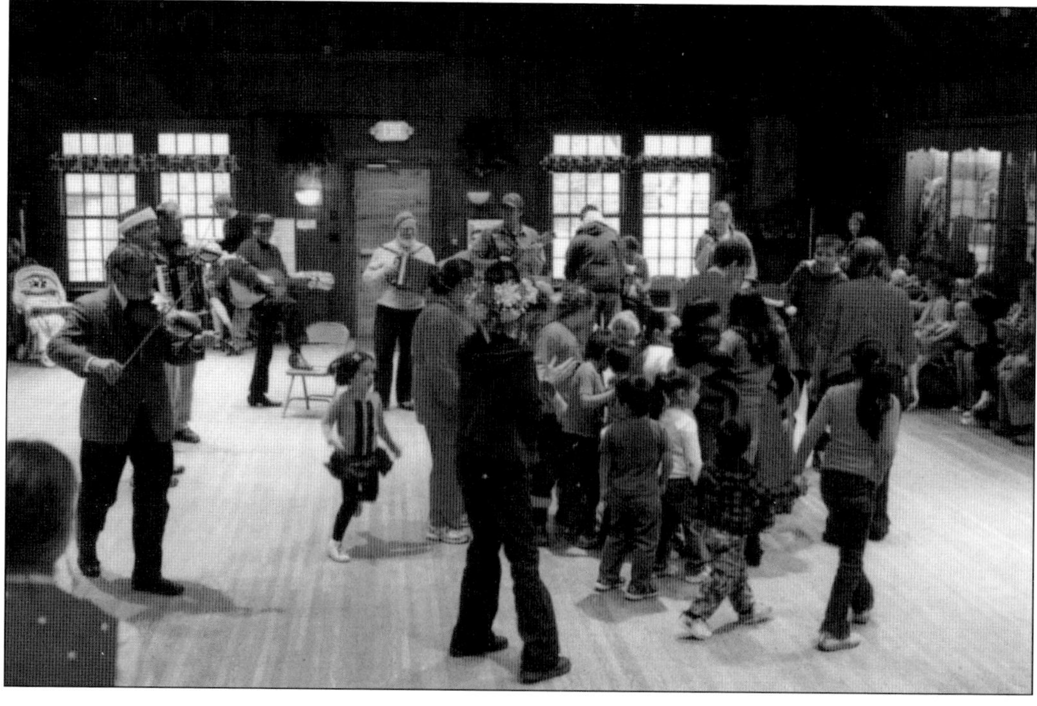

The Folk School Cookbook, a collection of more than 200 seasonal recipes, was published in 2018. The book features Southern Appalachian cooking as well as international cuisine. Many of the recipes have helped shape the school, from dishes served in the dining hall to meals prepared in cooking classes. Keather Gougler (left) provided photographs, Jerry Jackson (center) authored the foreword, and Nanette Davidson (right) collected and curated the selection of recipes.

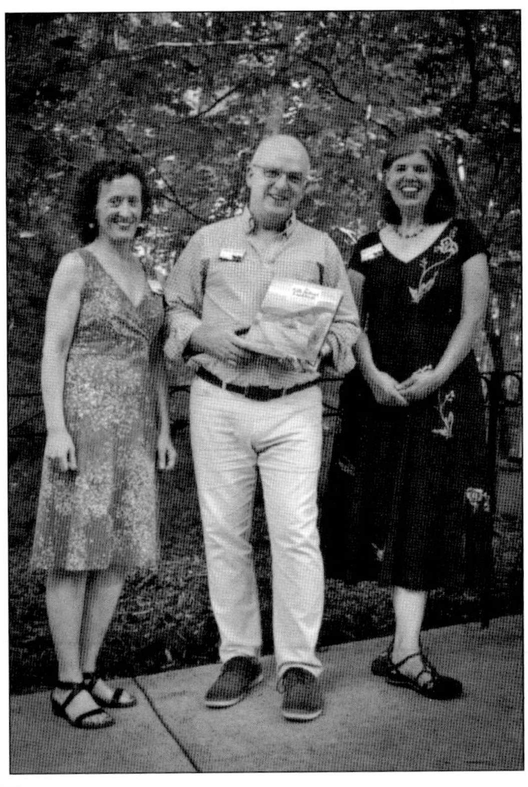

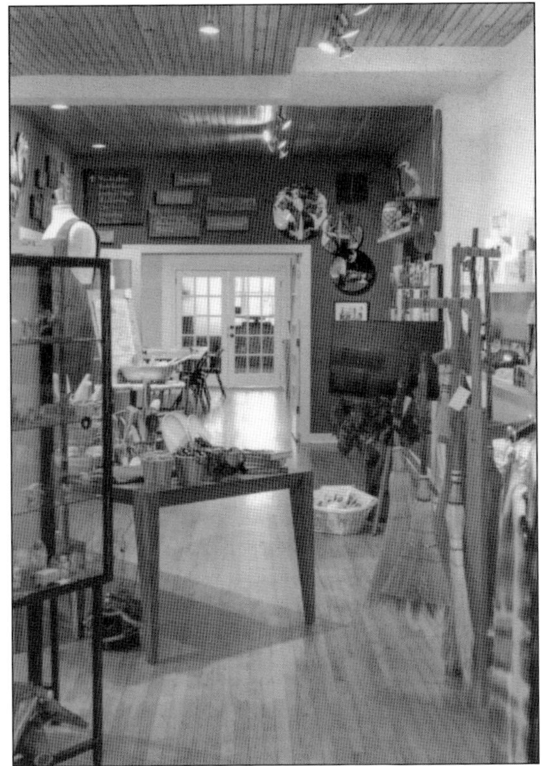

Olive's Porch, named for Folk School cofounder Olive Dame Campbell, opened in 2022. The space offers a Folk School experience in downtown Murphy, North Carolina, with workshops focused on crafts, music, dance, and community events and demonstrations designed for locals and visitors. Olive's Porch also includes a retail shop that showcases handmade work and provides high-quality art supplies.

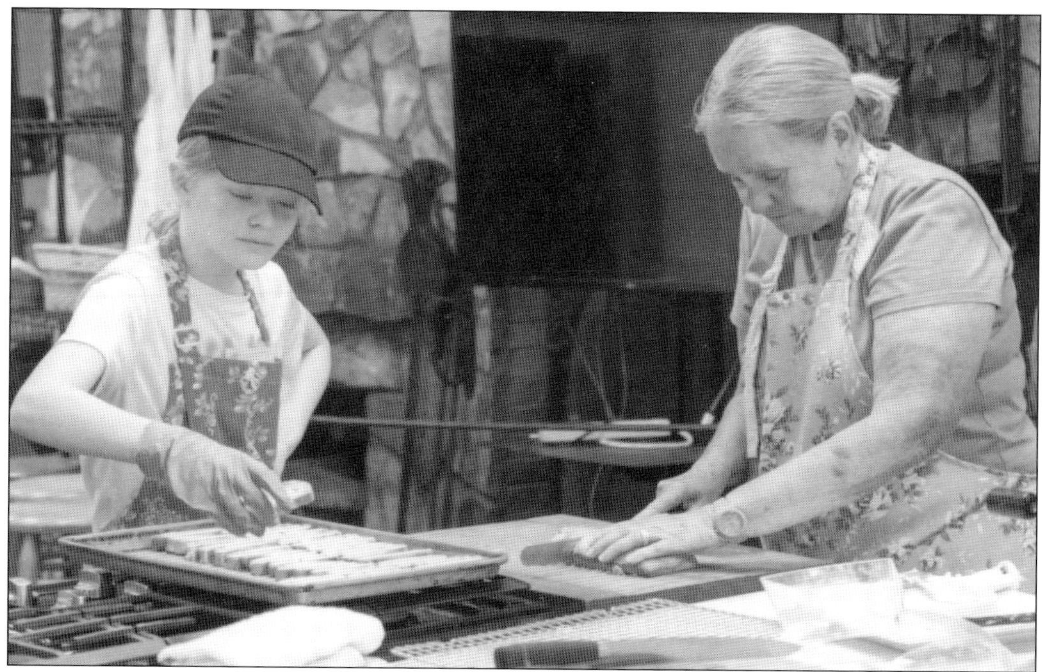

Intergenerational Week is a very special and cherished time in Brasstown. Youth between the ages of 12 and 17 take classes with a parent, grandparent, relative, or guardian. The experience brings loved ones together and introduces young people to art, music, and traditional and contemporary crafts, including baking and bead making. This youth program is one of the ways the school reaches the next group of makers and preserves traditions that have been practiced before the first Folk School classes were taught in 1925. Intergenerational classes often fill up quickly, and students of all ages enjoy creating alongside a special person in their lives.

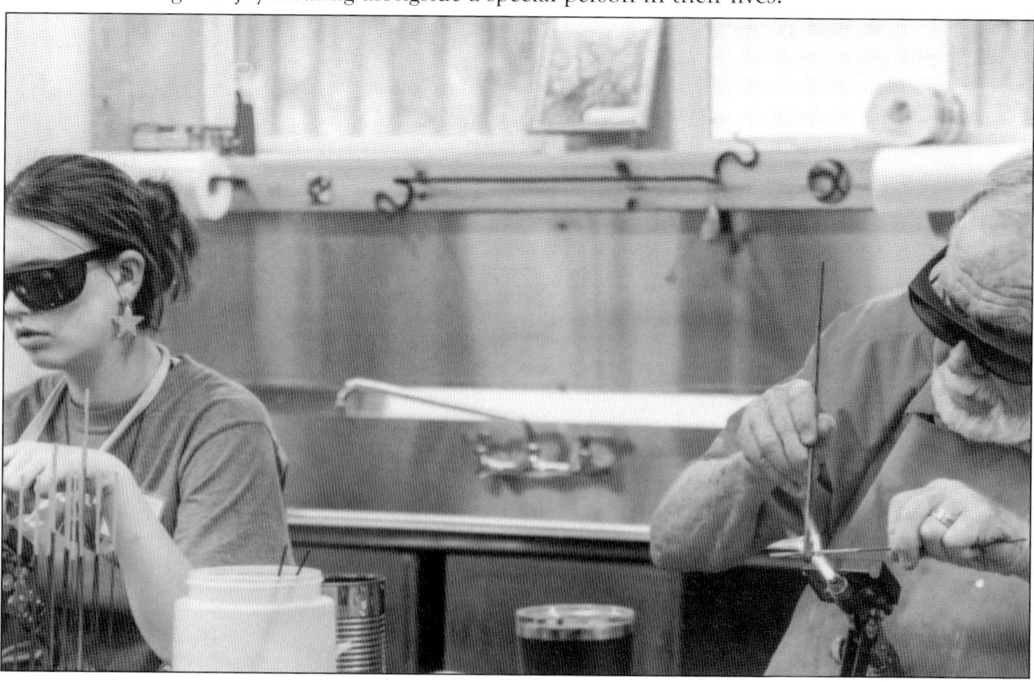

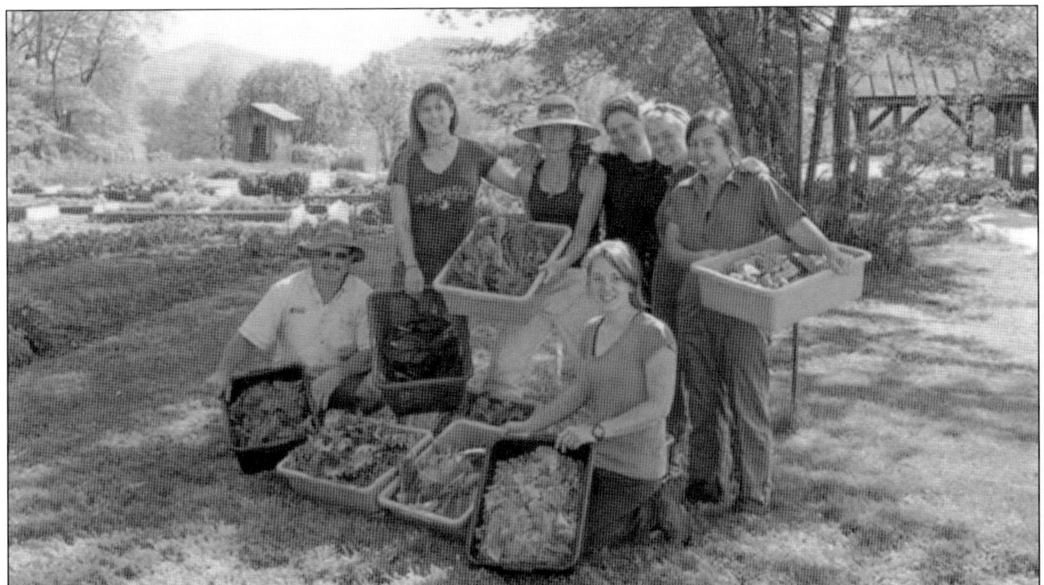

The work-study program offers participants the opportunity to learn, volunteer, and participate in the life of the Folk School for nine weeks. Many of these folks work on gardens and grounds projects, though others have spent time working with the marketing department and in archives. Housing and meals are provided for the entirety of their stay, and four tuition-free classes can be taken during the nine-week session.

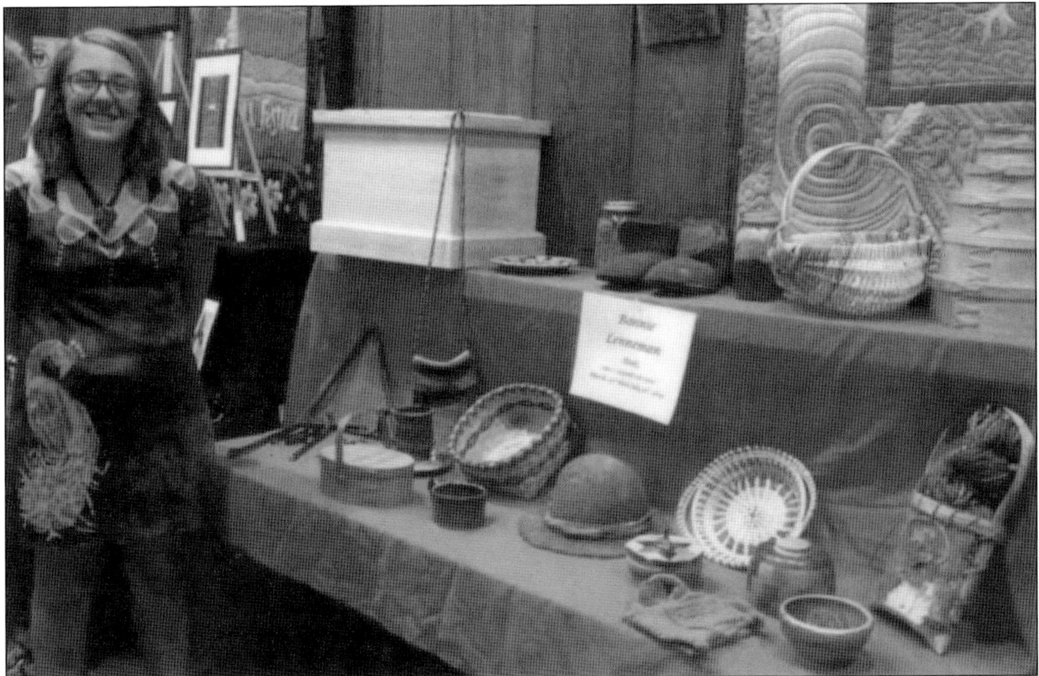

Folk School hosts hold a key role for their months-long stay, serving as a link between staff, students, and instructors. They are ambassadors for the school and help create a welcoming and comfortable environment for all. In exchange, hosts can take a class every week of their stay. Here, former host Bonnie Lennaman shares some of her finished pieces.

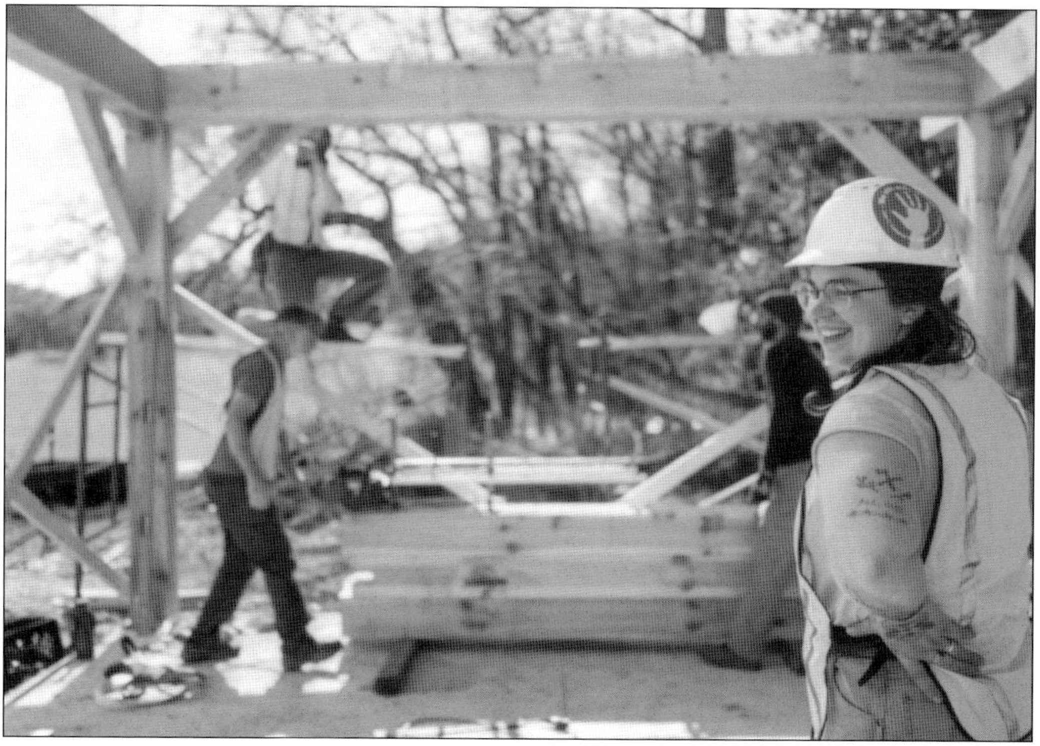

The Traditional Craft Mentorship, started in 2020, brings skilled practitioners of Appalachian craft together with emerging artists for focused study in small groups. The mentorship aims to support these artists through guidance from well-established makers, shared studio space, and relationship building. In 2024, the timber-framing mentorship started the construction of a shed for the garden that is now used to process and wash vegetables, dry herbs, and store materials.

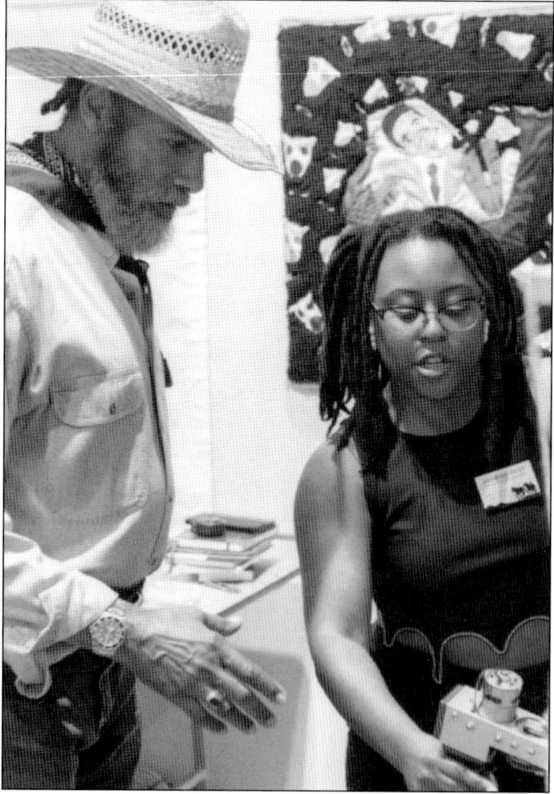

In 2023, Jasmine Best brought narratives from her North Carolina family and childhood to the artist-in-residence program. The grant-funded opportunity provided four months for early to mid-career artists to focus on their craft while working in the community. As a fiber artist, Best created dialogues about the Black female identity in the South and in predominantly White spaces.

In 2019, the Folk School hosted the first Friends & Family Day. Community members of all ages were invited to tour open studios, participate in hands-on making, watch demonstrations, and enjoy music and dance performances. Individuals and families from neighboring counties visited campus for the first time, establishing new and meaningful connections. Inside studios that were filled with energy and excitement, guests crafted small wooden boats, marbled paper, and enameled necklace pendants. All activities were family-friendly, and children were especially encouraged to try their hand at crafts. The event has continued to be a success, one that brings familiar faces to campus for a fun day of festivities.

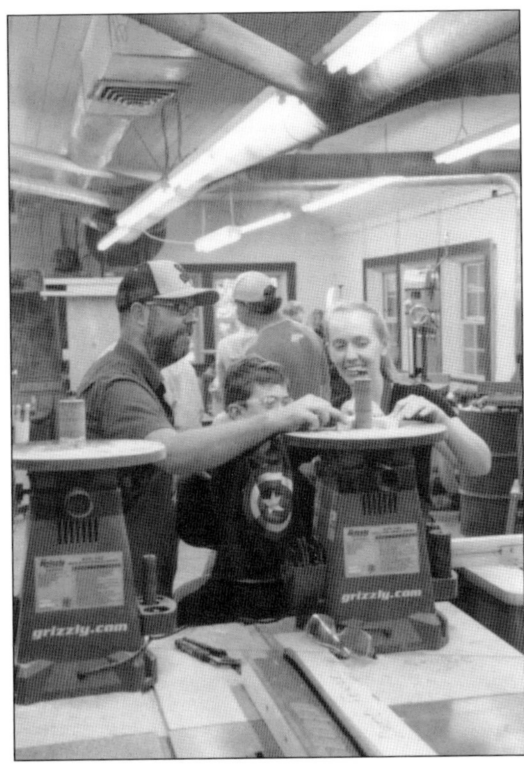

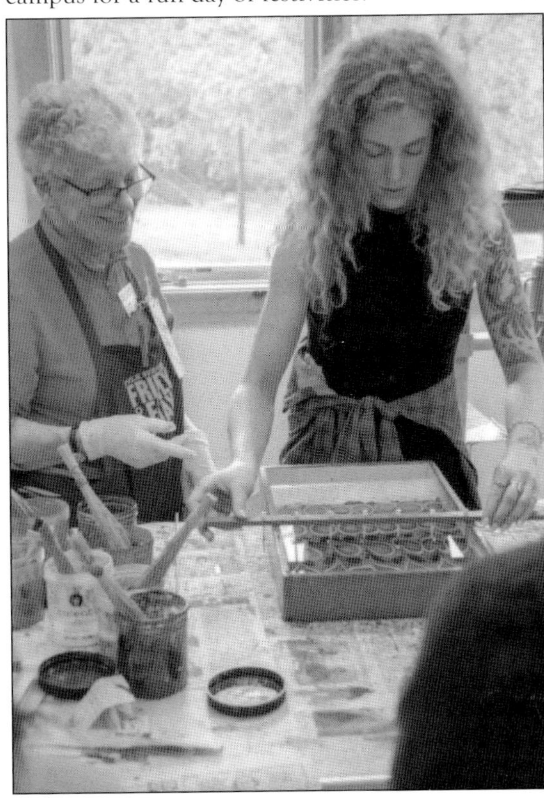

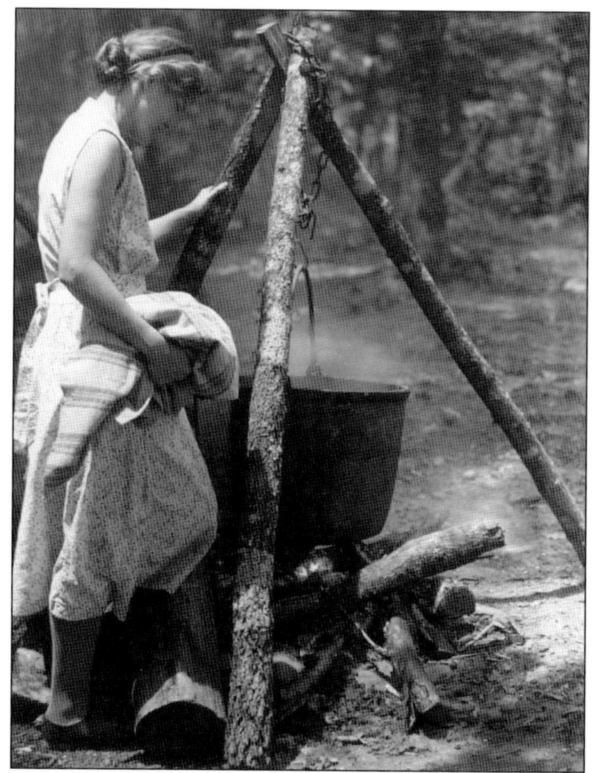

Louise Pitman (left) joined the Folk School staff in 1928 and was quickly placed in charge of the craft department. Due to the demand for quality, dyed yarn that would supply the weaving program, Pitman learned how to use vegetables to bring a variety of colors to spun wool. Folk School weavings became known for their colors, and Pitman documented the dying process for future use with yarn and other materials. Whether she intended to dye, wash, or finish the fabric is unknown, though by the time of this 1933 photograph, she was established in her natural dyeing methods. Almost 90 years later, fiber artist Lesley Darling (below) re-created the iconic Doris Ulmann photograph of Pitman standing over a cauldron with a large piece of cloth in her hand. Darling's image was taken during the 2020 Traditional Craft Mentorship.

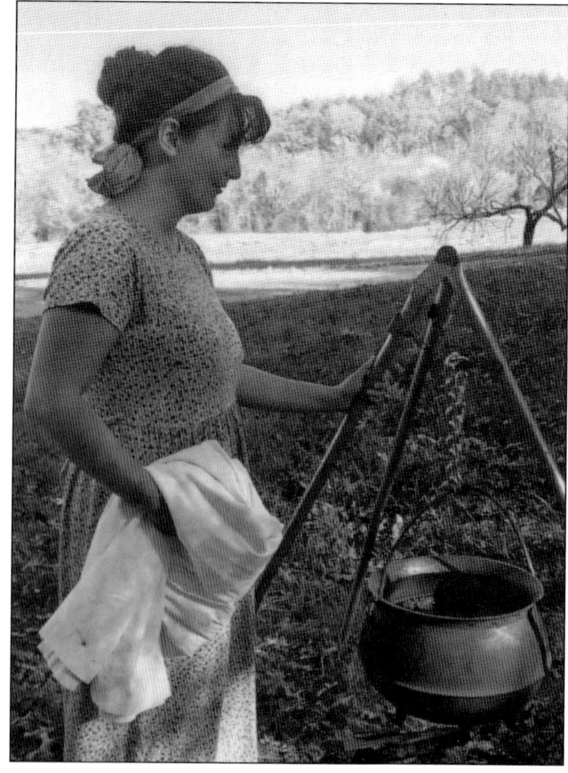

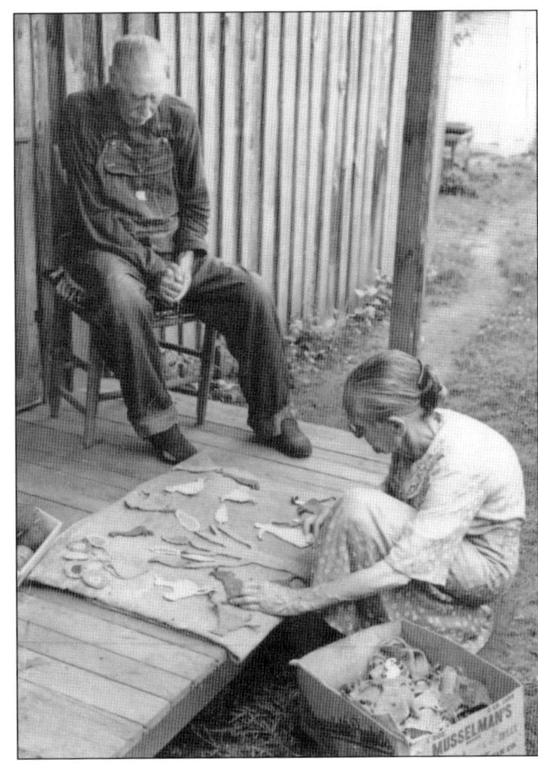

Kate Clayton Donaldson, known by many as "Granny Donaldson," was an early member of the Folk School staff who worked in the kitchen. She is now widely recognized for her cow blankets, a design she created by adding crocheted and dyed farm animal figures to an old baby blanket. Her ongoing work eventually caught the attention of Allen Eaton, a cofounder of the Southern Highland Craft Guild. Donaldson's great-great-great-granddaughter Jessica Penland attended a 2024 class, "Inspired by Granny Donaldson," and tried her hand at the family tradition. By the end of the week, Penland crocheted and added two mushroom tops to her own cow blanket design. The mushrooms were also a nod to Penland's great-grandfather and Brasstown Carver Hayden Hensley. Among his many carvings, mushrooms were a famous design.

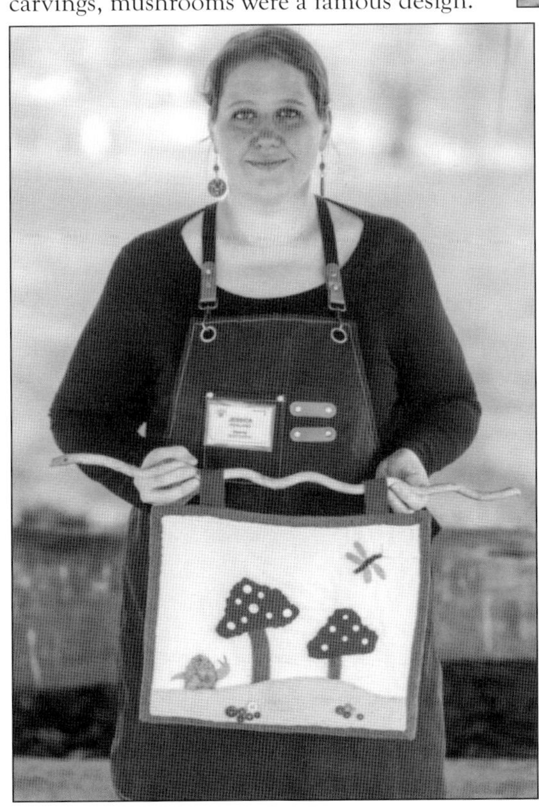

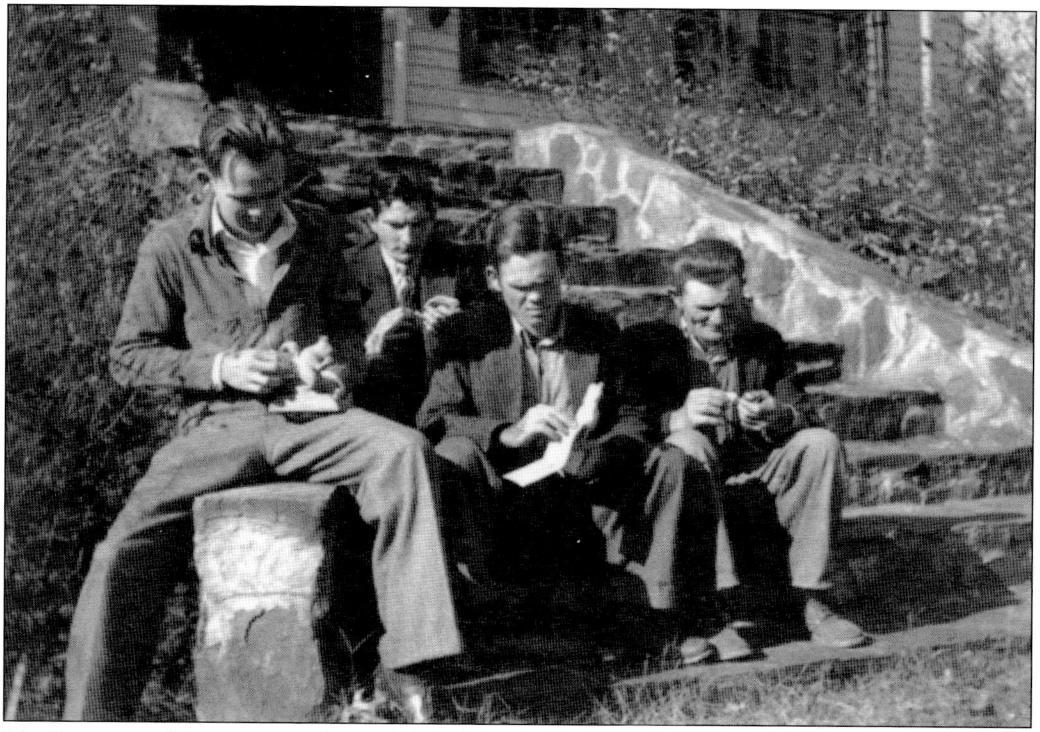

The Brasstown Carvers are a cohort of skilled wood-carvers whose rich history dates back to the early days of the John C. Campbell Folk School. These carvers have been instrumental in preserving and promoting the esteemed craft. For nearly 100 years, they have carried forward a tradition that once served as a key source of income for local folks who were supporting families during economically stressful times. Above, early carvers included, from left to right, Nolan Beaver, Jay A. Morris, Avery Beaver, and Pearlie Fleming, who were photographed with their work on the steps of Keith House in 1930. In 2024, Brasstown Carvers, from left to right, Carolyn Anderson, Richard Carter, Angela Wynn, and Helen Gibson carved on the same steps. The patterns and techniques that have been passed down through the years have created a rich tapestry of local history and craftsmanship.

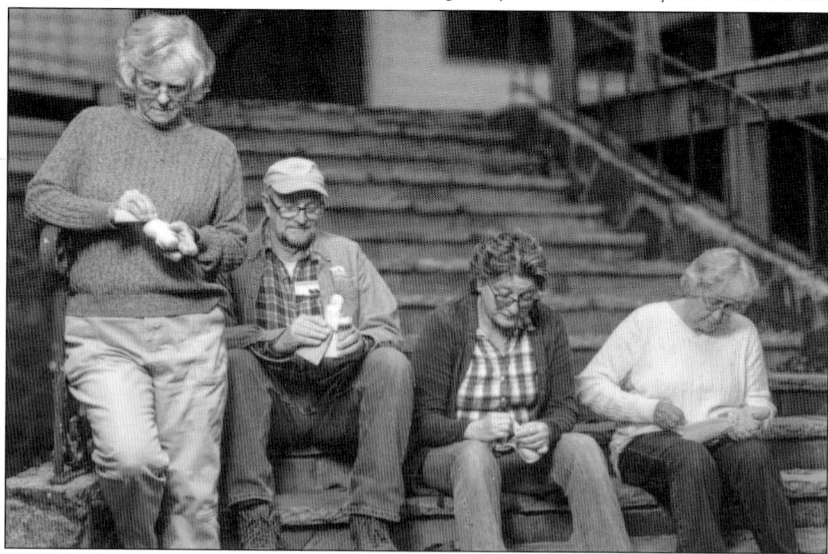

Ten

Brasstown Carvers
The Greenwood Side

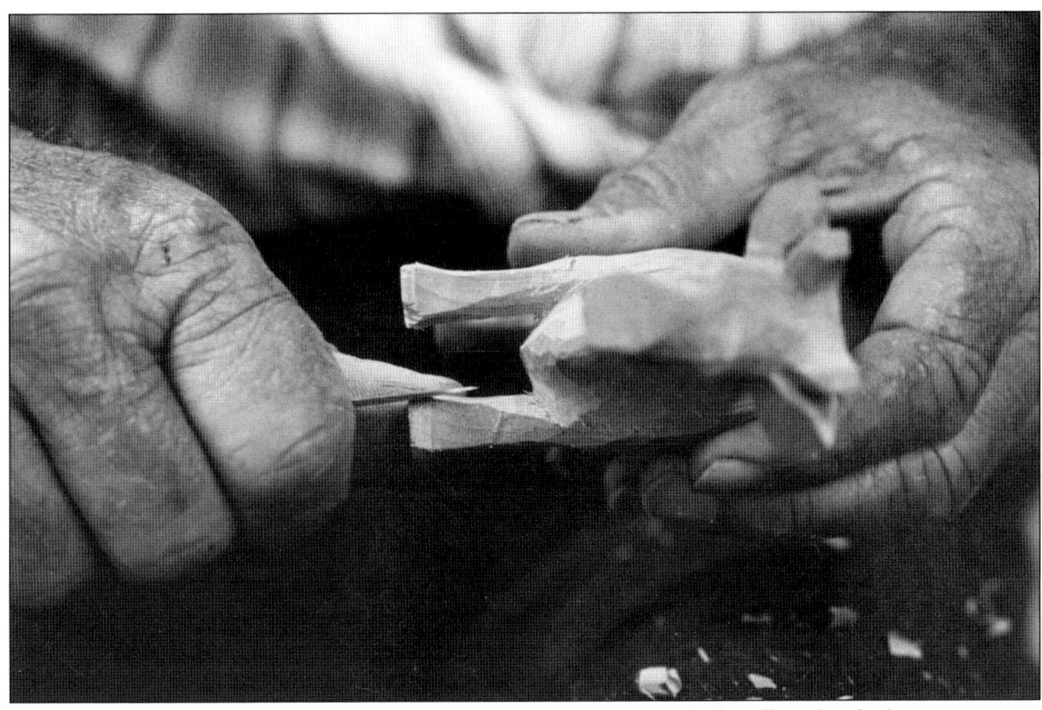

The Brasstown Carvers have been part of the John C. Campbell Folk School almost since its founding. In the early days, the cooperative provided an important source of income for many of the rural farming families in the area. The carvers flourished under the leadership of Murrial "Murray" Martin and were renowned for their animal figures and crèche (or nativity) scenes. The legacy continues today, keeping a treasured tradition alive.

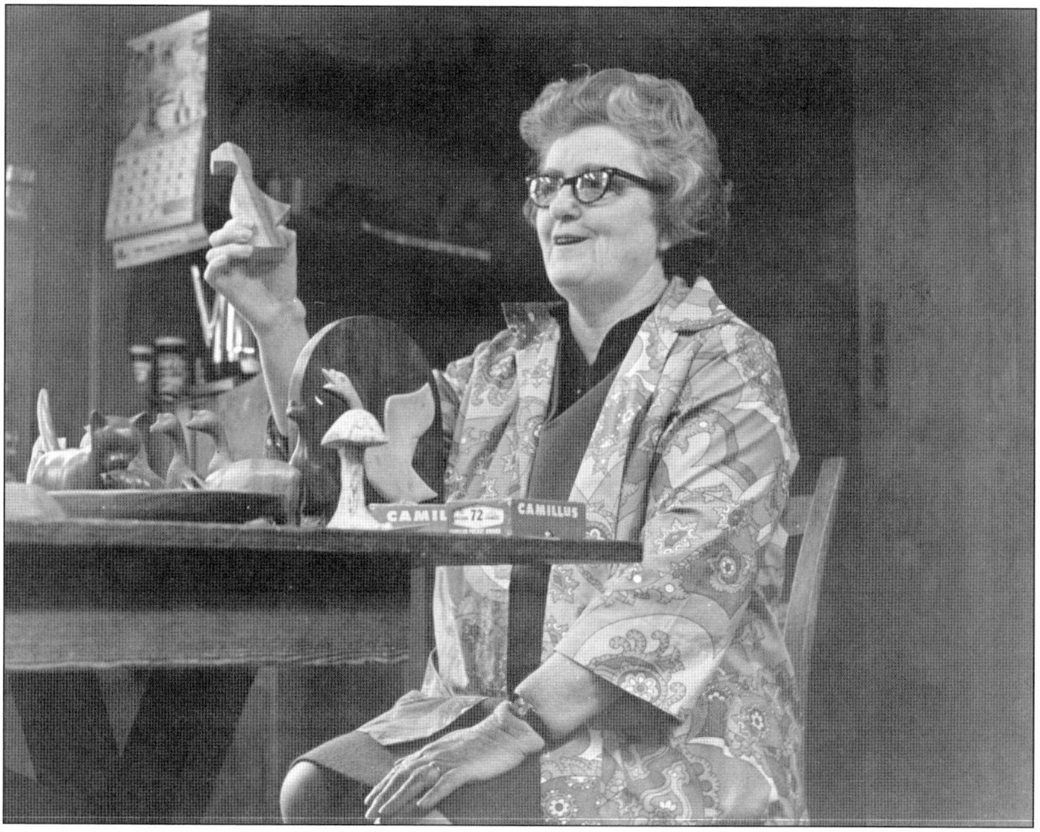

Murray Martin came to the Folk School in the early 1930s after teaching weaving as an occupational therapist at Walter Reed Hospital. In Brasstown, Martin originally taught a variety of crafts. By 1935, she was appointed as the carving instructor and was responsible for the carving program until 1973. She instructed students to observe, sometimes bringing animals to class so budding carvers could view them from different angles. She designed many patterns, including napkin rings and crèche figures, and her mentorship of the Brasstown Carvers took them to a place of national recognition. In the image below, Martin (standing) instructs, from left to right, carvers Talmadge Massey, John Hall, Ben Hall, Jack Hall, Ethel Hogsed, Ruth Hawkins, Sue McClure, and Lou Cable.

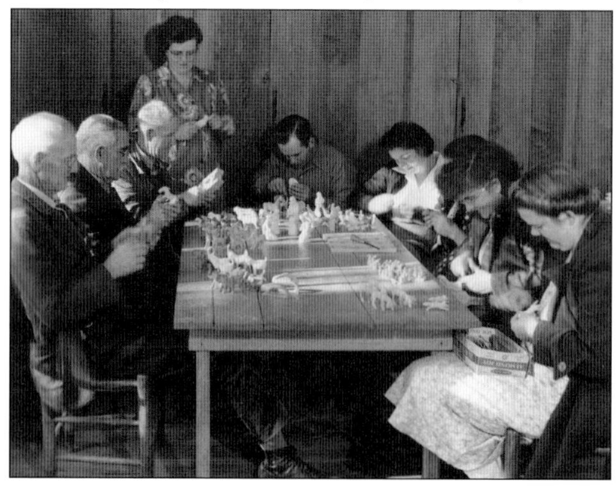

Hayden Hensley was among the first students at the Folk School. He was credited with making the first carving, a goose, that same year. He also met Bonnie Logan during his time as a student and married her in 1931. They created work together, with Hensley carving and his wife finishing his pieces. He became a member of the Southern Highland Craft Guild and spent many years teaching carving at Tri-County Community College in Murphy, North Carolina.

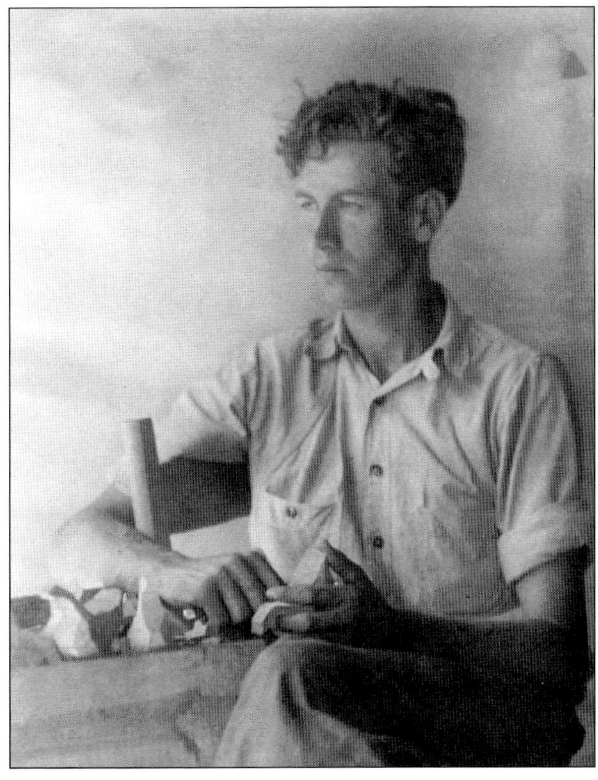

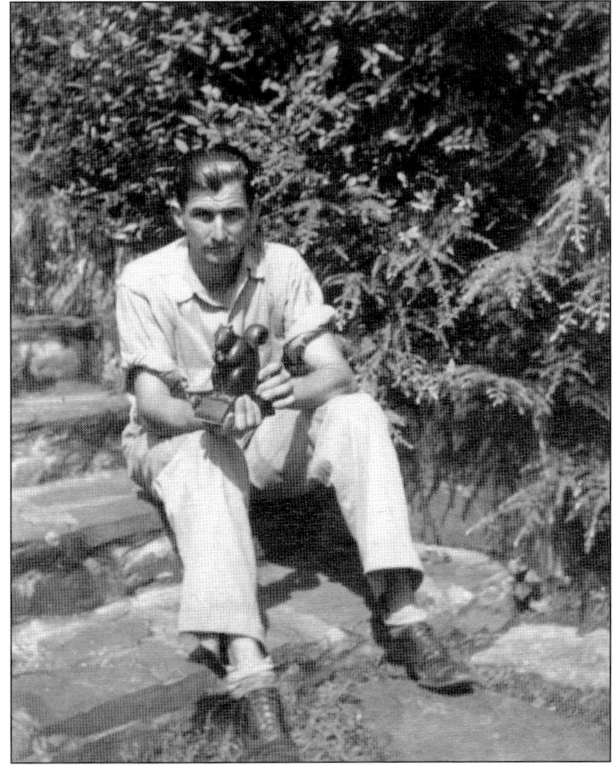

Jay A. Morris took up carving during the Great Depression, studying under Murray Martin. Morris was known for his rabbit and squirrel carvings, though during World War II, he also carved "GI Joe" figures with servicemen's caps. Among his many accomplishments, Morris later won a Tennessee Valley Authority (TVA) contest with a carved squirrel bookend.

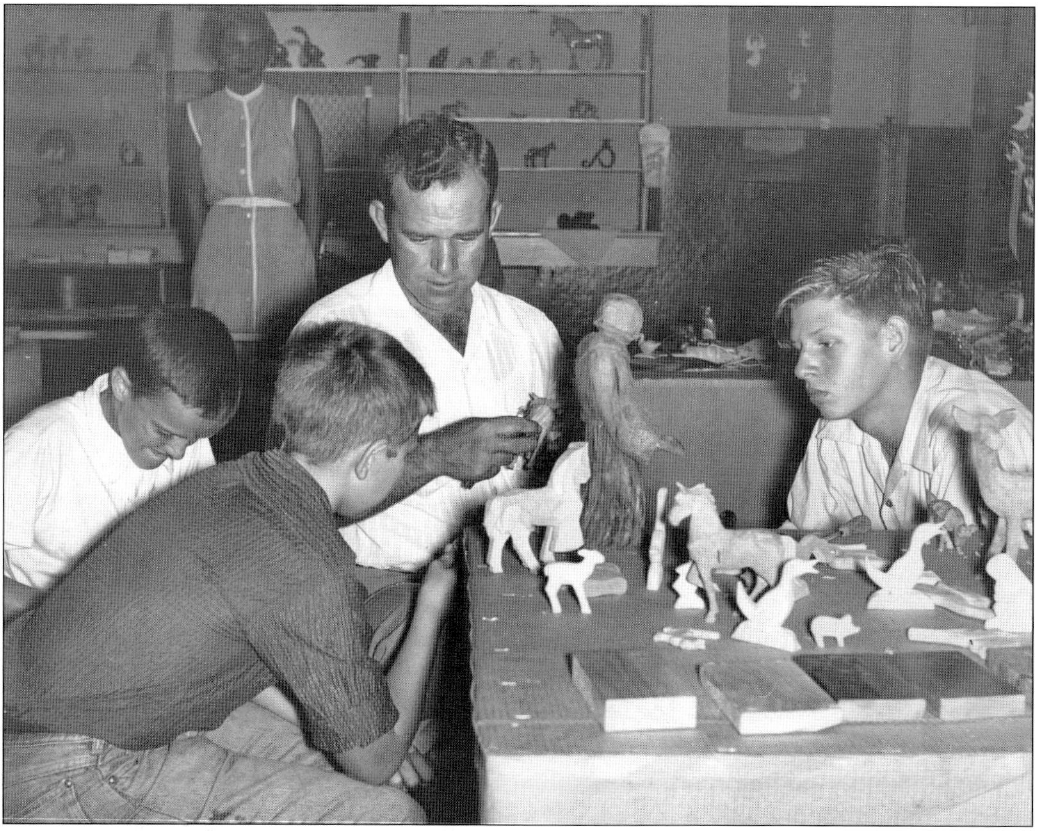

Jack Hall (center) was an especially renowned carver who led the Brasstown Carvers after Murray Martin's retirement. While under Martin's leadership, Hall helped bring the St. Francis figure into rotation. Martin designed them, Hall roughed them out, and the figure became a staple for the group. Seen here demonstrating at a craft fair, Hall also taught many well-known carvers, including Dexter Dockery, Helen Gibson, and Richard Carter.

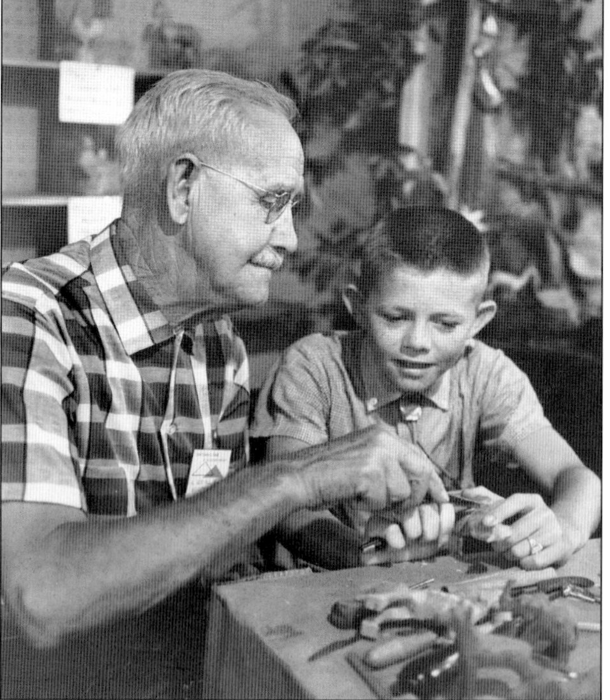

Another member of the Hall family, Ben Hall (left) was listed on the 1942 roster as the top earning Brasstown Carver. He brought home $758. Hall held a deep appreciation for the work, noting that it was his carving that enabled him to buy glasses for his son. Murray Martin described him as one of the more skilled carvers who often set high standards for others.

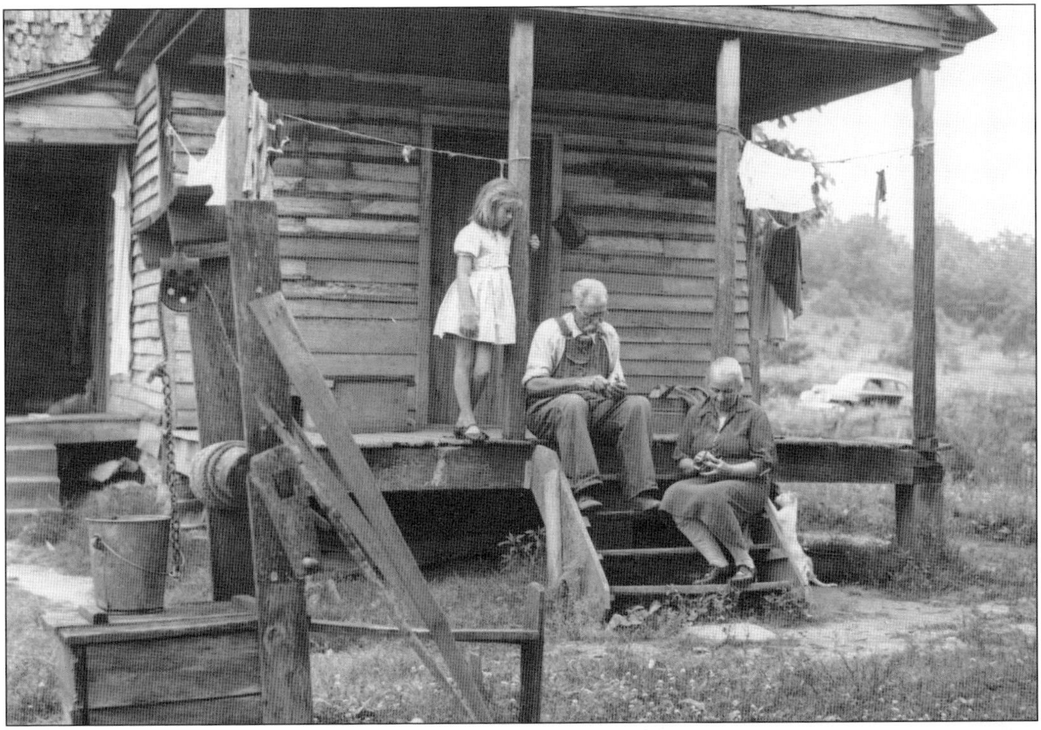

John Hall (center) was known for his "mad mules," inspired by one that took a hoof to his face. Along with his brothers and extended members of his family, Hall was a prolific carver. He and his wife, Bessie Wells Hall, are pictured on the porch of their home, both working on carvings while under the watchful eye of their granddaughter Loretta Miller.

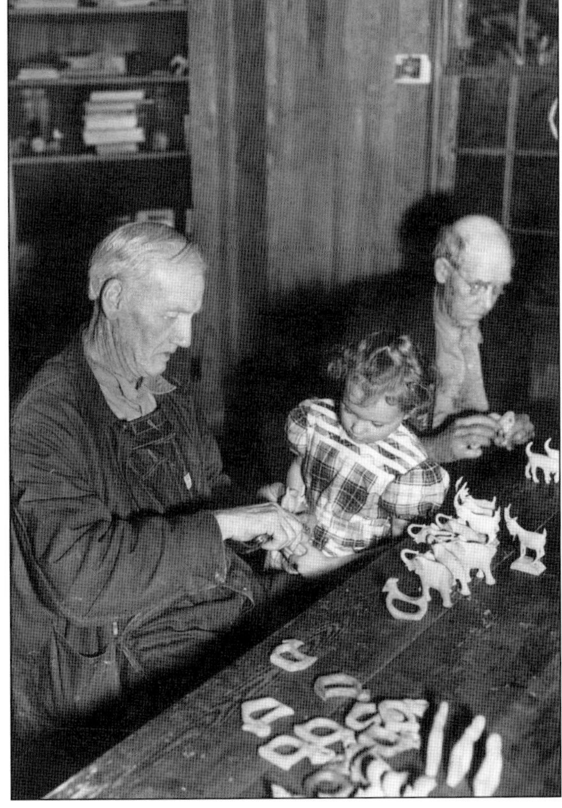

Talmadge Massey (left) was one of the first Brasstown Carvers, using the craft to supplement his income from farming. Elisha Hall (right) was one of many Hall family members who also picked up a knife and took to carving. Pictured here with an unidentified child, Massey and Hall worked on napkin rings, elephants, goats, and dogs.

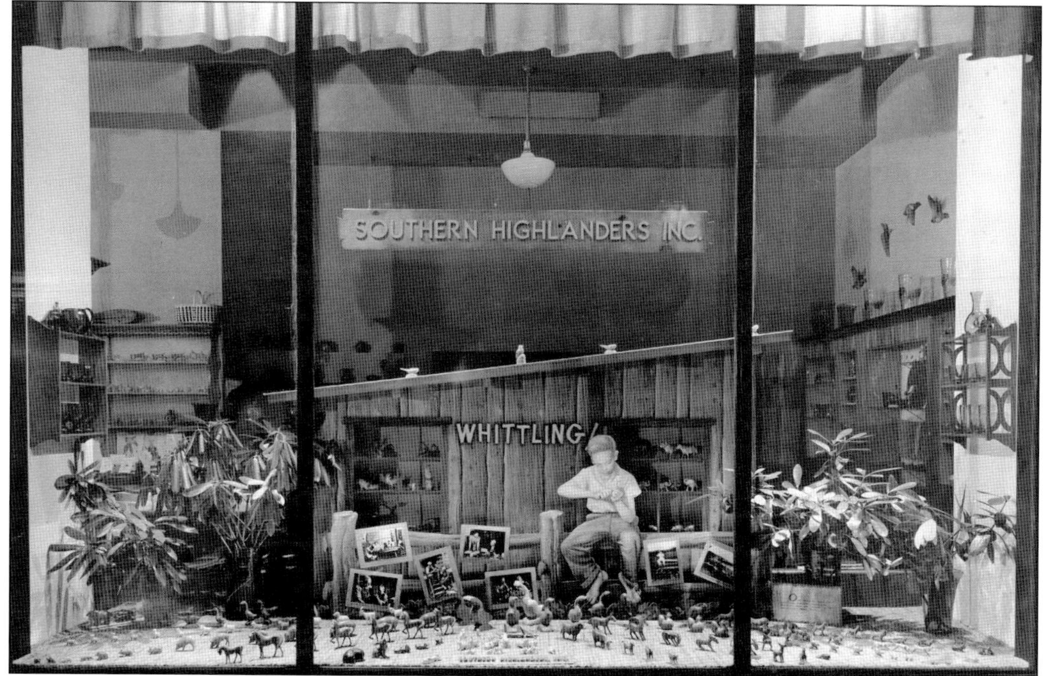

In the spring of 1947, the storefront of Southern Highlanders Inc. in New York City featured the Brasstown Carvers as well as other work from the Folk School. Southern Highlanders Inc. was a cooperative created by the Tennessee Valley Authority (TVA) that worked with residents who were displaced by TVA projects. From the 1930s to the 1950s, many North Carolina artists sold pieces through the cooperative.

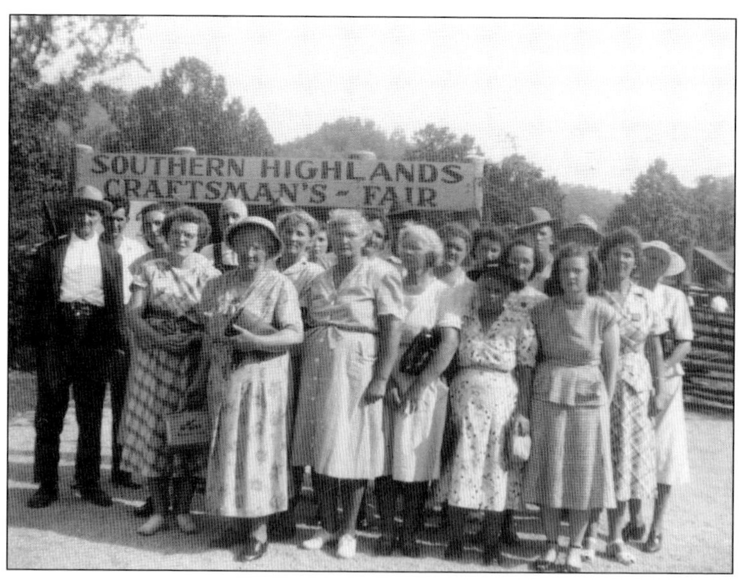

People in communities surrounding the Folk School, both in North Carolina and Georgia, were members of the Brasstown Carvers in the group's earlier decades. In 1949, a large group of those carvers attended the Southern Highlands Craftsman's Fair. Some carvers, including Ben Hall, also attended the inaugural fair in 1948. With the rise in guild membership and return of artisans from overseas, the fair was an especially meaningful celebration.

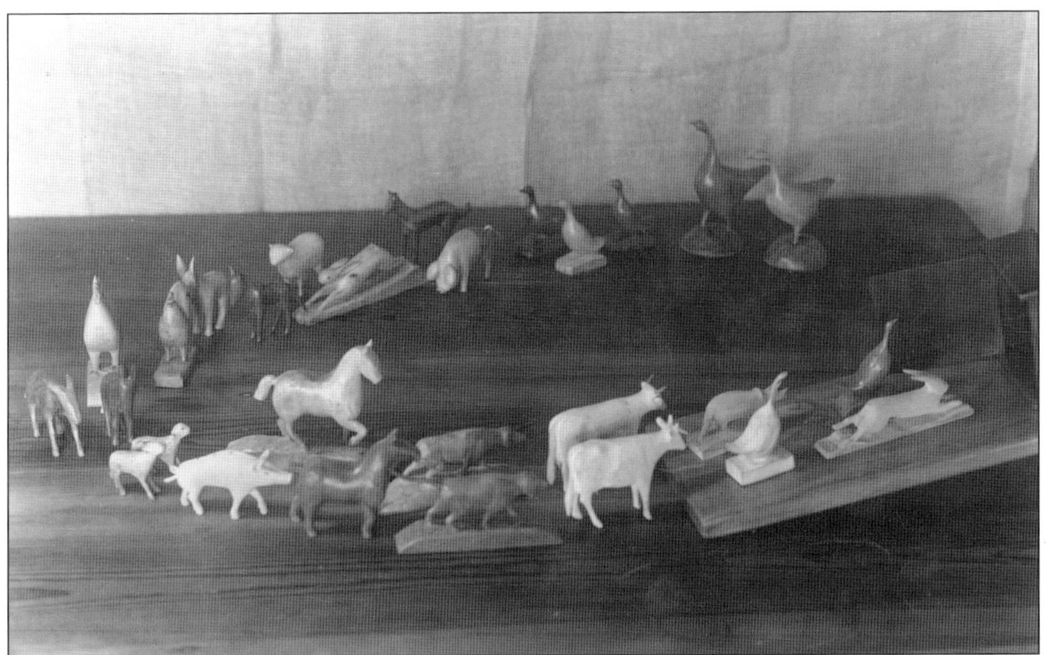

Much like the church played a significant role in the life of the Brasstown community, religious imagery eventually played a significant role in some of the Brasstown Carvers' work. From the figures of St. Francis of Assisi to the tender nativity scene, attention to detail was matched by shared belief. The scene of animals being processed into the ark was an ideal blend of the carvers' personal and professional lives.

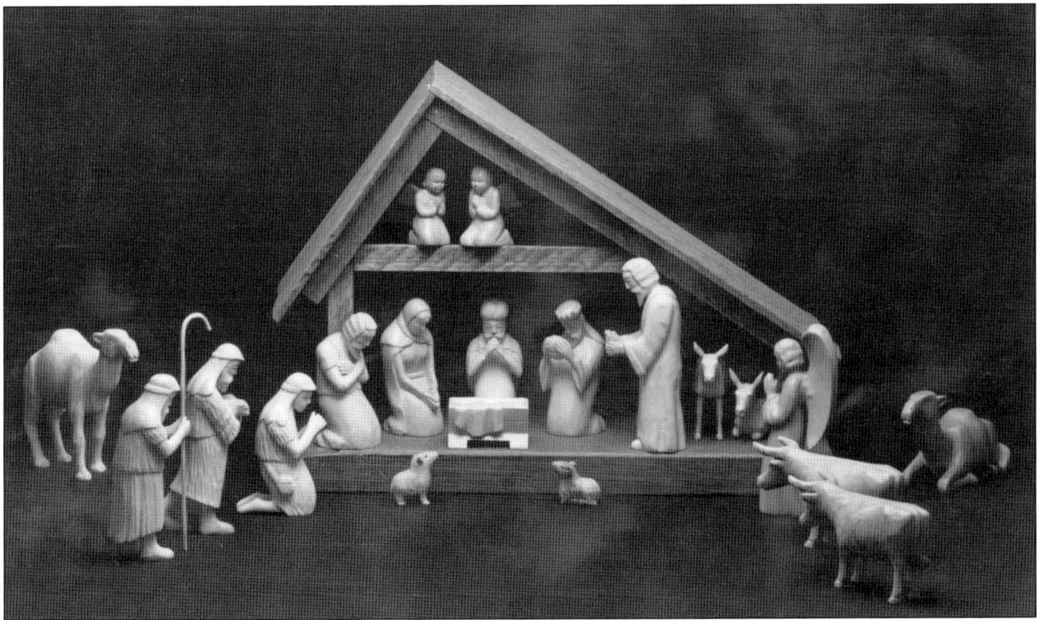

In the beginning, the carvers made only animal figures, largely farm and woodland creatures that were familiar to their lives. After evolving into carvings of human figures, nativity scenes were requested. They were originally sold only by mail order, and customers were willing to wait months or even years to collect all the pieces to complete their sets.

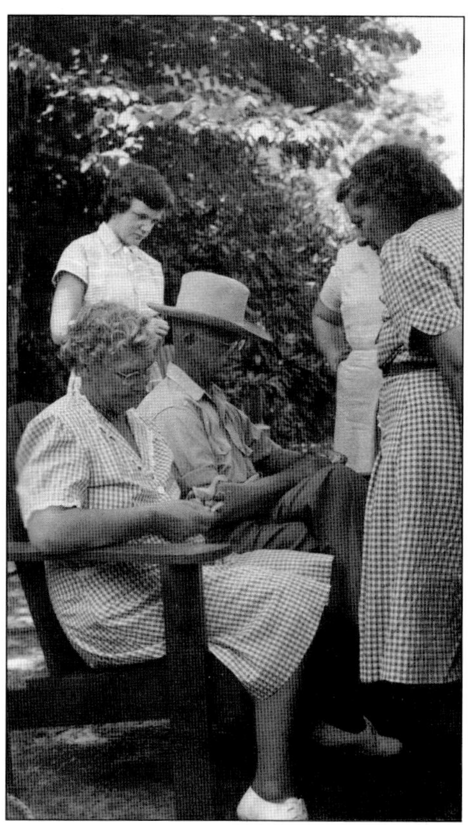

Sally (seated left) and Clarence Fleming (seated right) were also early Brasstown Carvers who were photographed carving together as early as 1935. In 1942, Clarence earned a sizeable amount of $230, while Sally earned a more modest $8. Both were recognized for their whimsical animals, and Clarence was best known for his pig carvings.

Dexter and Hazel Dockery were one of a few husband-and-wife members of the Brasstown Carvers. Dexter, a pastor, began carving around 1939, and Hazel sanded his work. By 1949, she was also a carver. He took much of his instruction from Murray Martin and Jack Hall, while Hazel learned directly from her husband. In the late 1980s, Dexter was recognized as a lifetime member of the Southern Highland Craft Guild.

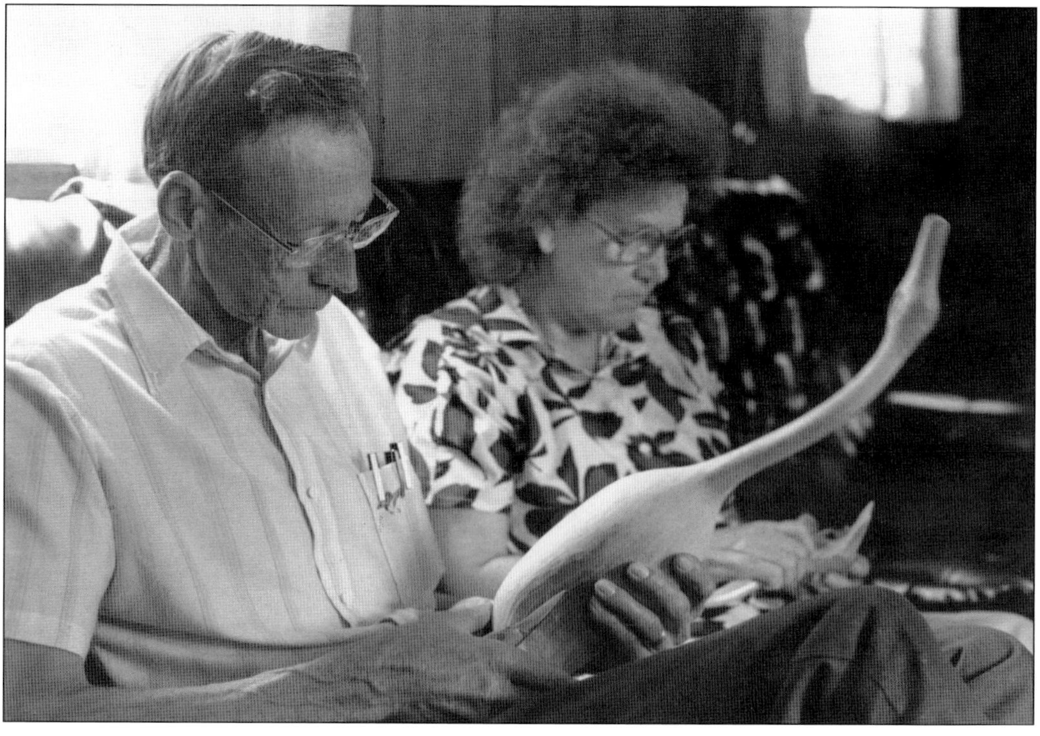

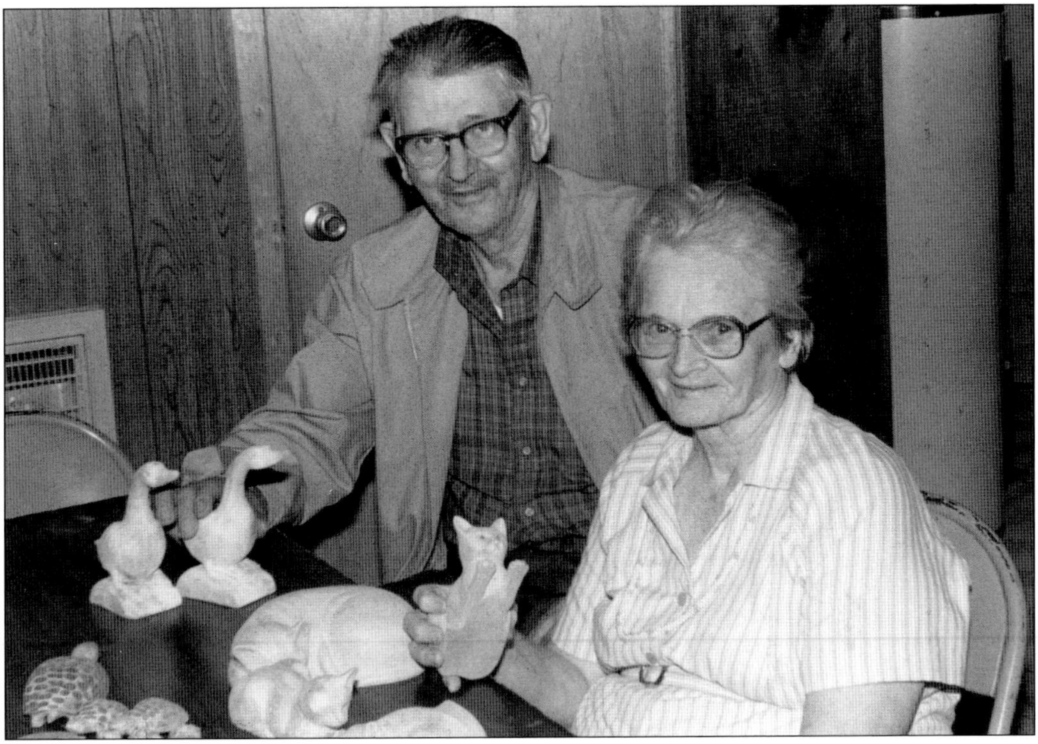

Glenn (above, left) and Hope Brown (above, right) both began carving around 1940. Hope was known for her cats, and Glenn was known for his birds. The couple were parents to eight daughters and sons, and Hope modeled her figurines of children on their own. She once said, "Often carving has meant the sole source of a doctor's bill . . . or food for my children. I am happy that I have the gift of carving and that the Folk School has given me the opportunity to use it." Her sentiments were shared by many of the carvers in the photograph below. From left to right are (sitting) Abalee Ivester, Betty Johnson, Jay A. Morris, an unidentified woman, Martha Coffey, and Nolan Beaver; (standing) Richard Carter, Max Johnson, Doris Reece, Verda Anderson, Helen Gibson, Hope Brown, Glenn Brown, and Nell Lee.

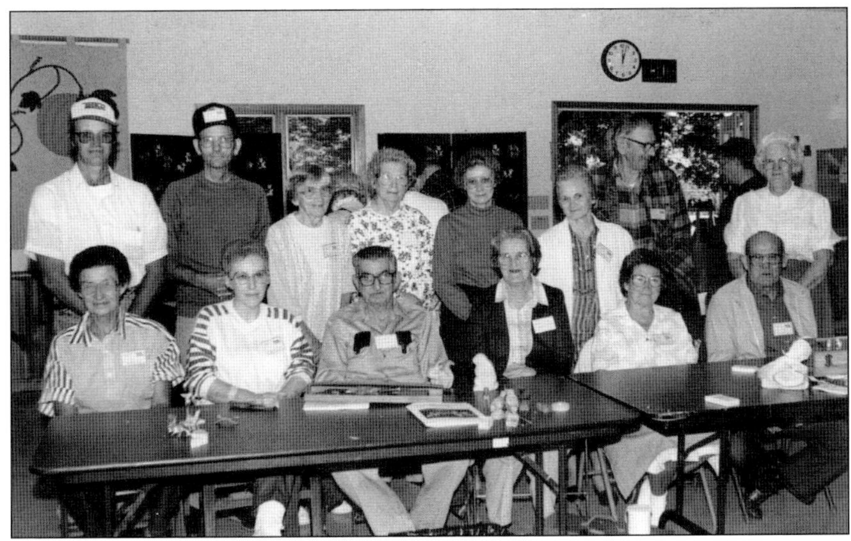

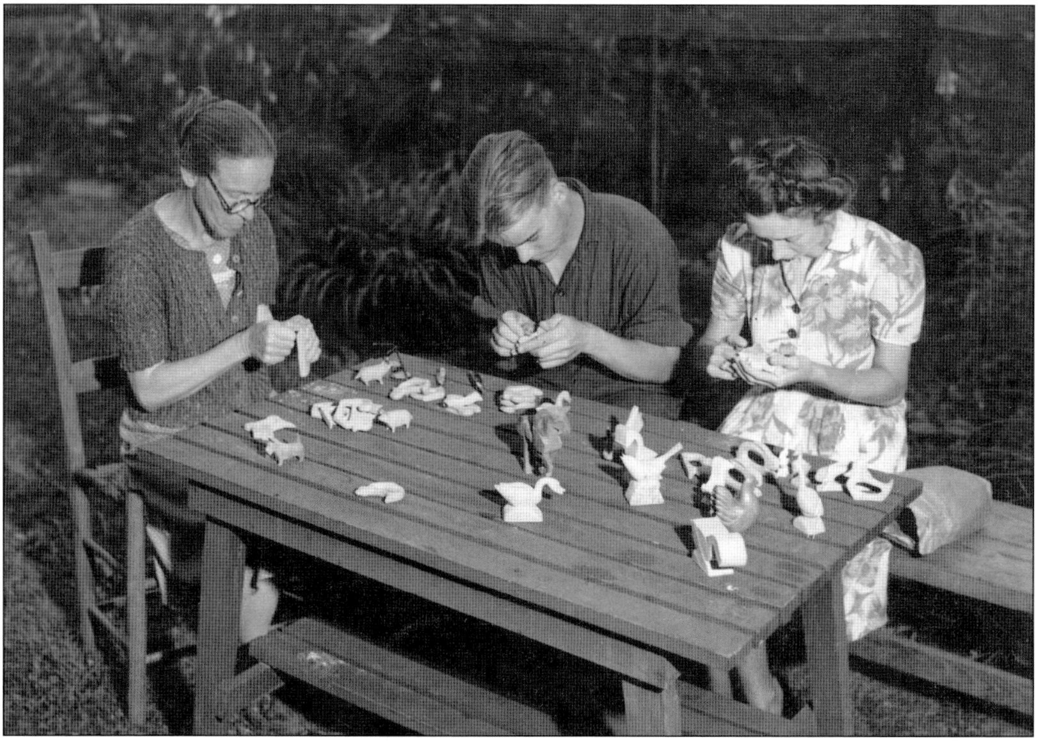

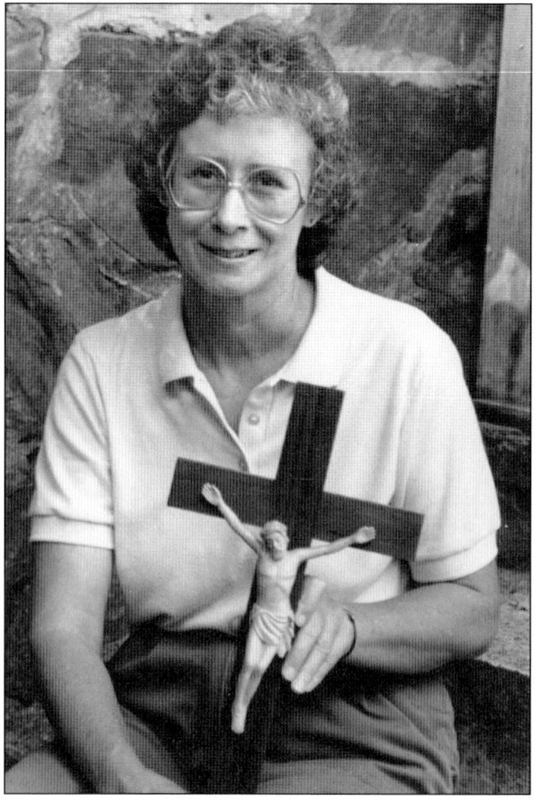

Helen Gibson (pictured at left) started carving as a child, learning from her mother, Dorothy "Dot" Payne McClure (above, right), as well as her neighbors Fannie Ivester and Martha Coffey. Gibson began teaching carving in 1989 through the Folk School's apprentice program and traveled regularly across the Southeast to teach at carving clubs. Gibson is one of the few remaining instructors to carve and teach the celebrated Brasstown nativity figures, which she has also illustrated in two of her books. In 2025, she was a recipient of the North Carolina Heritage Award, which honors artists for their contribution to the cultural lives of their communities.

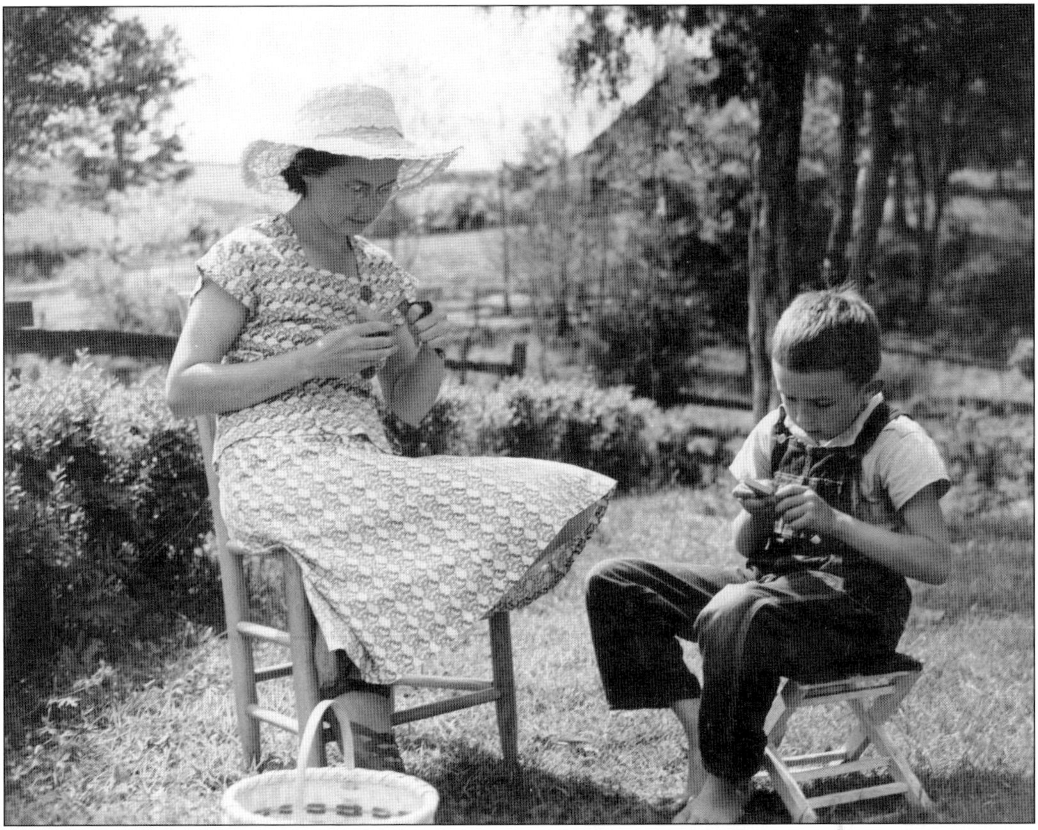

Ruth Fleming Hawkins began carving at age 20, at a time when there were few women among the Brasstown Carvers. Her attention to quality and detail brought great demand for her work. Hawkins started with napkin rings, progressed to animal figures—especially cats—and later carved Christmas ornaments and human figures. Her son Claude was also a member of the Brasstown Carvers.

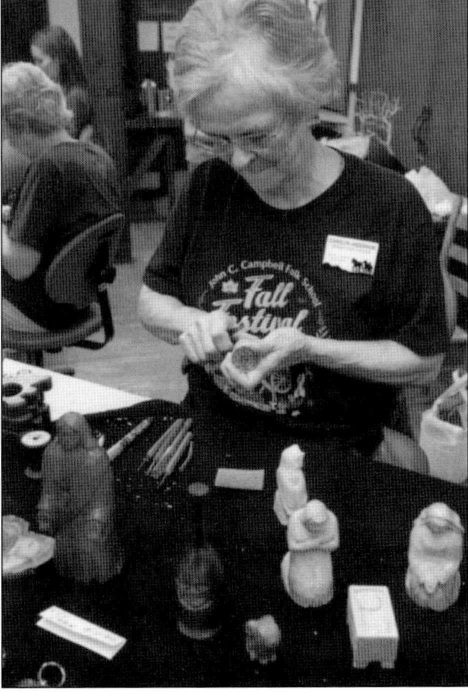

Carolyn Hall Anderson grew up in Warne, North Carolina, around several wood-carvers, including her relative Ruth Fleming Hawkins. Anderson started her own wood carving journey after her children left for college. She studied under Helen Gibson and started carving nativity figures and holiday ornaments. Anderson is a member of the Southern Highland Craft Guild and regularly assists Richard Carter with the Folk School's Thursday night carving class.

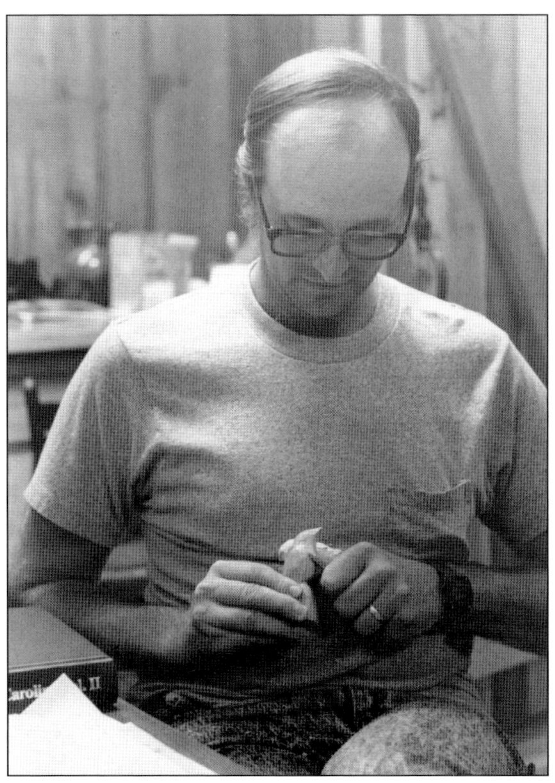

Richard Carter started working for the Folk School's dairy farm in the late 1960s. In the 1970s, he took a carving class at Tri-County Community College with Jack Hall. He went on to study with Helen Gibson, became a Brasstown Carver, and now manages the Thursday night carving class at the Folk School. Carter has mentored new carvers, including Terrence Fairies and Angela Wynn.

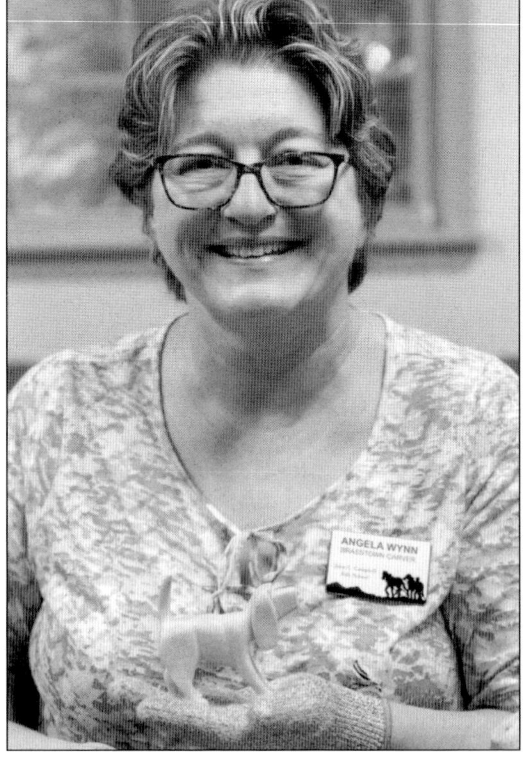

Angela Wynn grew up around multiple family members who were craftspeople, but she did not delve much into woodcraft until she met Richard Carter in October 2021. In 2023, Wynn was awarded a yearlong North Carolina Arts Council Folklife Apprenticeship grant to continue her mentorship with Carter. Under his guidance and encouragement, she joined the ranks of the Brasstown Carvers.

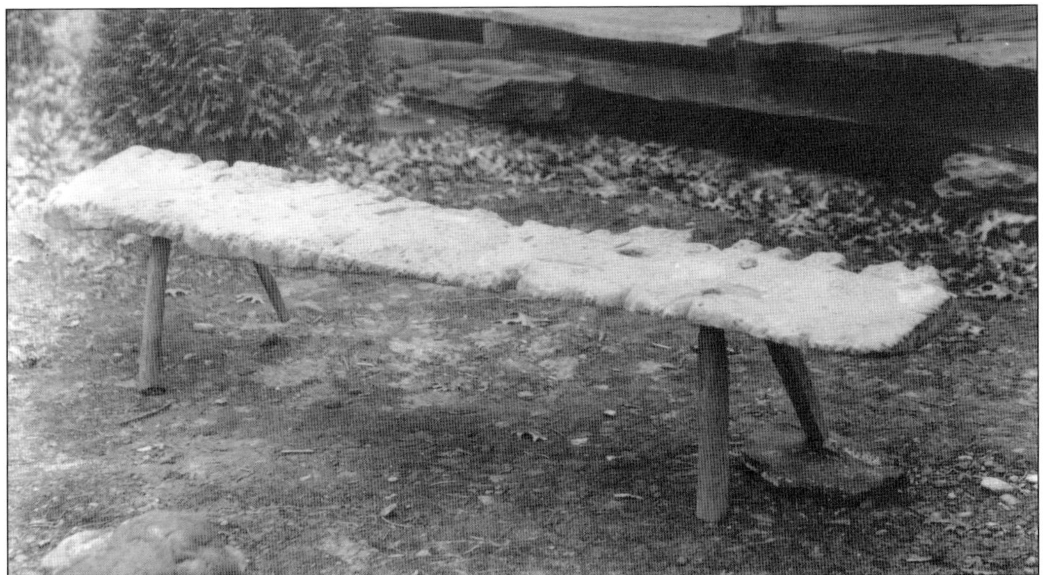

The bench that once graced the porch at Fred O. Scroggs's general store turned into a Brasstown Carvers' relic. Cofounders Olive Dame Campbell and Marguerite Butler Bidstrup recognized that a simple piece of furniture had itself become part of the story. Pictured outside the Log Cabin Museum in the late 1920s or early 1930s, it is now housed in the Folk School's History Center.

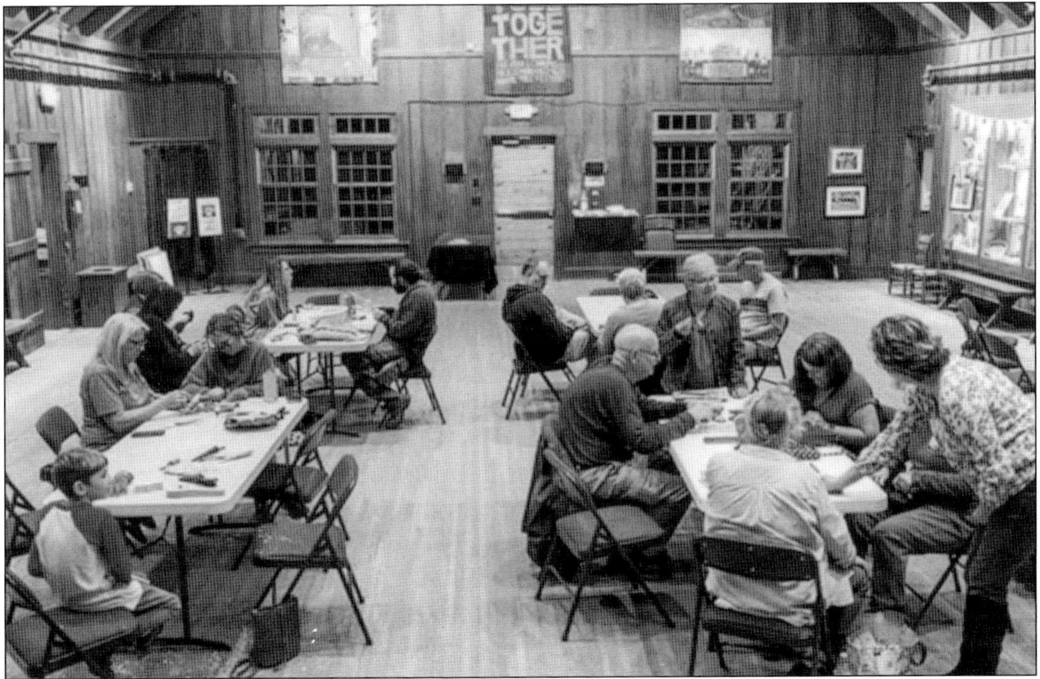

These days, aspiring carvers can be found on Thursday evenings in the Community Room. Richard Carter provides "blanks," pieces of wood cut into common animal patterns established generations ago, for all who attend. Much like the gathering space on Scroggs's porch, the room has become a place for carving and connection. It is a testament to the school's humble beginnings, revered traditions, and the immeasurable joy of making things.

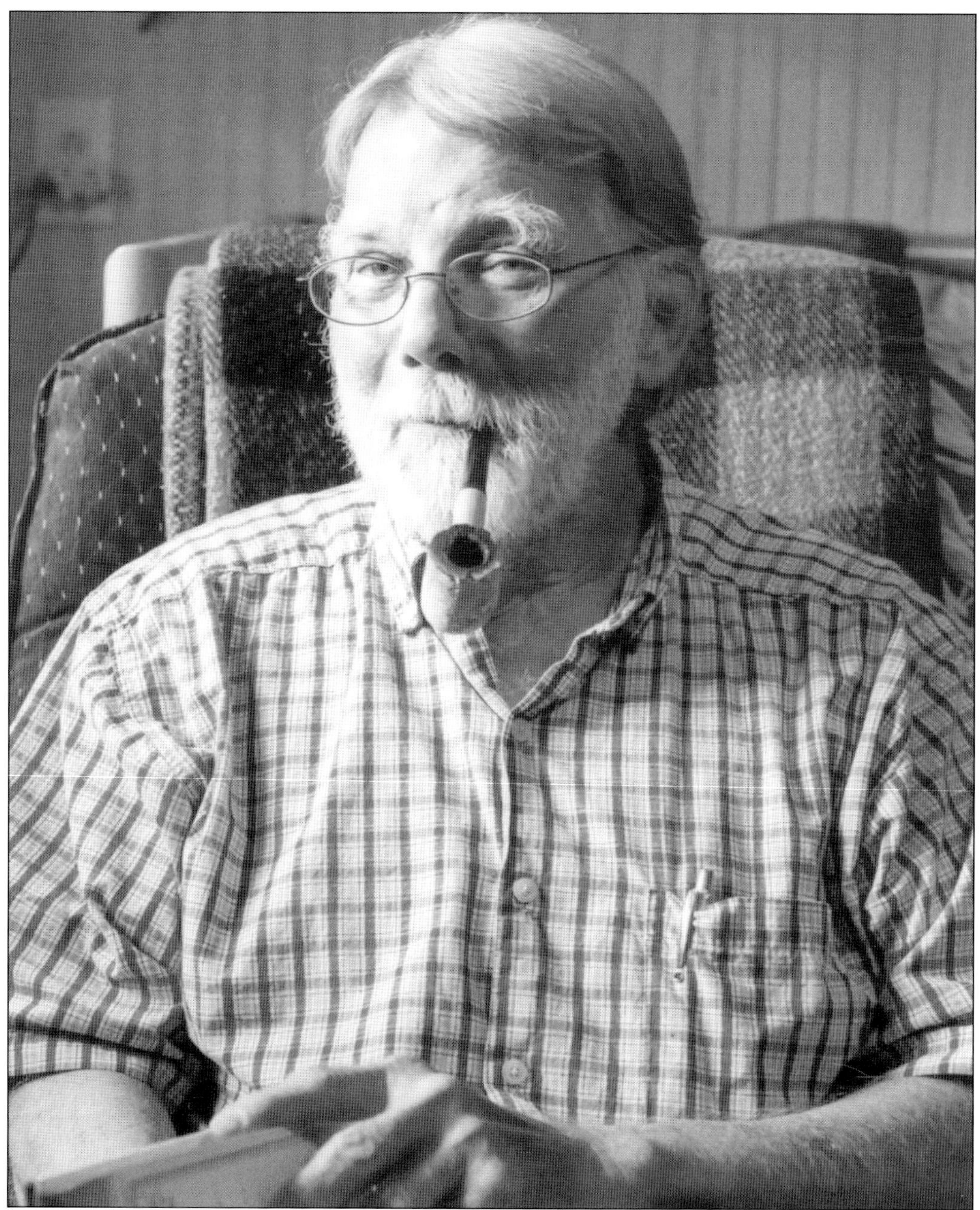

During the publication of this book, the community mourned the loss of a dear Folk School friend, Timothy Edmund Ryan (December 9, 1947–May 18, 2025). Ryan was a board member, staff member, donor, blacksmith, and beloved auctioneer. He served as the resident artist for gardening and homesteading for over 15 years and planned the initial designs for the herb and vegetable gardens. He contributed in so many ways, mentoring others through his love of the school and serving a regular Sunday brunch for work studies and hosts. His hospitality stretched as far as his book collection. Ryan will be remembered as an entertaining storyteller, a bonsai extraordinaire, and a connector of people. From glen to glen and down the mountainside, Tim Ryan will be missed. (Courtesy of Cory Marie Podielski.)

About the John C. Campbell Folk School

Tucked away in the mountains of Western North Carolina, the John C. Campbell Folk School offers weeklong and weekend classes for adults in craft, art, music, dance, cooking, gardening, nature studies, photography, writing, and more. Our noncompetitive and small-sized classes are offered year-round on a scenic 270-acre campus, attracting students from all over the world. The Folk School's peaceful environment and picturesque landscape provide inspiration for all our visitors, whether they are taking a class or stopping by for the day. Explore our campus by meandering through the woods on winding bark-chipped paths, walking alongside scenic pastures, or taking a stroll along Little Brasstown Creek. Guests are welcome to tour our studios and observe classes, where people just like you are creating and discovering in the heart of Appalachia.

John C. Campbell Folk School
1 Folk School Road
Brasstown, NC 28902

Olive's Porch
27 Peachtree Street
Murphy, NC 28906